Taste of Home

Make it!

TAKE IT | VOLUME 2

TASTE OF HOME BOOKS • RDA ENTHUSIAST BRANDS, LLC • MILWAUKEE, WI

PAGE 96

PAGE 40

PAGE 100

PAGE 8

CONTENTS

PAGE 98

PAGE 89

PAGE 33

PAGE 240

Executive Editor: Mark Hagen
Senior Art Director: Raeann Thompson
Editor: Christine Rukavena
Art Director: Maggie Conners
Designers: Jazmin Delgado, Arielle Jardine
Senior Copy Editor: Dulcie Shoener
Copy Editors: Chris McLaughlin, Ann Walter

Cover:
Photographer: Jim Wieland
Food Stylist: Josh Rink
Set Stylist: Stacey Genaw

Pictured on cover: Mamaw Emily's Strawberry Cake, p. 216; Summer Orzo, p. 113; Bacon Pea Salad, p. 131; Best Deviled Eggs, p. 8; Crispy Fried Chicken, p. 98

Pictured on title page: Bacon Cheeseburger Slider Bake, p. 12

Pictured on back cover: Garlic Garbanzo Bean Spread, p. 19; Debra's Cavatini, p. 87; Heavenly Filled Strawberries, p. 301; Taco Cornbread Casserole, p. 78

Pictured on spine: Cilantro Tomato Bruschetta, p. 30

© 2020 RDA Enthusiast Brands, LLC
1610 N. 2nd St., Suite 102, Milwaukee WI 53212-3906

International Standard Book Number:
978-1-61765-928-7

Library of Congress Control Number:
2643-6221

Printed in U.S.A.
1 3 5 7 9 10 8 6 4 2

GATHER THE GANG WITH GREAT FOODS FOR ALL SEASONS

PICNICS, PARTIES & POTLUCKS HAVE NEVER TASTED BETTER!

Savor the sweet taste of bring-a-dish victory. Just choose a recipe from these favorites shared by the family cooks at **Taste of Home.** And no matter where your celebrations take you, good times and great meals are guaranteed!

You'll find 365 amazing dishes in this edition of **Make It, Take It!** Whether you're attending an Easter brunch, summer reunion, spaghetti dinner or holiday fete, the best

recipes to feed a crowd on the go are right here! Sample the goodness with smart choices like these.

SPRING AHEAD

Discover overnight stratas, sweet rolls and other morning jump-starts, such as Patricia Quinn's impressive **Blueberry-Mascarpone French Toast (p. 40).** These and dozens of other **MAKE AHEAD** dishes let you do most of the work in advance and pop the dish into the fridge or freezer for simple serving on a moment's notice. Aren't you smart?

PACK A PICNIC

Reunions, picnics, block parties and pig roasts...summer is prime time for get-togethers. The freewheeling favorites you'll find here include heat-on-the-grill-and-serve **Saucy Grilled Baby Back Ribs (p. 95)**, frosting-free **Pineapple Upside-Down Cupcakes (p. 241)** that can take the heat, and mayo-free salads like Shayna Marmar's delectable **Summer Orzo (p. 113),** featured on the cover.

PAGE 241

PAGE 211

CELEBRATE FALL

The return of football season calls out for simple **Spicy Nacho Bake (p. 176)** or **Beefy Taco Dip (p. 14)**. And **Pretty Pumpkin Cinnamon Buns (p. 44)** make an autumnal morning even more glorious.

KEEP IT COZY

Slow cookers are a potluck partygoer's best friend, and you'll find an entire chapter dedicated to dishes prepared in them! From Cathy Johnson's perfect **So-Easy Spaghetti Sauce (p. 200)** to crowd-sized holiday sides like **Rich & Creamy Mashed Potatoes (p. 211)**, you'll find over three dozen keep-warm delights.

PAGE 176

Chocolate brownie meets peanut butter meets crispy treats in Dawn Pasco's irresistible **Peanut Butter Brownie Crispy Bars**. Get the recipe on p. 244.

MAKE A PLAN FOR FOOD SAFETY

✔ **Set up in the shade.** If possible, keep your outdoor buffet in a cool area—like a garage, in the shade of a building or under a big tree. Stash your coolers in the shade to keep drinks colder, too.

✔ **Have plenty of ice to pack around dishes and keep things cold.** Not only will food taste better when it's properly chilled, but you won't have to worry about the risk of foodborne illness.

✔ **Likewise, keep hot foods hot.** Foods should not be out at room temperature for more than two hours (less if it's hotter than that). Chafing dishes, slow cookers, and grills or ovens set on low all help to keep things safe.

✔ **Designate a meal time—and stick to it.** Set aside two hours for the meal and serve hot and cold foods only during that time. Afterward, put leftovers in the fridge or pack 'em up in well-iced coolers.

Party Pesto
Pinwheels
page 15

Appetizers & Dips

Invited to a holiday party or a game-day get-together? Find the perfect nibble, bite and nosh among these tasty and totable appetizers, snacks, dips and spreads!

BEST DEVILED EGGS

Herbs lend amazing flavor, making these the best deviled eggs you can make!
—Jesse and Anne Foust, Bluefield, WV

Takes: 15 min. • **Makes:** 2 dozen

- ½ cup mayonnaise
- 2 Tbsp. 2% milk
- 1 tsp. dried parsley flakes
- ½ tsp. dill weed
- ½ tsp. minced chives
- ½ tsp. ground mustard
- ¼ tsp. salt
- ¼ tsp. paprika
- ⅛ tsp. garlic powder
- ⅛ tsp. pepper
- 12 hard-boiled large eggs
  Minced fresh parsley and additional paprika

In a bowl, combine the first 10 ingredients. Cut eggs lengthwise in half; remove yolks and set whites aside. In another bowl, mash yolks; add to mayonnaise mixture, mixing well. Spoon or pipe filling into egg whites. Sprinkle with parsley and additional paprika. Refrigerate until serving.

1 stuffed egg half: 73 cal., 6g fat (1g sat. fat), 108mg chol., 81mg sod., 0 carb. (0 sugars, 0 fiber), 3g pro.

Deviled Eggs with Bacon: To mayonnaise, mix in 3 crumbled, cooked bacon strips, 3 Tbsp. finely chopped red onion, 3 Tbsp. sweet pickle relish and ¼ tsp. smoked paprika.

Smokin' Hot Deviled Eggs: To mayonnaise, mix in 3 finely chopped chipotle peppers in adobo sauce, 1 Tbsp. drained capers, 1 Tbsp. stone-ground mustard, ¼ tsp. salt and ¼ tsp. white pepper. Sprinkle stuffed eggs with minced fresh cilantro.

Crabby Deviled Eggs: Increase mayonnaise to ⅔ cup. Mix in 1 cup finely chopped imitation crabmeat, ½ cup finely chopped celery, ½ cup chopped slivered almonds, 2 Tbsp. finely chopped green pepper and ½ tsp. salt.

ROASTED VEGETABLE DIP

While my children were always very good eaters, I came up with this recipe to get them to enjoy eating more veggies. The dip doesn't last long in our house!
—Sarah Vasques, Milford, NH

Prep: 15 min. • **Bake:** 25 min. + cooling
Makes: 20 servings

- 2 large sweet red peppers
- 1 large zucchini
- 1 medium onion
- 1 Tbsp. olive oil
- ½ tsp. salt
- ¼ tsp. pepper
- 1 pkg. (8 oz.) reduced-fat cream cheese
  Assorted crackers or fresh vegetables

1. Preheat oven to 425°. Cut vegetables into 1-in. pieces. Place in a 15x10x1-in. baking pan coated with cooking spray; toss with oil, salt and pepper. Roast until tender, stirring occasionally, 25-30 minutes. Cool mixture completely.

2. Place vegetables and cream cheese in a food processor; process until blended. Transfer to a bowl; refrigerate, covered, until serving. Serve dip with crackers or fresh vegetables.

2 Tbsp. dip: 44 cal., 3g fat (2g sat. fat), 8mg chol., 110mg sod., 3g carb. (2g sugars, 1g fiber), 2g pro.

TEST KITCHEN TIP
Roasted veggies account for more than half the volume of this blended dip, which means more nutrients, fewer calories, and less saturated fat. Not to mention amazing flavor!

MAKE AHEAD

SAUSAGE WONTON CUPS

Here's a tasty hot appetizer for all those gatherings that feature fun finger foods. I've made this recipe several times, and these bites always disappear so fast. It's really easy.
—Shirley Van Allen, High Point, NC

....

Takes: 30 min. • **Makes:** 2 dozen

1   **lb. Italian turkey sausage links, casings removed**
1   **can (15 oz.) tomato sauce**
½   **tsp. garlic powder**
½   **tsp. dried basil**
24   **wonton wrappers**
1   **cup shredded Italian cheese blend**

1. In a large skillet, cook sausage over medium heat until no longer pink; drain. Stir in the tomato sauce, garlic powder and basil. Bring to a boil. Reduce the heat; simmer, uncovered, until thickened, for 8-10 minutes.

2. Meanwhile, press wonton wrappers into miniature muffin cups coated with cooking spray. Bake at 350° until lightly browned, about 8-9 minutes.

3. Spoon the sausage mixture into wonton cups. Sprinkle with cheese. Bake appetizers until the cheese is melted, 5-7 minutes longer. Serve warm.

Freeze option: Freeze cooled filled wonton cups in freezer containers, separating layers with waxed paper. To use, reheat wonton cups in coated muffin pans in a preheated 350° oven until crisp and heated through.

1 wonton cup: 68 cal., 3g fat (1g sat. fat), 15mg chol., 270mg sod., 6g carb. (0 sugars, 0 fiber), 5g pro. **Diabetic exchanges:** ½ starch, ½ fat.

★ ★ ★ ★ ★   **READER REVIEW**

"Everyone loved these! They were gone almost as fast as I put them out! Very easy to make."

TKOELZER TASTEOFHOME.COM

in 2 greased 13x9-in. baking pans. Sprinkle each pan of rolls with 1 cup cheese. Bake until cheese is melted, 3-5 minutes.

2. In a large skillet, cook beef and onion over medium heat until beef is no longer pink and onion is tender, breaking up beef into crumbles, 6-8 minutes; drain. Stir in tomatoes, mustard, Worcestershire sauce, salt and pepper. Cook and stir until mixture is combined, 1-2 minutes.

3. Spoon beef mixture evenly over rolls; sprinkle with remaining cheese. Top with bacon. Replace tops. For the glaze, in a microwave-safe bowl, combine butter, brown sugar, Worcestershire sauce and mustard. Microwave, covered, on high until butter is melted, stirring occasionally. Pour over the rolls; sprinkle with sesame seeds. Bake, uncovered, until golden brown and heated through, 20-25 minutes.

Freeze option: Cover and freeze unbaked sandwiches; prepare and freeze glaze. To use, partially thaw in refrigerator overnight. Remove from refrigerator 30 minutes before baking. Preheat oven to 350°. Pour glaze over buns and sprinkle with sesame seeds. Bake sandwiches as directed, increasing time by 10-15 minutes, until cheese is melted and a thermometer inserted in center reads 165°.

1 slider: 380 cal., 24g fat (13g sat. fat), 86mg chol., 628mg sod., 21g carb. (9g sugars, 2g fiber), 18g pro.

TEST KITCHEN TIP
Here in our Test Kitchen, we adore this sweet and savory combination! If you want a more classic burger flavor, just use a package of dinner rolls in place of the Hawaiian rolls.

MAKE AHEAD

BACON CHEESEBURGER SLIDER BAKE

I created this dish to fill two pans because these sliders disappear fast. Just cut the recipe in half if you only want to make one batch.
—Nick Iverson, Denver, CO

Prep: 20 min. • **Bake:** 25 min.
Makes: 2 dozen

- 2 pkg. (17 oz. each) Hawaiian sweet rolls
- 4 cups shredded cheddar cheese, divided
- 2 lbs. ground beef
- 1 cup chopped onion
- 1 can (14½ oz.) diced tomatoes with garlic and onion, drained
- 1 Tbsp. Dijon mustard
- 1 Tbsp. Worcestershire sauce
- ¾ tsp. salt
- ¾ tsp. pepper
- 24 bacon strips, cooked and crumbled

GLAZE
- 1 cup butter, cubed
- ¼ cup packed brown sugar
- 4 tsp. Worcestershire sauce
- 2 Tbsp. Dijon mustard
- 2 Tbsp. sesame seeds

1. Preheat the oven to 350°. Without separating rolls, cut each package of rolls horizontally in half; arrange bottom halves

THREE-PEPPER BEAN DIP

My husband's great-grandmother and I spent time together creating this recipe after trying a similar version from his aunt. So it not only tastes delicious, it also has a lot of sentimental value.
—Amber Massey, Argyle, TX

Prep: 15 min. • **Bake:** 30 min.
Makes: 5 cups

- 1 **can (16 oz.) refried beans**
- 1½ **cups reduced-fat sour cream**
- 1 **cup salsa**
- 4 **green onions, chopped**
- 1 **can (4 oz.) chopped green chiles**
- 3 **oz. reduced-fat cream cheese**
- 1 **jalapeno pepper, seeded and chopped**
- 2 **Tbsp. chopped chipotle peppers in adobo sauce**
- 1½ **tsp. ground cumin**
- ½ **tsp. chili powder**
- 1 **cup shredded Colby-Monterey Jack cheese**
  Tortilla chips or assorted fresh vegetables

1. Preheat oven to 325°. In a large bowl, combine the first 10 ingredients. Transfer to a greased 1½-qt. baking dish. Cover and bake at for 25 minutes.

2. Sprinkle with cheese. Bake, uncovered, until bubbly, 5-10 minutes longer. Serve warm with chips.

Note: Wear disposable gloves when cutting hot peppers; the oils can burn skin. Avoid touching your face.

¼ cup: 84 cal., 4g fat (3g sat. fat), 16mg chol., 211mg sod., 7g carb. (2g sugars, 2g fiber), 4g pro. **Diabetic exchanges:** 1 fat, ½ starch.

BEEFY TACO DIP

Here's a taco dip that combines several of my friends' recipes. I experimented until I came up with my favorite. It's always a hit, no matter where I take it.
—Faye Parker, Bedford, NS

Prep: 30 min. + chilling
Makes: 20 servings

- 1 pkg. (8 oz.) cream cheese, softened
- 1 cup sour cream
- ¾ cup mayonnaise
- 1 lb. ground beef
- 1 envelope taco seasoning
- 1 can (8 oz.) tomato sauce
- 2 cups shredded cheddar or Mexican cheese blend
- 4 cups shredded lettuce
- 2 medium tomatoes, diced
- 1 small onion, diced
- 1 medium green pepper, diced
  Tortilla chips

1. In a small bowl, beat the cream cheese, sour cream and mayonnaise until smooth. Spread on a 12- to 14-in. pizza pan or serving dish. Refrigerate for 1 hour.
2. In a saucepan over medium heat, brown beef; drain. Add the taco seasoning and tomato sauce; cook and stir for 5 minutes. Cool completely. Spread over the cream cheese layer. Chill.
3. Just before serving, sprinkle with cheese, lettuce, tomatoes, onion and green pepper. Serve with chips.
1 serving: 216 cal., 18g fat (8g sat. fat), 47mg chol., 383mg sod., 5g carb. (2g sugars, 1g fiber), 8g pro.

PARTY PESTO PINWHEELS

I took a few of my favorite recipes and combined them into these delicious hors d'oeuvres. The colorful spirals come together easily with refrigerated crescent roll dough, prepared pesto and a jar of roasted red peppers.
—Kathleen Farrell, Rochester, NY

....

Takes: 30 min. • **Makes:** 20 pinwheels

- 1 tube (8 oz.) refrigerated crescent rolls
- ⅓ cup prepared pesto sauce
- ¼ cup roasted sweet red peppers, drained and chopped
- ¼ cup grated Parmesan cheese
- 1 cup pizza sauce, warmed

1. Unroll crescent dough into two long rectangles; seal seams and perforations. Spread each with pesto; sprinkle with red peppers and cheese.

2. Roll each up jelly-roll style, starting with a short side. With a sharp knife, cut each roll into 10 slices. Place cut side down 2 in. apart on two ungreased baking sheets.

3. Bake at 400° until pinwheels are golden brown, 8-10 minutes. Serve warm with pizza sauce.

1 pinwheel: 76 cal., 5g fat (1g sat. fat), 2mg chol., 201mg sod., 6g carb. (2g sugars, 0 fiber), 2g pro.

FIESTA BITES

When a friend at the office shared these rolled tortilla appetizers with me, I knew in one bite I'd be taking her recipe home for the holidays.
—Diane Martin, Brown Deer, WI

Prep: 15 min. + chilling
Makes: about 5 dozen

 1 **pkg. (8 oz.) cream cheese, softened**
½ **cup sour cream**
¼ **cup picante sauce**
 2 **Tbsp. taco seasoning**
    Dash garlic powder
 1 **can (4½ oz.) chopped ripe olives, drained**
 1 **can (4 oz.) chopped green chiles**
 1 **cup finely shredded cheddar cheese**
½ **cup thinly sliced green onions**
 8 **flour tortillas (10 in.)**
    Salsa

1. In a small bowl, beat cream cheese, sour cream, picante sauce, taco seasoning and garlic powder until smooth. Stir in olives, chiles, cheese and onions. Spread about ½ cup on each tortilla.
2. Roll up jelly-roll style; wrap. Refrigerate for 2 hours or overnight. Slice rolls into 1-in. pieces. Serve with salsa.
Freeze Option: Slices may be prepared ahead and frozen. Thaw in refrigerator.
1 piece: 59 cal., 3g fat (2g sat. fat), 6mg chol., 154mg sod., 6g carb. (1g sugars, 0 fiber), 2g pro.

QUICK & EASY SWEDISH MEATBALLS

Rich and creamy, this classic meatball sauce is a must in your recipe box.
—*Taste of Home* Test Kitchen

Takes: 30 min. • **Makes:** 20 servings

 1 **pkg. (22 oz.) frozen fully cooked Angus beef meatballs**
 2 **Tbsp. butter**
 2 **Tbsp. all-purpose flour**
 1 **cup beef broth**
½ **cup heavy whipping cream**
¼ **tsp. dill weed**
¼ **cup minced fresh parsley, optional**

1. Prepare the meatballs according to package directions.
2. Meanwhile, in a large saucepan, melt butter. Stir in flour until smooth; gradually add broth. Bring to a boil; cook and stir until thickened, 1-2 minutes. Stir in cream and dill; simmer for 1 minute. Stir in the meatballs; heat through. Garnish with parsley if desired.
1 meatball: 115 cal., 10g fat (5g sat. fat), 26mg chol., 253mg sod., 2g carb. (1g sugars, 0 fiber), 4g pro.

GARLIC GARBANZO BEAN SPREAD

My friends and family always ask me to make this. I guarantee you'll be asked for the recipe. You can serve it as an appetizer or a filling for sandwiches.
—Lisa Moore, North Syracuse, NY

Takes: 10 min. • **Makes:** 1½ cups

1 can (15 oz.) garbanzo beans or chickpeas, rinsed and drained
½ cup olive oil
2 Tbsp. minced fresh parsley
1 Tbsp. lemon juice
1 green onion, cut into three pieces
1 to 2 garlic cloves, peeled
¼ tsp. salt
Assorted fresh vegetables and baked pita chips

In a food processor, combine the first 7 ingredients; cover and process until blended. Transfer to a bowl. Refrigerate until serving. Serve dip with vegetables and pita chips.
2 Tbsp. dip: 114 cal., 10g fat (1g sat. fat), 0 chol., 96mg sod., 6g carb. (1g sugars, 1g fiber), 1g pro. **Diabetic exchanges:** 2 fat, ½ starch.

CHICKEN FAJITA PIZZA

Pizza takes a southwest turn in this version. I made this recipe on the first date I had with my husband, Gary—an evening of cooking at my apartment.
—Tricia Longo, Spencer, MA

Prep: 20 min. • **Bake:** 20 min.
Makes: 12 slices

1 tube (13.8 oz.) refrigerated pizza crust
½ lb. boneless skinless chicken breasts, cut into strips
2 Tbsp. olive oil
½ cup sliced onion
½ cup julienned green pepper
3 garlic cloves, minced
1 tsp. chili powder
¼ tsp. salt
⅛ tsp. pepper
1 cup salsa
2 cups shredded Mexican cheese blend

1. Unroll crust into a greased 15x10x1-in. baking pan; flatten dough and build up edges slightly. Bake at 400° until lightly browned, 8-10 minutes.
2. Meanwhile, in a large skillet, saute the chicken in oil until lightly browned. Add onion, green pepper, garlic, chili powder, salt and pepper. Cook and stir until the vegetables are tender and chicken is no longer pink.
3. Spread salsa over crust. Top with 1 cup of cheese, chicken mixture and remaining cheese. Bake at 400° until cheese is bubbly and golden brown, 10-15 minutes.
1 slice: 191 cal., 8g fat (2g sat. fat), 24mg chol., 505mg sod., 18g carb. (3g sugars, 1g fiber), 12g pro. **Diabetic exchanges:** 1½ lean meat, 1 starch, 1 vegetable.

SMOKED GOUDA & BACON POTATOES

Creme fraiche gives these hearty, special bites a really rich flavor.
—Cheryl Perry, Hertford, NC

Prep: 50 min. • **Bake:** 10 min.
Makes: 2½ dozen (2 cups sauce)

- 2 whole garlic bulbs
- 1 Tbsp. olive oil
- 15 small red potatoes, halved
- 15 bacon strips
- 2 cups shredded smoked Gouda cheese
- 1 tsp. coarsely ground pepper
- 2 cups creme fraiche or sour cream
- ¼ cup fresh cilantro leaves

1. Remove papery outer skin from garlic (do not peel or separate cloves). Cut tops off of garlic bulbs. Brush with oil. Wrap each bulb in heavy-duty foil. Bake at 425° until softened, 30-35 minutes. Cool.

2. Meanwhile, place potatoes in a large saucepan; cover with water. Bring to a boil. Reduce heat; cover and simmer just until tender, 8-10 minutes. Cut bacon strips in half widthwise. In a large skillet, cook bacon over medium heat until partially cooked but not crisp. Remove to paper towels to drain; keep warm.

3. Preheat oven to 375°. Place 1 Tbsp. of cheese on the cut side of a potato half. Wrap with a half-strip of bacon and secure with a toothpick. Place on an ungreased baking sheet. Repeat. Sprinkle appetizers with pepper. Bake until the bacon is crisp, 10-15 minutes.

4. For sauce, squeeze softened garlic into a food processor. Add creme fraiche and cilantro; cover and process until blended. Serve with potatoes.

1 potato: 161 cal., 13g fat (7g sat. fat), 30mg chol., 169mg sod., 5g carb. (0 sugars, 0 fiber), 4g pro.

CHOCOLATE CHIP CHEESE BALL

Your guests are in for a sweet surprise when they try this unusual cheese ball. It tastes just like cookie dough! Rolled in chopped pecans, the chip-studded spread is just as wonderful on regular or chocolate graham crackers.
—Kelly Glascock, Syracuse, MO

Prep: 15 min. + chilling
Makes: 16 servings (2 Tbsp. each)

1 pkg. (8 oz.) cream cheese, softened
½ cup butter, softened
¼ tsp. vanilla extract
¾ cup confectioners' sugar
2 Tbsp. brown sugar
¾ cup miniature semisweet chocolate chips
¾ cup finely chopped pecans
Graham crackers

1. Beat the cream cheese, butter and vanilla until smooth; beat in both sugars just until blended. Stir in the miniature chocolate chips. Refrigerate mixture, covered, until it is firm enough to shape, about 2 hours.

2. Place mixture on a large sheet of plastic wrap; shape into a ball. Wrap; refrigerate ball at least 1 hour.

3. To serve, roll cheese ball in pecans. Serve with graham crackers.

2 Tbsp. cheese: 202 cal., 17g fat (8g sat. fat), 31mg chol., 99mg sod., 14g carb. (12g sugars, 1g fiber), 2g pro.

CRAB CRESCENTS

Good and quick are two words that describe this appetizer. The little bites also are delicious and decadent.
—Stephanie Howard, Oakland, CA

Takes: 25 min. • **Makes:** 16 appetizers

- 1 tube (8 oz.) refrigerated crescent rolls
- 3 Tbsp. prepared pesto
- ½ cup fresh crabmeat

1. Unroll the crescent dough; separate into 8 triangles. Cut each triangle in half lengthwise, forming 2 triangles. Spread ½ tsp. pesto over each triangle; place 1 rounded tsp. of crab along the wide end of each triangle.

2. Roll up triangles from the wide ends; place point side down 1 in. apart on an ungreased baking sheet.

3. Bake at 375° until golden brown, about 10-12 minutes. Serve warm.

1 serving: 74 cal., 4g fat (1g sat. fat), 5mg chol., 144mg sod., 6g carb. (1g sugars, 0 fiber), 2g pro.

★ ★ ★ ★ ★ **READER REVIEW**

"Made this for New Year's Eve. Used tiny shrimp instead of crab, and the results were outstanding."

BEEMA TASTEOFHOME.COM

BAKED ONION DIP

Some people like this cheesy dip so much that they can't tear themselves away from the appetizer table to eat their dinner.

—Mona Zignego, Hartford, WI

Prep: 5 min. • **Bake:** 40 min.
Makes: 16 servings (2 cups)

- 1 cup mayonnaise
- 1 cup chopped sweet onion
- 1 Tbsp. grated Parmesan cheese
- ¼ tsp. garlic salt
- 1 cup shredded Swiss cheese
  Minced fresh parsley, optional
  Assorted crackers

1. In a large bowl, combine mayonnaise, onion, Parmesan cheese and garlic salt; stir in Swiss cheese. Spoon into a 1-qt. baking dish.

2. Bake, uncovered, at 325° until golden brown, about 40 minutes. If desired, sprinkle with parsley. Serve with crackers.

2 Tbsp. dip: 131 cal., 13g fat (3g sat. fat), 11mg chol., 127mg sod., 1g carb. (1g sugars, 0 fiber), 2g pro.

golden brown, 12-15 minutes. Remove from pan to a wire rack.

4. Meanwhile, in a microwave, warm sauce ingredients, stirring to combine. Serve with the empanadas.

Freeze option: Cover and freeze unbaked empanadas on waxed paper-lined baking sheets until firm. Transfer to a freezer container; return to freezer. To use, bake empanadas as directed, increasing time as necessary. Prepare sauce as directed.

Note: This recipe was tested with McCormick Gourmet Moroccan Seasoning (ras el hanout).

1 empanada with about 2 tsp. sauce: 215 cal., 11g fat (5g sat. fat), 30mg chol., 256mg sod., 25g carb. (8g sugars, 0 fiber), 5g pro.

EASY BUFFALO CHICKEN DIP

Everyone will simply devour this savory and delicious dip. The spicy kick makes it perfect football-watching food, and the recipe always brings raves.
—Janice Foltz, Hershey, PA

Takes: 30 min. • **Makes:** 4 cups

- 1 pkg. (8 oz.) reduced-fat cream cheese
- 1 cup reduced-fat sour cream
- ½ cup Louisiana-style hot sauce
- 3 cups shredded cooked chicken breast
  Assorted crackers

1. Preheat oven to 350°. In a large bowl, beat cream cheese, sour cream and hot sauce until smooth; stir in chicken.

2. Transfer to an 8-in. square baking dish coated with cooking spray. Cover and bake until heated through, 18-22 minutes. Serve warm with crackers.

3 Tbsp. dip: 77 cal., 4g fat (2g sat. fat), 28mg chol., 71mg sod., 1g carb. (1g sugars, 0 fiber), 8g pro.

MAKE AHEAD

MOROCCAN EMPANADAS

My family really goes for Moroccan flavors, so I make empanada pastries using apricot preserves and beef. A spicy dipping sauce adds to the appeal of these flaky hand pies.
—Arlene Erlbach, Morton Grove, IL

Prep: 30 min. • **Bake:** 15 min.
Makes: 20 servings

- ¾ lb. ground beef
- 1 medium onion, chopped
- 3 oz. cream cheese, softened
- ⅓ cup apricot preserves
- ¼ cup finely chopped carrot
- ¾ tsp. Moroccan seasoning (ras el hanout) or ½ tsp. ground cumin plus ¼ tsp. ground coriander and dash cayenne pepper
- ¼ tsp. salt
- 3 sheets refrigerated pie crust
- 1 large egg yolk, beaten
- 1 Tbsp. sesame seeds

SAUCE
- ½ cup apricot preserves
- ½ cup chili sauce

1. Preheat oven to 425°. In a large skillet, cook beef and onion over medium heat until beef is no longer pink, breaking up beef into crumbles, 5-7 minutes; drain. Stir in cream cheese, preserves, carrot and seasonings. Cool slightly.

2. On a floured surface, unroll pie crust. Cut 40 circles with a floured 3-in. cookie cutter, rerolling crusts as necessary. Place half of the circles 2 in. apart on parchment-lined baking sheets. Top each circle with 1 rounded Tbsp. beef mixture. Top with remaining crusts; press with a fork to seal.

3. Brush tops with egg yolk; sprinkle with sesame seeds. Cut slits in tops. Bake until

TEXAS TACO PLATTER

When I'm entertaining, this colorful dish is usually my top menu choice. My friends can't resist the hearty appetizer topped with cheese, lettuce, tomatoes and olives.
—Kathy Young, Weatherford, TX

Prep: 20 min. • **Cook:** 1½ hours
Makes: 20 servings

- 2 lbs. ground beef
- 1 large onion, chopped
- 1 can (14½ oz.) diced tomatoes, undrained
- 1 can (12 oz.) tomato paste
- 1 can (15 oz.) tomato puree
- 2 Tbsp. chili powder
- 1 tsp. ground cumin
- ½ tsp. garlic powder
- 2 tsp. salt
- 2 cans (15 oz. each) Ranch Style beans (pinto beans in seasoned tomato sauce)
- 1 pkg. (10½ oz.) corn chips
- 2 cups hot cooked rice

TOPPINGS
- 2 cups shredded cheddar cheese
- 1 medium onion, chopped
- 1 medium head iceberg lettuce, shredded
- 3 medium tomatoes, chopped
- 1 can (2¼ oz.) sliced ripe olives, drained
- 1 cup picante sauce, optional

1. In a large skillet or Dutch oven, cook beef and onion over medium heat until the meat is no longer pink; drain. Add the next 7 ingredients; cover and simmer for 1½ hours.

2. Add beans and heat through. On a platter, layer the corn chips, rice, meat mixture, cheese, onion, lettuce, tomatoes and olives. If desired, serve platter with picante sauce.

1 serving: 522 cal., 24g fat (9g sat. fat), 56mg chol., 1200mg sod., 47g carb. (9g sugars, 8g fiber), 27g pro.

TEST KITCHEN TIP
Cooking spices in a bit of fat for a minute or two (known as blooming them) helps take off the raw edges and encourages flavors to meld. After draining meat, try cooking it with seasonings for a minute before adding other ingredients.

MAKE AHEAD

ALMOND CHEDDAR APPETIZERS

I always try to have a supply of these appetizers in the freezer. If guests drop in, I just pull some out and reheat them to serve. They work great as a snack, for brunch or along with a lighter lunch.
—Linda Thompson, Southampton, ON

Takes: 25 min. • **Makes:** about 4 dozen

- 1 cup mayonnaise
- 2 tsp. Worcestershire sauce
- 1 cup shredded sharp cheddar cheese
- 1 medium onion, chopped
- ¾ cup slivered almonds, chopped
- 6 bacon strips, cooked and crumbled
- 1 loaf (1 lb.) French bread

1. In a bowl, combine the mayonnaise and Worcestershire sauce; stir in the cheese, onion, almonds and bacon.
2. Cut bread into ½-in. slices; spread with cheese mixture. Cut slices in half; place on a greased baking sheet. Bake at 400° until bubbly, 8-10 minutes.

Freeze option: Place unbaked appetizers in a single layer on a baking sheet; freeze for 1 hour. Remove from pan and store in an airtight container for up to 2 months. When ready to use, place thawed appetizers on a greased baking sheet. Bake at 400° for 10 minutes or until bubbly.

1 piece: 81 cal., 6g fat (1g sat. fat), 4mg chol., 116mg sod., 6g carb. (1g sugars, 0 fiber), 2g pro.

STUFFED BABY RED POTATOES

This recipe just says "party" to me! The ingredients are basic, but the finished appetizer looks like you worked a lot harder than you really did.
—Carole Bess White, Portland, OR

Prep: 45 min. • **Bake:** 15 min.
Makes: 2 dozen

24	small red potatoes (about 2½ lbs.)
¼	cup butter, cubed
½	cup shredded Parmesan cheese, divided
½	cup crumbled cooked bacon, divided
⅔	cup sour cream
1	large egg, beaten
½	tsp. salt
⅛	tsp. pepper
⅛	tsp. paprika

1. Scrub the potatoes; place in a large saucepan and cover with water. Bring to a boil. Reduce heat; cover and cook until tender, 15-20 minutes. Drain.

2. When cool enough to handle, cut a thin slice off the top of each potato. Scoop out pulp, leaving a thin shell. (Cut thin slices from potato bottoms to level if necessary.)

3. In a large bowl, mash the potato tops and pulp with butter. Set aside 2 Tbsp. each of cheese and bacon for garnish; add remaining cheese and bacon to potatoes. Stir in the sour cream, egg, salt and pepper. Spoon mixture into potato shells. Top with the remaining cheese and bacon; sprinkle with paprika.

4. Place in an ungreased 15x10x1-in. baking pan. Bake at 375° until a thermometer reads 160°, 12-18 minutes.

1 stuffed potato: 82 cal., 4g fat (3g sat. fat), 21mg chol., 135mg sod., 8g carb. (1g sugars, 1g fiber), 3g pro. **Diabetic exchanges:** 1 fat, ½ starch.

CILANTRO TOMATO BRUSCHETTA

This is an easy tomato appetizer that all of my family and friends love. Ingredients meld together for a great-tasting hors d'oeuvre, and it goes so well with many different main dishes.
—Lisa Kane, Milwaukee, WI

Takes: 25 min. • **Makes:** about 2 dozen

- 1 loaf (1 lb.) French bread, cut into 1-in. slices
- ½ cup olive oil, divided
- 1 Tbsp. balsamic vinegar
- 3 small tomatoes, seeded and chopped
- ¼ cup finely chopped onion
- ¼ cup fresh cilantro leaves, coarsely chopped
- ¼ tsp. salt
- ¼ tsp. pepper
- ¼ cup shredded part-skim mozzarella cheese

1. Preheat oven to 325°. Place bread on ungreased baking sheets; brush the slices with ¼ cup oil. Bake until golden brown, 10-12 minutes.
2. In a small bowl, whisk together vinegar and remaining oil. Stir in tomatoes, onion, cilantro, salt and pepper.
3. To serve, spoon a scant 1 Tbsp. of the tomato mixture onto each slice of bread. Top with cheese.
1 piece: 98 cal., 5g fat (1g sat. fat), 1mg chol., 147mg sod., 11g carb. (1g sugars, 1g fiber), 2g pro. **Diabetic exchanges:** 1 starch, 1 fat.

DIJON-BACON DIP FOR PRETZELS

With just 4 ingredients that you probably already have in your pantry, this quick appetizer comes together in a snap. If you like the zip of horseradish, start with 1 or 2 teaspoons and add more to your taste.
—Isabelle Rooney, Summerville, SC

Takes: 5 min. • **Makes:** 1½ cups

- 1 cup mayonnaise
- ½ cup Dijon mustard
- ¼ cup bacon bits or crumbled cooked bacon
- 1 to 3 tsp. prepared horseradish Pretzels

In a small bowl, combine the mayonnaise, mustard, bacon and horseradish. Cover and chill until serving. Serve with pretzels.
2 Tbsp. dip: 154 cal., 16g fat (2g sat. fat), 8mg chol., 428mg sod., 1g carb. (0 sugars, 0 fiber), 2g pro.

SPICY CRAB DIP

With cayenne pepper and hot sauce (both optional), this delicious dip doubles up on the heat. Chock-full of crabmeat, this appetizer seems special, yet it only takes minutes to prepare.
—Carol Forcum, Marion, IL

Takes: 15 min. • **Makes:** 4 cups

- ⅓ cup mayonnaise
- 2 Tbsp. dried minced onion
- 2 Tbsp. lemon juice
- 2 Tbsp. white wine or white grape juice
- 1 Tbsp. minced garlic
- ½ tsp. cayenne pepper, optional
- ½ tsp. hot pepper sauce, optional
- 2 pkg. (8 oz. each) cream cheese, cubed
- 1 lb. imitation crabmeat, chopped
  Assorted crackers or fresh vegetables

1. In a food processor, combine the first 8 ingredients. Cover and process until smooth. Transfer to a large microwave-safe bowl. Stir in crab; mix well.

2. Cover and microwave on high until bubbly, 2-3 minutes. Serve warm with crackers or vegetables.

2 Tbsp. dip: 82 cal., 7g fat (3g sat. fat), 18mg chol., 133mg sod., 3g carb. (0 sugars, 0 fiber), 2g pro.

BUFFALO CHICKEN MEATBALLS

I like to make these game-day appetizer meatballs with blue cheese or ranch salad dressing for dipping. If I make them for a meal, I often skip the dressing and serve the meatballs with blue cheese polenta on the side. Yum.
—Amber Massey, Argyle, TX

Prep: 15 min. • **Bake:** 20 min.
Makes: 2 dozen

- ¾ cup panko (Japanese) bread crumbs
- ⅓ cup plus ½ cup Louisiana-style hot sauce, divided
- ¼ cup chopped celery
- 1 large egg white
- 1 lb. lean ground chicken
  Reduced-fat blue cheese or ranch salad dressing, optional

1. Preheat oven to 400°. In a large bowl, combine bread crumbs, ⅓ cup hot sauce, celery and egg white. Add chicken; mix lightly but thoroughly.
2. Shape into twenty-four 1-in. balls. Place on a greased rack in a shallow baking pan. Bake until cooked through, 20-25 minutes.
3. Toss meatballs with the remaining hot sauce. If desired, drizzle meatballs with salad dressing just before serving.

1 meatball: 35 cal., 1g fat (0 sat. fat), 14mg chol., 24mg sod., 2g carb. (0 sugars, 0 fiber), 4g pro.

BACON-STUFFED MUSHROOMS

I first tried these broiled treats at my sister-in-law's house. The juicy mushroom caps and creamy filling were so fabulous that I had to get the recipe. It's hard to believe how simple, fast and easy they are.
—Angela Coffman, KS City, MO

Takes: 25 min. • **Makes:** about 2 dozen

- 1 pkg. (8 oz.) cream cheese, softened
- ¼ tsp. garlic powder
- 8 bacon strips, cooked and crumbled
- 1 Tbsp. chopped green onion
- 1 lb. whole fresh mushrooms, stems removed

1. Preheat broiler. Mix cream cheese and garlic powder. Stir in bacon and chopped green onion.
2. Place mushrooms in an ungreased 15x10x1-in. pan, stem side up. Fill with cream cheese mixture. Broil 4-6 in. from heat until heated through, 4-6 minutes.
1 stuffed mushroom: 51 cal., 4g fat (2g sat. fat), 12mg chol., 79mg sod., 1g carb. (1g sugars, 0 fiber), 2g pro.

SALTED CARAMEL & DARK CHOCOLATE FIGS

Here's a special appetizer that won't last long! Honey, caramel and rich dark chocolate add a sweet touch to this grown-up dipped fruit.
—Taste of Home Test Kitchen

Prep: 30 min. + standing • **Makes:** 1 dozen

- 12 large toothpicks
- 12 dried figs
- 4 oz. fresh goat cheese
- 1 tsp. honey
- 1 tsp. balsamic vinegar
- 1 pkg. (11 oz.) Kraft caramel bits
- 2 Tbsp. water
- ⅓ cup finely chopped almonds
- 1½ cups dark chocolate chips, melted
  Coarse sea salt

1. Line a baking sheet with waxed paper and grease the paper; set aside.
2. Insert a toothpick into each fig. Make a ½-in. cut on the side of each fig. Combine the cheese, honey and vinegar in a small bowl. Transfer to a heavy-duty resealable plastic bag; cut a small hole in a corner of bag. Pipe cheese mixture into figs.
3. Melt caramels and water in a microwave; stir until smooth. Dip each fig into caramel; turn to coat. Place on the prepared pan; let stand until set.
4. Place almonds in a small shallow bowl. Dip bottom third of each fig into melted chocolate; allow excess to drip off. Dip into almonds and sprinkle with salt. Return to pan; let stand until set.
1 fig: 308 cal., 15g fat (9g sat. fat), 6mg chol., 124mg sod., 47g carb. (40g sugars, 3g fiber), 4g pro.

MAKE AHEAD

CRANBERRY BRIE PINWHEELS

People will think you really worked hard when you present these crisp, flaky pinwheels...but they're easy to do. The filling is bursting with savory goodness and a touch of sweetness.
—Marcia Kintz, South Bend, IN

Prep: 20 min. • **Bake:** 15 min.
Makes: 1 dozen

- 1 **sheet frozen puff pastry, thawed**
- 2 **Tbsp. Dijon mustard**
- 2 **Tbsp. honey**
- 1 **cup finely chopped fresh spinach**
- ½ **cup finely chopped Brie cheese**
- ½ **cup finely chopped walnuts**
- ¼ **cup dried cranberries, finely chopped**

1. Unfold pastry. Combine mustard and honey; spread over pastry. Layer with spinach, cheese, walnuts and cranberries. Roll up jelly-roll style; cut into 12 slices. Place cut side down on an ungreased baking sheet.
2. Bake at 400° until golden brown, about 15-20 minutes.
Freeze option: Freeze cooled appetizers in a freezer container. To use, preheat oven to 400° and reheat appetizers on a parchment-lined baking sheet until pinwheels are crisp and heated through.
1 piece: 173 cal., 10g fat (3g sat. fat), 6mg chol., 167mg sod., 18g carb. (5g sugars, 2g fiber), 4g pro.

FRESH PEACH SALSA

Whether scooped up on chips or spooned over tacos, this peachy salsa packs the bright taste of summer into every juicy bite. It's also a tasty garnish for chicken or fish. Make it in the food processor in almost no time at all.
—Shawna Laufer, Fort Meyers, FL

Takes: 15 min.
Makes: 16 servings (¼ cup each)

- 4 **medium peaches, peeled and quartered**
- 2 **large tomatoes, seeded and cut into wedges**
- ⅔ **cup chopped sweet onion**
- ½ **cup fresh cilantro leaves**
- 2 **garlic cloves, peeled and sliced**
- 2 **cans (4 oz. each) chopped green chiles**
- 4 **tsp. cider vinegar**
- 1 **tsp. lime juice**
- ¼ **tsp. pepper**
  Baked tortilla chip scoops

1. Place the first 5 ingredients in a food processor; pulse until peaches are coarsely chopped. Add chiles, vinegar, lime juice and pepper; pulse just until blended.
2. Remove to a bowl; refrigerate, covered, until serving. Serve with chips.
¼ cup: 25 cal., 0 fat (0 sat. fat), 0 chol., 58mg sod., 6g carb. (4g sugars, 1g fiber), 1g pro.
Diabetic exchanges: ½ starch.

SHRIMP SPREAD

This tasty appetizer is always a crowd-pleaser. People will never know that you used lower-fat ingredients.
—Norene Wright, Manilla, IN

Takes: 15 min.
Makes: 20 servings (3¾ cups)

- 1 pkg. (8 oz.) reduced-fat cream cheese
- ½ cup reduced-fat sour cream
- ¼ cup reduced-fat mayonnaise
- 1 cup seafood cocktail sauce
- 2 cups shredded part-skim mozzarella cheese
- 1 can (6 oz.) small shrimp, rinsed and drained
- 3 green onions, sliced
- 1 medium tomato, finely chopped
  Sliced Italian bread or assorted crackers

1. In a small bowl, beat the cream cheese, sour cream and mayonnaise until smooth. Spread onto a 12-in. round serving plate; top with cocktail sauce. Sprinkle with cheese, shrimp, onions and tomato.

2. Chill until serving. Serve with bread or crackers.

3 Tbsp. spread: 93 cal., 6g fat (3g sat. fat), 35mg chol., 312mg sod., 4g carb. (3g sugars, 0 fiber), 6g pro.

Rainbow Quiche
page 61

Breakfast For a Bunch

Whether you prefer sweet French toast in the morning or you're a big meat-and-potatoes breakfast fan, you'll find family-pleasing, crowd-sized brunch dishes here.

NO-TURN OMELET

It's a snap to put together this colorful casserole. I like to make it a day ahead, then refrigerate and bake the next morning. It's like a strata—except it uses crackers rather than traditional bread cubes.
—Helen Clem, Creston, IA

Prep: 10 min. • **Bake:** 45 min. + standing
Makes: 10 servings

- 8 large eggs, lightly beaten
- 2 cups cooked crumbled sausage or cubed fully cooked ham
- 2 cups cubed process cheese (Velveeta)
- 2 cups milk
- 1 cup crushed saltines (about 24 crackers)
- ¼ cup chopped onion
- ¼ cup chopped green pepper
- ¼ cup chopped sweet red pepper
- ½ to 1 tsp. salt

1. Combine all ingredients. Pour into a greased shallow 3-qt. baking dish.
2. Bake, uncovered, at 350° until a knife inserted in center comes out clean, for 45 minutes. Let omelet stand 5 minutes before serving.
1 cup: 272 cal., 18g fat (8g sat. fat), 213mg chol., 767mg sod., 10g carb. (5g sugars, 0 fiber), 18g pro.

MAKE AHEAD

BLUEBERRY-MASCARPONE FRENCH TOAST

When I want something special to serve my guests for a brunch, this recipe never fails. It's wonderful during the spring and early summer when the blueberries shine.
—Patricia Quinn, Omaha, NE

Prep: 15 min. + chilling
Bake: 1 hour
Makes: 10 servings

- 4 cups cubed French bread (about eight ½-in. slices)
- 2 cups fresh or frozen blueberries
- 2 cartons (8 oz. each) mascarpone cheese
- ½ cup confectioners' sugar
- 10 slices French bread (1 in. thick)
- 8 large eggs
- 2 cups half-and-half cream
- 1 cup whole milk
- ⅓ cup sugar
- 1 tsp. vanilla extract
  Additional confectioners' sugar
- 1 cup sliced almonds, toasted
  Additional fresh blueberries, optional

1. In a greased 13x9-in. baking dish, layer bread cubes and blueberries. In a small bowl, beat mascarpone cheese and confectioners' sugar until smooth; drop by tablespoonfuls over blueberries. Top with bread slices. Whisk eggs, cream, milk, granulated sugar and vanilla; pour over bread. Refrigerate, covered, overnight.
2. Preheat oven to 350°. Remove French toast from refrigerator while oven heats. Bake, covered, 30 minutes. Uncover; bake until puffed and golden and a knife inserted in the center comes out clean, for about 30-40 minutes longer.
3. Let stand 10 minutes before serving. Dust with additional confectioners' sugar; sprinkle with almonds. If desired, serve with additional blueberries.
Note: To toast nuts, bake in a shallow pan in a 350° oven for 5-10 minutes or cook in a skillet over low heat until lightly browned, stirring the nuts occasionally.
1 piece: 575 cal., 37g fat (17g sat. fat), 232mg chol., 368mg sod., 45g carb. (20g sugars, 3g fiber), 17g pro.

PINEAPPLE & CREAM CHEESE BREAD PUDDING

Every time I take this creamy bread pudding to church or school, people ask for the recipe. You can change up the fruit or add maple syrup to make it your own.
—Laura Ellis, Saucier, MS

Prep: 20 min. + chilling • **Bake:** 25 min.
Makes: 12 servings

- 1 **can (20 oz.) unsweetened pineapple chunks, undrained**
- 10 **cups cubed dinner rolls (about 17 rolls)**
- 1 **pkg. (8 oz.) cream cheese, softened**
- 3 **Tbsp. confectioners' sugar**
- 5 **large eggs**
- 1 **can (14 oz.) sweetened condensed milk**
- ½ **cup heavy whipping cream**
- 2 **tsp. vanilla extract**

SAUCE
- 1 **can (14 oz.) sweetened condensed milk**
- ¼ **cup butter, cubed**
- 1½ **tsp. vanilla extract**

1. Drain pineapple, reserving ⅓ cup juice. Place half of the bread cubes in a greased 13x9-in. baking dish. In a small bowl, beat cream cheese and confectioners' sugar until smooth; drop by tablespoonfuls over bread cubes. Top with remaining bread cubes and pineapple.

2. In a large bowl, whisk eggs, milk, cream, vanilla and reserved pineapple juice until blended; pour over pineapple. Refrigerate, covered, several hours or overnight.

3. Preheat oven to 350°. Remove bread pudding from refrigerator while oven heats. Bake pudding, uncovered, until lightly browned, 25-35 minutes.

4. In a small saucepan, heat milk and butter until butter is melted. Remove from heat; stir in vanilla. Just before serving, drizzle over warm bread pudding.

1 serving: 566 cal., 25g fat (14g sat. fat), 165mg chol., 487mg sod., 71g carb. (47g sugars, 2g fiber), 14g pro.

PRETTY PUMPKIN CINNAMON BUNS

I make sticky buns and cinnamon rolls quite often because my husband loves them. One day, I had some fresh pumpkin on hand and decided to try pumpkin cinnamon buns. We liked the results; it's such a natural combination.
—Glenda Joseph, Chambersburg, PA

Prep: 45 min. + rising • **Bake:** 25 min.
Makes: 2 dozen

2 Tbsp. active dry yeast
½ cup warm water (110° to 115°)
4 large eggs
1 cup shortening
1 cup canned pumpkin
1 cup warm whole milk (110° to 115°)
½ cup sugar
½ cup packed brown sugar
⅓ cup instant vanilla pudding mix
⅓ cup instant butterscotch pudding mix
1 tsp. salt
8 to 9 cups all-purpose flour
FILLING
¼ cup butter, melted
1 cup packed brown sugar
2 tsp. ground cinnamon
ICING
3 Tbsp. water
2 Tbsp. butter, softened
1 tsp. ground cinnamon
2 cups confectioners' sugar
1½ tsp. vanilla extract

1. In a large bowl, dissolve yeast in warm water. Add the eggs, shortening, pumpkin, milk, sugars, pudding mixes, salt and 6 cups flour. Beat until smooth. Stir in enough of the remaining flour to form a soft dough (dough will be sticky).

2. Turn onto a floured surface; knead until smooth and elastic, 6-8 minutes. Place in a greased bowl, turning once to grease top. Cover and let rise in a warm place until doubled, about 1 hour.

3. Punch dough down; divide in half. Roll each portion into a 12x8-in. rectangle; brush with butter. Combine brown sugar and cinnamon; sprinkle over dough to within ½ in. of edges.

4. Roll up jelly-roll style, starting with a long side; pinch seams to seal. Cut each into 12 slices. Place cut side down in 2 greased 13x9-in. baking pans. Cover and let rise until doubled, about 30 minutes.

5. Bake at 350° until golden brown, for 22-28 minutes. In a small bowl, combine the water, butter and cinnamon. Add confectioners' sugar and vanilla; beat until smooth. Spread over buns. Serve warm.

1 bun: 399 cal., 13g fat (4g sat. fat), 40mg chol., 188mg sod., 65g carb. (31g sugars, 2g fiber), 6g pro.

★ ★ ★ ★ ★ **READER REVIEW**

"So moist and yummy. They came out perfectly! The pumpkin flavor is not strong, but there's a lot of cinnamon flavor. They are perfect, and I would not alter the recipe in any way."
KENGRANTS TASTEOFHOME.COM

MUSHROOM & SMOKED SALMON TARTS

This recipe came from a "what's-in-the-fridge?" moment, and it's so good. It makes two tarts for brunch or appetizers.
—Jacquelyn Benson, South Berwick, ME

Prep: 30 min. + chilling • **Bake:** 15 min.
Makes: 2 tarts (6 servings each)

- 2 **sheets refrigerated pie crust**
- 1 **Tbsp. olive oil**
- 1 **medium red onion, thinly sliced**
- 1 **Tbsp. butter**
- 4 **cups sliced fresh mushrooms (about 10 oz.)**
- ⅔ **cup smoked salmon or lox**
- ⅓ **cup crumbled feta cheese**
- 8 **large eggs, divided use**
- 4 **tsp. drained capers, divided**
- ½ **tsp. salt, divided**
- ½ **tsp. pepper, divided**
- 2 **tsp. snipped fresh dill, optional, divided**

1. Unroll crusts into two 9-in. fluted tart pans with removable bottoms; trim edges. Chill 30 minutes. Preheat oven to 400°.
2. Line the unpricked crusts with a double thickness of foil. Fill with pie weights, dried beans or uncooked rice. Bake on a lower oven rack until edges are golden brown, 10-15 minutes. Remove foil and weights; bake until the bottom is golden brown, 2-4 minutes longer. Cool on a wire rack. Reduce oven setting to 375°.
3. In a large skillet, heat oil over medium-high heat. Add onion; cook and stir until tender and lightly browned, 5-7 minutes. Remove from pan. Add the butter and mushrooms; cook and stir mixture until the mushrooms are tender, 6-8 minutes. Cool slightly.
4. Place tart pans on separate baking sheets. Divide onion and mushrooms between crusts; top with salmon and cheese. In a bowl, whisk 4 eggs, 2 tsp. capers and ¼ tsp. each salt and pepper; if desired, stir in 1 tsp. dill. Pour over one of the tarts. Repeat for second tart.
5. Bake until a knife inserted in the center comes out clean, 15-20 minutes. Let stand 5 minutes before cutting.
Note: Tarts may also be prepared in two 9-in. springform pans or pie plates; bake as directed.
1 piece: 239 cal., 15g fat (6g sat. fat), 136mg chol., 382mg sod., 18g carb. (2g sugars, 1g fiber), 8g pro.

MAKE AHEAD

REUBEN & RYE STRATA

This make-ahead dish is wonderful for brunch, lunch, supper or as a potluck meal that is so easy to prepare. If you prefer, substitute turkey pastrami for the corned beef.

—Mary-Louise Lever, Rome, GA

Prep: 25 min. + chilling
Bake: 50 min.
Makes: 10 servings

- 10 slices rye bread, cubed (about 6 cups)
- 1¼ lbs. thinly sliced deli corned beef, chopped
- 2 cups shredded Gruyere cheese or Swiss cheese
- 1 cup sauerkraut, rinsed, drained and patted dry
- ¼ cup chopped dill pickles
- 6 large eggs
- 2 cups 2% milk
- ⅔ cup Thousand Island salad dressing
  Dash garlic powder
- ¼ cup shredded Parmesan cheese
  Chopped fresh parsley

1. Place bread cubes in a greased 13x9-in. baking dish. Top with the corned beef, Gruyere, sauerkraut and pickles. In a large bowl, whisk eggs, milk, dressing and garlic powder. Pour over bread. Refrigerate, covered, overnight.

2. Preheat oven to 350°. Remove strata from refrigerator while oven heats. Bake, uncovered, 45 minutes. Sprinkle with Parmesan. Bake until a knife inserted in the center comes out clean, 5-10 minutes longer. Let stand 10-15 minutes before cutting. Sprinkle with parsley.

1 piece: 382 cal., 22g fat (9g sat. fat), 175mg chol., 1377mg sod., 21g carb. (6g sugars, 2g fiber), 25g pro.

BANANA OAT BREAKFAST COOKIES

I used to buy breakfast cookies from the supermarket, but since I found this recipe I've enjoyed making my cookies more than buying them.
—Linda Burciaga, *tasteofhome.com*

Prep: 20 min. • **Bake:** 15 min./batch
Makes: 1 dozen

1	cup mashed ripe bananas (about 2 medium)
½	cup chunky peanut butter
½	cup honey
1	tsp. vanilla extract
1	cup old-fashioned oats
½	cup whole wheat flour
¼	cup nonfat dry milk powder
2	tsp. ground cinnamon
½	tsp. salt
¼	tsp. baking soda
1	cup dried cranberries or raisins

1. Preheat oven to 350°. Beat banana, peanut butter, honey and vanilla until blended. In another bowl, combine next six ingredients; gradually beat into wet mixture. Stir in dried cranberries.

2. Drop dough by ¼ cupfuls 3 in. apart onto greased baking sheets; flatten to ½-in. thickness.

3. Bake until golden brown, 14-16 minutes. Cool on pans 5 minutes. Remove to wire racks to finish cooling. Serve warm or at room temperature. To reheat, microwave each cookie on high just until warmed, 15-20 seconds.

1 cookie: 212 cal., 6g fat (1g sat. fat), 0 chol., 186mg sod., 38g carb. (25g sugars, 4g fiber), 5g pro.

CRAN-APPLE MUFFINS

I like to pile a fresh batch of these muffins on a plate when friends drop in for coffee. Even my grandkids enjoy the cranberry and apple flavor combination.
—Millie Westland, Hayward, MN

Prep: 20 min. • **Bake:** 20 min.
Makes: 1 dozen

- ½ cup whole-berry cranberry sauce
- ½ tsp. grated orange zest
- 1½ cups all-purpose flour
- ½ cup sugar
- 1 tsp. ground cinnamon
- ½ tsp. baking soda
- ¼ tsp. baking powder
- ¼ tsp. salt
- 1 large egg, room temperature
- ⅓ cup 2% milk
- ⅓ cup canola oil
- 1 cup shredded peeled tart apple
- ½ cup confectioners' sugar
- 1 Tbsp. orange juice

1. In a bowl, combine cranberry sauce and orange zest; set aside.
2. In a large bowl, combine the flour, sugar, cinnamon, baking soda, baking powder and salt. Beat the egg, milk and oil; stir into dry ingredients just until moistened. Fold in the apple.
3. Fill greased or paper-lined muffin cups half full. Make a well in the center of each muffin; fill with about 2 tsp. of reserved cranberry mixture.
4. Bake at 375° until a toothpick inserted in muffin comes out clean, 18-20 minutes. Cool for 5 minutes before removing from pan to a wire rack. Combine confectioners' sugar and orange juice; drizzle glaze over warm muffins.
1 muffin: 195 cal., 7g fat (1g sat. fat), 19mg chol., 122mg sod., 32g carb. (17g sugars, 1g fiber), 2g pro.

ASPARAGUS HAM STRATA

You can easily prepare this the night before for a luncheon or brunch. I serve it year-round, for large groups like my card club or garden club, at picnics and at other occasions. When I do, just about always someone requests the recipe! I've enjoyed cooking since I was a girl. My mother was an excellent cook, and she passed along many of the Pennsylvania Dutch recipes that are popular in this part or our state.
—Ethel Pressel, New Oxford, PA

Prep: 20 min. + chilling
Bake: 55 min.
Makes: 8 servings

- 12 slices white bread
- 12 oz. process cheese (Velveeta), diced
- 1½ lbs. fresh asparagus, trimmed
- 2 cups diced cooked ham
- 6 large eggs
- 3 cups milk
- 2 Tbsp. finely chopped onion
- ½ tsp. salt
- ¼ tsp. ground mustard

1. Using a doughnut cutter, cut 12 circles and holes from bread; set aside. Tear the remaining bread in pieces and place in a greased 13x9-in. baking dish.
2. Layer with cheese, asparagus and ham; arrange bread circles and holes on top. Lightly beat eggs with milk. Add onion, salt and mustard; mix well. Pour egg mixture over bread circles and holes. Cover and refrigerate at least 6 hours or overnight.
3. Bake, uncovered, at 325° until the top is light golden brown, for 55 minutes. Let stand for 10 minutes before serving.
1 piece: 420 cal., 21g fat (10g sat. fat), 211mg chol., 1427mg sod., 32g carb. (10g sugars, 2g fiber), 27g pro.

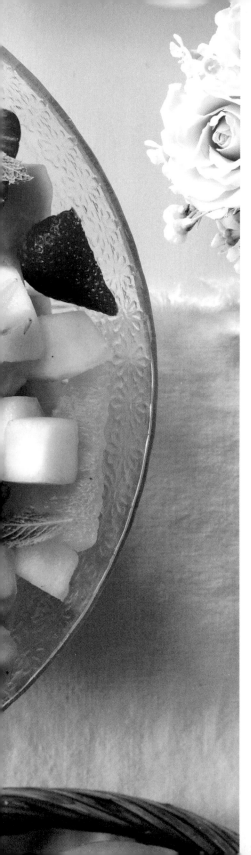

MAKE AHEAD

FRESH FRUIT BOWL

The glorious colors used here make this a great summer salad. Slightly sweet and chilled, it's lovely with almost any entree.
—Marion Kirst, Troy, MI

....

Prep: 15 min. + chilling
Makes: 16 servings

- 8 to 10 cups fresh melon cubes
- 1 to 2 Tbsp. white corn syrup
- 1 pint fresh strawberries, halved
- 2 cups fresh pineapple chunks
- 2 oranges, sectioned
  Fresh mint leaves, optional

In a large bowl, combine melon cubes and corn syrup. Cover and refrigerate overnight. Just before serving, stir in remaining fruit. Garnish with fresh mint leaves if desired.

¾ cup: 56 cal., 0 fat (0 sat. fat), 0 chol., 14mg sod., 14g carb. (11g sugars, 2g fiber), 1g pro.
Diabetic exchanges: 1 fruit.

★ ★ ★ ★ ★ **READER REVIEW**

"Wonderfully fresh and tasty addition to any meal."

GRANNYGOURMET TASTEOFHOME.COM

.CARAMEL NUT BREAKFAST CAKE

I first tasted this incredible coffee cake when a kind neighbor brought it by. It was so good, my brother-in-law tried hiding it from us so he wouldn't have to share.
—Arlene Isaac, Crooked Creek, AB

....

Prep: 25 min. • **Bake:** 25 min.
Makes: 18 servings

- 1 pkg. white cake mix (regular size)
- 2 large eggs, room temperature
- ⅔ cup water
- ½ cup all-purpose flour
- ¼ cup canola oil

TOPPING
- 1 cup packed brown sugar
- ¾ cup chopped pecans
- ¼ cup butter, melted

DRIZZLE
- 1 cup confectioners' sugar
- 1 Tbsp. light corn syrup
- 1 Tbsp. water

1. Preheat oven to 350°. Reserve 1 cup cake mix for topping. In a large bowl, combine eggs, water, flour, oil and remaining cake mix; beat on low speed 30 seconds. Beat on medium 2 minutes. Transfer to a greased 13x9-in. baking pan.
2. In a small bowl, combine brown sugar, pecans and reserved cake mix; stir in butter until crumbly. Sprinkle over batter. Bake until a toothpick inserted in center comes out clean, 25-30 minutes. In a small bowl, mix confectioners' sugar, corn syrup and water until smooth; drizzle over warm cake. Serve warm.

1 piece: 281 cal., 12g fat (3g sat. fat), 27mg chol., 208mg sod., 43g carb. (30g sugars, 1g fiber), 3g pro.

4. Spoon egg mixture, chorizo and cheese across wide end of triangles. Fold pointed end of triangles over filling, tucking points under to form a ring (filling will be visible). Bake until golden brown ,15-20 minutes. Serve with salsa.

1 serving: 477 cal., 32g fat (11g sat. fat), 255mg chol., 1149mg sod., 25g carb. (5g sugars, 0 fiber), 20g pro.

CRAN-APPLE BAKED OATMEAL

Enjoy the fall flavors of cranberries, apples and walnuts in this comforting baked oatmeal. I also serve it at my church's breakfast potlucks.
—Sharon Gerst, North Liberty, IA

Prep: 15 min. • **Bake:** 30 min.
Makes: 8 servings

- 4 cups old-fashioned oats
- 2 tsp. baking powder
- 1 tsp. salt
- 1 tsp. ground cinnamon
- 3 large eggs
- 2 cups 2% milk
- ⅔ cup sugar
- ⅔ cup canola oil
- 1 medium apple, chopped
- 1 cup fresh cranberries, chopped
- 1 cup chopped walnuts, toasted
- ½ cup packed brown sugar

1. Preheat oven to 350°. In a large bowl, mix the oats, baking powder, salt and cinnamon. Whisk eggs, milk, sugar and oil until blended; stir into oat mixture. Stir in apple, cranberries and walnuts.
2. Transfer to a greased 13x9-in. baking dish. Sprinkle with brown sugar. Bake, uncovered, until set and edges are lightly browned, 30-35 minutes.

1 serving: 401 cal., 23g fat (3g sat. fat), 50mg chol., 317mg sod., 44g carb. (25g sugars, 4g fiber), 8g pro.

CHORIZO & EGG BREAKFAST RING

Friends always flip for this loaded crescent ring when I bring it to brunch. It's the happy result of my love for both Mexican dishes and quick-fix recipes.
—Frances Blackwelder, Grand Junction, CO

Prep: 25 min. • **Bake:** 15 min.
Makes: 8 servings

- 2 tubes (8 oz. each) refrigerated crescent rolls
- ½ lb. uncooked chorizo, casings removed, or bulk spicy pork sausage
- 8 large eggs
- ¼ tsp. salt
- ¼ tsp. pepper
- 1 Tbsp. butter
- 1 cup shredded pepper Jack cheese
- 1 cup salsa

1. Preheat oven to 375°. Unroll crescent dough and separate into triangles. On an ungreased 12-in. pizza pan, arrange triangles in a ring with points toward the outside and wide ends overlapping. Press overlapping dough to seal.
2. In a large skillet, cook the chorizo over medium heat 6-8 minutes or until cooked through, breaking into crumbles. Remove with a slotted spoon; drain on paper towels. Discard drippings and wipe the skillet clean.
3. Whisk eggs, salt and pepper until blended. In the same skillet, heat butter over medium heat. Pour in egg mixture; cook and stir until eggs are thickened and no liquid egg remains.

CHEESY POTATO EGG BAKE

I whipped up this cozy egg bake with potato crowns for an easy "brinner," as I like to call it. Use add-ins you like—sweet peppers, onions, broccoli, carrots. The possibilities are endless.
—Amy Lents, Grand Forks, ND

Prep: 20 min. • **Bake:** 45 min.
Makes: 12 servings

1 lb. bulk lean turkey breakfast sausage
1¾ cups sliced baby portobello mushrooms, chopped
4 cups fresh spinach, coarsely chopped
6 large eggs
1 cup 2% milk
Dash seasoned salt
2 cups shredded cheddar cheese
6 cups frozen potato crowns

1. Preheat oven to 375°. In a large skillet, cook sausage over medium heat until no longer pink, 5-7 minutes, breaking into crumbles. Add mushrooms and spinach; cook until mushrooms are tender and spinach is wilted, 2-4 minutes longer.

2. Spoon sausage mixture into a greased 13x9-in. baking dish. In a large bowl, whisk eggs, milk and seasoned salt until blended; pour over sausage mixture. Layer with cheese and potato crowns.

3. Bake, uncovered, until set and top is crisp, 45-50 minutes.

1 serving: 315 cal., 20g fat (7g sat. fat), 154mg chol., 910mg sod., 16g carb. (2g sugars, 2g fiber), 20g pro.

MIXED BERRY FRENCH TOAST BAKE

I love this recipe! Perfect for fuss-free holiday breakfasts or for company, it's scrumptious and so easy to put together the night before.

—Amy Berry, Poland, ME

....

Prep: 20 min. + chilling • **Bake:** 45 min.
Makes: 8 servings

6	large eggs
1¾	cups fat-free milk
1	tsp. sugar
1	tsp. ground cinnamon
1	tsp. vanilla extract
¼	tsp. salt
1	loaf (1 lb.) French bread, cubed
1	pkg. (12 oz.) frozen unsweetened mixed berries
2	Tbsp. cold butter
⅓	cup packed brown sugar

1. Whisk together first six ingredients. Place bread cubes in a 13x9-in. or 3-qt. baking dish coated with cooking spray. Pour egg mixture over top. Refrigerate, covered, 8 hours or overnight.

2. Preheat oven to 350°. Remove berries from freezer and French toast from the refrigerator; let stand while oven heats. Bake, covered, 30 minutes.

3. In a small bowl, cut butter into brown sugar until crumbly. Top French toast with berries; sprinkle with the brown sugar mixture. Bake, uncovered, until a knife inserted in the center comes out clean, 15-20 minutes.

1 serving: 310 cal., 8g fat (3g sat. fat), 148mg chol., 517mg sod., 46g carb. (17g sugars, 3g fiber), 13g pro.

MOUNTAIN HAM SUPREME

Little kids think it's neat how the ham sandwiches make "mountains" in the pan. The mountains are very tasty, too.
—Keri Cotton, Lakeville, MN

Prep: 20 min. + chilling • **Bake:** 45 min.
Makes: 12 servings

12	slices bread
1	lb. ground fully cooked ham
2	cups shredded cheddar cheese
½	cup mayonnaise
1	tsp. ground mustard
6	large eggs
2¼	cups 2% milk
¼	tsp. salt
¼	tsp. pepper

1. Toast the bread. Mix ham, cheese, mayonnaise and ground mustard. Spread the ham mixture over 6 slices of bread; top with the remaining bread slices to make 6 sandwiches. Cut each sandwich into 2 triangles.

2. In a greased 13x9-in. baking dish, arrange sandwich triangles cut side down, with points facing up, pressing together as needed to fit in 2 rows. Whisk eggs, milk, salt and pepper until well blended. Pour over the sandwich triangles. Refrigerate, covered, overnight.

3. Remove casserole from refrigerator 30 minutes before baking. Preheat oven to 300°. Bake, uncovered, until a knife inserted in center comes out clean, 45-50 minutes.

1 serving: 366 cal., 24g fat (9g sat. fat), 137mg chol., 903mg sod., 17g carb. (4g sugars, 1g fiber), 19g pro.

BERRIES IN YOGURT CREAM

Yogurt, cream, brown sugar and fresh fruit are all you need to wake up your taste buds on mornings you'd rather sleep in. Have guests assemble their own parfaits to save time.
—Michelle Stillman, Lancaster, PA

....

Prep: 10 min. + chilling
Makes: 10 servings

1½ cups (12 oz.) plain yogurt
1¼ cups heavy whipping cream
½ cup packed brown sugar
5 cups assorted fresh berries

1. Place yogurt in a large bowl; whisk in cream. Sprinkle with brown sugar but do not stir. Cover and refrigerate for at least 3 hours.

2. Just before serving, stir cream mixture. Divide among 10 dessert dishes. Top with the berries.

½ cup berries with ¼ cup cream mixture: 208 cal., 12g fat (8g sat. fat), 46mg chol., 33mg sod., 24g carb. (20g sugars, 2g fiber), 2g pro.

MAKE AHEAD
HAM & BRIE STRATA

There's nothing quite like comfy strata made with Brie, ham and mushrooms. Put it together and bake it now, or hold it overnight to pop into the oven tomorrow.
—Elisabeth Larsen, Pleasant Grove, UT

....

Prep: 20 min. • **Bake:** 35 min.
Makes: 12 servings

1 Tbsp. canola oil
8 oz. sliced fresh mushrooms
½ cup chopped onion
2 cups fresh baby spinach
2 garlic cloves, minced
12 cups (about 8 oz.) cubed day-old French bread
2 cups cubed deli ham
8 oz. Brie cheese, rind removed, chopped
8 large eggs
3 cups 2% milk
2 Tbsp. Dijon mustard
⅛ tsp. salt
⅛ tsp. pepper

1. Preheat oven to 375°. In a large skillet, heat oil over medium-high heat. Add mushrooms and onion; cook and stir 5-7 minutes or until the mushrooms are golden brown and onion is tender. Add spinach and garlic; cook 1-2 minutes longer or until spinach is wilted.
2. Transfer the mushroom mixture to a greased 13x9-in. baking dish. Add bread, ham and cheese.
3. In a large bowl, whisk the eggs, milk, mustard, salt and pepper. Pour over bread. Bake, uncovered, until a knife inserted in center comes out clean, 35-40 minutes. Let stand 5-10 minutes before serving.
To Make Ahead: Refrigerate unbaked strata, covered, several hours or overnight. To use, preheat oven to 375°. Remove strata from refrigerator while oven heats. Bake as directed.
1 serving: 243 cal., 12g fat (6g sat. fat), 162mg chol., 680mg sod., 15g carb. (5g sugars, 1g fiber), 18g pro.

TEST KITCHEN TIP
Not a fan of Brie? Swiss cheese would make a tasty substitute in this dish.

MEDITERRANEAN VEGGIE BRUNCH PUFF

I make breakfast casseroles with whatever I have, and that's often spinach, sweet red pepper and cheddar. I like to give this puff a burst of flavor with a spoonful of Greek vinaigrette topping.
—Angela Robinson, Findlay, OH

Prep: 25 min. + chilling • **Bake:** 25 min.
Makes: 8 servings

- 6 **large eggs**
- 2 **large egg whites**
- 1 **cup whole milk**
- 1 **garlic cloves, minced**
- ½ **tsp. salt**
- ¼ **tsp. pepper**
- 5 **cups cubed croissants (about 6 oz.)**
- ¾ **cup chopped roasted sweet red peppers, divided**
- ½ **cup finely chopped sweet onion**
- 1 **pkg. (10 oz.) frozen chopped spinach, thawed and squeezed dry**
- 1 **cup shredded cheddar cheese**
- ½ **cup crumbled feta cheese**
- 3 **Tbsp. Greek vinaigrette**

1. In a bowl, whisk the first 6 ingredients until blended. Place croissant pieces in a single layer in a greased 11x7-in. baking dish; top with ½ cup red pepper, onion and spinach. Pour the egg mixture over top. Sprinkle with cheddar and feta cheeses. Refrigerate, covered, overnight.

2. Finely chop the remaining red pepper; place in a jar with a tight-fitting lid. Add the vinaigrette; shake jar to combine and refrigerate until serving.

3. Preheat oven to 350°. Remove casserole from refrigerator while oven heats. Bake, uncovered, until a knife inserted in the center comes out clean, 25-30 minutes. Let stand 5-10 minutes before cutting. Serve with vinaigrette mixture.

Freeze option: Cover and freeze unbaked casserole and remaining chopped sweet red pepper separately. To use, partially thaw both in refrigerator overnight. Remove from refrigerator 30 minutes before baking. Preheat oven to 350°. Bake casserole as directed, increasing time as necessary to heat through and for a thermometer inserted in center to read 165°. Combine vinaigrette and chopped sweet red pepper; serve with casserole.

1 serving with 1½ tsp. vinaigrette: 281 cal., 17g fat (8g sat. fat), 175mg chol., 656mg sod., 16g carb. (6g sugars, 2g fiber), 14g pro.

2. In a large bowl, whisk eggs, milk, melted butter, vanilla and cinnamon until blended; pour over waffles. Refrigerate casserole, covered, overnight.

3. Preheat oven to 350°. Remove casserole from refrigerator while oven heats. In a small bowl, mix brown sugar, flour and cinnamon; cut in the butter until crumbly. Stir in pecans; sprinkle over top. Bake, uncovered, until set and top is golden, 40-45 minutes. Let stand for 10 minutes before serving.

1 serving: 446 cal., 27g fat (12g sat. fat), 179mg chol., 490mg sod., 41g carb. (20g sugars, 2g fiber), 10g pro.

CABIN HASH

My family named this dish that I served them when we vacationed at our cabin on the Mississippi River. Now it's become such a favorite that I often make it when we're home.

—Lyman Hein, Rochester, MN

Takes: 30 min. • **Makes:** 10 servings

- 12 medium potatoes (about 4 lbs.), peeled, cooked and cubed
- 3 cups cubed fully cooked ham (about 1 lb.)
- ½ cup chopped onion
- ½ cup butter, cubed
- 3 cups frozen chopped broccoli, thawed
  Salt and pepper to taste
  Sour cream, optional

In a large skillet, cook the potatoes, ham and onion in butter, stirring frequently, until potatoes are lightly browned. Add broccoli; heat through. Season with salt and pepper. Serve hash with sour cream if desired.

1 cup: 308 cal., 13g fat (7g sat. fat), 47mg chol., 641mg sod., 38g carb. (4g sugars, 3g fiber), 12g pro.

MAKE AHEAD

STREUSEL-TOPPED BLUEBERRY WAFFLE CASSEROLE

I had company coming and needed a new breakfast casserole, so I made up this nutty idea using waffles. My neighbors and husband all approved of it.

—Joan Hallford, North Richland Hills, TX

Prep: 30 min. + chilling
Bake: 40 min.
Makes: 12 servings

- 1 pkg. (8 oz.) cream cheese, softened
- ¼ cup packed brown sugar
- 15 frozen waffles, thawed and cut into 1-in. pieces
- 1½ cups fresh or frozen blueberries
- 8 large eggs
- 1½ cups 2% milk
- 6 Tbsp. butter, melted
- 1 tsp. vanilla extract
- ½ tsp. ground cinnamon

STREUSEL
- ½ cup packed brown sugar
- ⅓ cup all-purpose flour
- 1 tsp. ground cinnamon
- ¼ cup butter, softened
- ½ cup chopped pecans

1. In a small bowl, beat cream cheese and brown sugar until blended. Place half of the waffle pieces in a greased 13x9-in. baking dish. Drop the cream cheese mixture by tablespoonfuls over waffles. Layer with blueberries and remaining waffles.

EGGNOG FRENCH TOAST

This recipe is a favorite of our family not only at Christmas but any time of the year. It makes a hearty breakfast.
—Robert Northrup, Las Cruces, NM

Prep: 10 min. **Cook:** 30 min.
Makes: 8 servings

- 8 large eggs
- 2 cups eggnog
- ¼ cup sugar
- ½ tsp. vanilla or rum extract
- 24 slices English muffin bread
  Confectioners' sugar, optional
  Maple syrup

In a bowl, beat eggs, eggnog, sugar and extract; soak bread for 2 minutes per side. Cook on a greased hot griddle until golden brown on both sides and cooked through. Dust with confectioners' sugar if desired. Serve with syrup.

3 slices: 541 cal., 10g fat (4g sat. fat), 223mg chol., 832mg sod., 87g carb. (18g sugars, 6g fiber), 24g pro.

MAKE AHEAD

RAINBOW QUICHE

With plenty of veggies and a creamy egg-cheese filling, this tasty quiche gets two thumbs up.
—Lilith Fury, Adena, OH

Prep: 30 min. • **Bake:** 40 min. + standing
Makes: 8 servings

- Pastry for single-crust pie (9 in.)
- 2 Tbsp. butter
- 1 small onion, finely chopped
- 1 cup sliced fresh mushrooms
- 1 cup small fresh broccoli florets
- ½ cup finely chopped sweet orange pepper
- ½ cup finely chopped sweet red pepper

- 3 large eggs, lightly beaten
- 1⅓ cups half-and-half cream
- ¾ tsp. salt
- ½ tsp. pepper
- 1 cup shredded Mexican cheese blend, divided
- 1 cup fresh baby spinach

1. Preheat oven to 425°. Unroll pastry sheet onto a lightly floured surface, roll to a 12-in. circle. Transfer to a 9-in. deep-dish pie plate; trim and flute edge. Refrigerate while preparing filling.

2. In a skillet, heat butter over medium-high heat; saute onion, mushrooms, broccoli and peppers until mushrooms are lightly browned, 6-8 minutes. Cool slightly.

3. Whisk together eggs, cream and salt and pepper. Sprinkle ½ cup cheese over crust; top with spinach and vegetable mixture. Sprinkle with remaining cheese. Pour in egg mixture.

Freeze option: Bake on a lower oven rack 15 minutes. Reduce oven setting to 350°; bake until a knife inserted in the center comes out clean, 25-30 minutes. (Cover edge loosely with foil if necessary to prevent overbrowning.) Let stand 10 minutes before cutting.

1 piece: 347 cal., 25g fat (15g sat. fat), 140mg chol., 537mg sod., 20g carb. (3g sugars, 1g fiber), 10g pro.

Quick Quiche for 12: Use this recipe to fill 2 frozen deep-dish pie shells. Bake quiches for 40-45 minutes. Each yields 6 servings.

Rich Rainbow Quiche: Substitute heavy whipping cream for the half-and-half cream.

Italian Sausage Quiche: Omit broccoli and butter. Substitute Italian cheese blend for the Mexican cheese blend. In a large skillet, saute 1 pound bulk of Italian sausage, onion, mushrooms and peppers until tender; drain. Add ½ tsp. dried basil, ½ tsp. dried parsley and ⅛ tsp. crushed red pepper to the egg mixture.

SWEET POTATO DUMPLINGS WITH CARAMEL SAUCE

When family stays over after a holiday dinner, we make these sweet potato dumplings, bacon and eggs for breakfast. Then later, we even serve the dumplings for dessert.
—Mary Leverette, Columbia, SC

Prep: 40 min. • **Bake:** 30 min.
Makes: 10 servings

- 2 tubes (12 oz. each) refrigerated buttermilk biscuits
- 1½ cups mashed sweet potatoes
- 1½ tsp. ground cinnamon, divided
- 1 cup sugar
- 1 cup packed brown sugar
- 1 cup water
- ½ cup butter, cubed

1. Preheat oven to 350°. Roll out each biscuit into a 3-in. circle. In a small bowl, mix sweet potatoes and ¾ tsp. cinnamon. Place 1 Tbsp. sweet potato mixture on one side of each circle. Fold dough over filling. Press edges with a fork to seal. Transfer dumplings to a greased 13x9-in. baking pan, overlapping slightly.
2. In a small heavy saucepan, combine sugars, water, butter and remaining cinnamon. Bring to a boil; cook and stir until sugar is dissolved, 2-3 minutes.
3. Pour over dumplings. Bake, uncovered, until golden brown, 30-35 minutes.

2 dumplings: 482 cal., 17g fat (9g sat. fat), 24mg chol., 653mg sod., 81g carb. (48g sugars, 1g fiber), 5g pro.

SAUSAGE-VEGETABLE EGG BAKE

When we were kids, our mom tucked homegrown Swiss chard inside this comfy casserole. Now I grow the chard, make the dish and savor the memories.
—Cathy Banks, Encinitas, CA

Prep: 25 min. • **Bake:** 1 hour
Makes: 8 servings

- 1 pkg. (19½ oz.) Italian turkey sausage links, casings removed
- 1 Tbsp. butter
- ¾ lb. sliced fresh mushrooms
- 3 cups thinly sliced Swiss chard
- ¼ cup white wine
- 3 garlic cloves, minced
- 9 large eggs
- 1¼ cups 2% milk
- ¼ tsp. salt
- ¼ tsp. pepper
- 1 cup shredded part-skim mozzarella cheese
- ¼ cup grated Parmesan or shredded fontina cheese
  Minced fresh parsley

1. Preheat oven to 350°. In a large skillet, cook sausage over medium heat until no longer pink, 5-7 minutes, breaking into crumbles. Using a slotted spoon, transfer sausage to a greased 13x9-in. baking dish, spreading evenly. Remove the drippings from the pan.

2. In same skillet, heat the butter over medium-high heat. Add mushrooms; cook and stir until tender, for 3-5 minutes. Add Swiss chard, wine and garlic; cook and stir until chard is tender and liquid is almost evaporated, 1-2 minutes longer. Add to the baking dish.

3. In a large bowl, whisk eggs, milk, salt and pepper until blended; pour over the vegetable mixture. Sprinkle mozzarella cheese over top.

4. Bake, uncovered, 45 minutes. Sprinkle with Parmesan cheese. Bake until a knife inserted in the center comes out clean, about 10-15 minutes longer. Let stand for 5 minutes before serving. Sprinkle with parsley.

1 serving: 248 cal., 15g fat (6g sat. fat), 253mg chol., 640mg sod., 6g carb. (3g sugars, 1g fiber), 21g pro.

MAKE AHEAD

CRANBERRY HONEY BUTTER

If you are traveling to a friend's or loved one's for the holidays, bring them something that's even better than a bottle of wine—this easy-to-whip-up treat!
—Arisa Cupp, Warren, OR

Takes: 10 min. • **Makes:** 24 servings

- 1   cup butter, softened
- ⅓   cup finely chopped dried cranberries
- ¼   cup honey
- 2   tsp. grated orange zest
- ⅛   tsp. kosher salt

In a small bowl, beat all ingredients until blended. Store in an airtight container in the refrigerator up to 2 weeks or freeze up to 3 months.

1 Tbsp. spread: 75 cal., 8g fat (5g sat. fat), 20mg chol., 71mg sod., 2g carb. (2g sugars, 0 fiber), 0 pro.

TEST KITCHEN TIP

If you replace the honey with maple syrup, this butter pairs perfectly with a stack of fluffy pancakes. For a variation, use dried blueberries and lemon zest instead of cranberries and orange zest.

MAKE AHEAD

HOMEMADE BREAKFAST SAUSAGE PATTIES

Buttermilk is the secret ingredient that keeps these pork patties moist, while a seasoning blend creates a wonderful flavor.
—Harvey Keeney, Mandan, ND

Prep: 30 min. • **Cook:** 10 min./batch
Makes: 20 patties

- ¾   cup buttermilk
- 2¼   tsp. kosher salt
- 1½   tsp. rubbed sage
- 1½   tsp. brown sugar
- 1½   tsp. pepper
- ¾   tsp. dried marjoram
- ¾   tsp. dried savory
- ¾   tsp. cayenne pepper
- ¼   tsp. ground nutmeg
- 2½   lbs. ground pork

1. In a bowl, combine first 9 ingredients. Add pork; mix lightly but thoroughly. Shape into twenty 3-in. patties.

2. In a large skillet coated with cooking spray, cook the patties in batches over medium heat until a thermometer reads 160°, 5-6 minutes on each side. Remove to paper towels to drain.

Freeze option: Wrap each cooked, cooled patty; transfer to an airtight container. May be frozen for up to 3 months. To use, unwrap patties and place on a baking sheet coated with cooking spray. Bake at 350° until heated through, turning once, about 15 minutes on each side.

1 sausage patty: 126 cal., 8g fat (3g sat. fat), 38mg chol., 251mg sod., 1g carb. (1g sugars, 0 fiber), 11g pro.

HAM & CHEESE QUICHE

When I was expecting our daughter, I made and froze these cheesy quiches as well as several other dishes. After her birth, it was nice to have dinner in the freezer when my husband and I were too tired to cook.

—Christena Palmer, Green River, WY

Prep: 20 min. • **Bake:** 35 min.
Makes: 2 quiches (6 servings each)

- 1 pkg. (14.1 oz.) refrigerated pie crust
- 2 cups diced fully cooked ham
- 2 cups shredded sharp cheddar cheese
- 2 tsp. dried minced onion
- 4 large eggs
- 2 cups half-and-half cream
- ½ tsp. salt
- ¼ tsp. pepper

1. Preheat oven to 400°. Unroll pie crust sheets into two 9-in. pie plates; flute edges. Line unpricked pie crusts with a double thickness of heavy-duty foil. Fill with pie weights, dried beans or uncooked rice. Bake crust until light golden brown, about 10-12 minutes. Remove foil and weights; bake until bottom is golden brown, for 3-5 minutes longer. Cool on wire racks.

2. Divide ham, cheese and onion between shells. In a large bowl, whisk eggs, cream, salt and pepper until blended. Pour into shells. Cover edges loosely with foil. Bake until a knife inserted in the center comes out clean, 35-40 minutes. Let stand for 5-10 minutes before cutting.

Note: Let pie weights cool before storing. Beans and rice may be reused for pie weights, but not for cooking.

Freeze option: Cover and freeze unbaked quiche. To use, remove from the freezer 30 minutes before baking (do not thaw). Preheat oven to 350°. Place quiche on a baking sheet; cover edge loosely with foil. Bake as directed, increasing time as necessary for a knife inserted in the center to come out clean.

1 piece: 349 cal., 23g fat (12g sat. fat), 132mg chol., 596mg sod., 20g carb. (3g sugars, 0 fiber), 13g pro.

MAKE AHEAD

SPARKLING ORANGES

We were living in Texas when I found the recipe for this simple yet elegant salad. I was thrilled— we had a surplus of fresh oranges! Since it's prepared ahead, all you do at the last minute is garnish and serve.
—Janie Bush, Weskan, KS

Prep: 35 min. + chilling
Makes: 8 servings

- ½ cup sugar
- ½ cup orange marmalade
- 1 cup white grape juice
- ½ cup lemon-lime soda
- 8 large oranges, peeled and sectioned
- 3 Tbsp. slivered almonds, toasted
- 3 Tbsp. sweetened shredded coconut, toasted

1. In a small saucepan over medium heat, combine sugar and marmalade; cook and stir until sugar is dissolved. Remove from heat. Stir in grape juice and soda. Pour over orange sections; toss to coat. Refrigerate, covered, overnight.

2. Using a slotted spoon, remove oranges to a serving dish. Sprinkle with almonds and coconut.

Note: To toast nuts and coconut, bake in separate shallow pans in a 350° oven for until golden brown, 5-10 minutes, stirring nuts or coconut occasionally.

1 serving: 234 cal., 2g fat (1g sat. fat), 0 chol., 21mg sod., 55g carb. (49g sugars, 5g fiber), 3g pro.

SPICED PUMPKIN FRENCH TOAST CASSEROLE

I make this breakfast dish anytime, but it's especially useful for those very busy holiday mornings—just pop it in the oven.
—Joanne Wessel, Greenwood, IN

Prep: 20 min. + chilling • **Bake:** 65 min.
Makes: 12 servings

- 8 **large eggs**
- 2 **cups whole milk**
- 2 **cups heavy whipping cream**
- 1 **can (15 oz.) solid-pack pumpkin**
- 1½ **cups sugar**
- 2 **tsp. vanilla extract**
- 1½ **tsp. ground cinnamon**
- ½ **tsp. salt**
- ½ **tsp. ground ginger**
- ¼ **tsp. ground nutmeg**
- 14 **cups cubed challah or egg bread (about 28 oz.)**
- ½ **cup raisins**
  Confectioners' sugar and maple syrup, optional

1. In a bowl, whisk the first 10 ingredients until blended. Add bread cubes and raisins; gently stir to combine. Transfer mixture to a greased 13x9-in. baking dish. Chill dish, covered, several hours or overnight.

2. Preheat oven to 350°. Remove casserole from refrigerator while oven heats. Bake, uncovered, until edges of bread are golden brown and a knife inserted in the center comes out clean, 65-75 minutes.

3. Let stand 5-10 minutes before serving. If desired, serve with confectioners' sugar and syrup.

1 serving: 529 cal., 23g fat (12g sat. fat), 207mg chol., 428mg sod., 68g carb. (34g sugars, 3g fiber), 13g pro.

WHOLE WHEAT PANCAKES

To fix a large batch of tender pancakes for my five children, I rely on this quick and wholesome recipe. It calls for whole wheat flour and buttermilk, which make the pancakes filling but also light. Serve them with hot chocolate for a breakfast that's sure to delight little ones.
—Line Walter, Wayne, PA

Takes: 25 min. • **Makes:** 20 pancakes

- 2 **cups whole wheat flour**
- ½ **cup toasted wheat germ**
- 1 **tsp. baking soda**
- ½ **tsp. salt**
- 2 **large eggs, room temperature**
- 3 **cups buttermilk**
- 1 **Tbsp. canola oil**

1. In a large bowl, combine the flour, wheat germ, baking soda and salt. In another bowl, whisk the eggs, buttermilk and oil. Stir into dry ingredients just until blended.
2. Pour batter by ¼ cupfuls onto a hot griddle coated with cooking spray; turn when bubbles form on top. Cook until the second side is golden brown.

Freeze option: Freeze cooled pancakes between layers of waxed paper in an airtight freezer container. To use, place pancakes on an ungreased baking sheet, cover with foil, and reheat in a preheated 375° oven 6-10 minutes. Or place a stack of 3 pancakes on a microwave-safe plate and microwave on high until heated through, 45-90 seconds.

2 pancakes: 157 cal., 4g fat (1g sat. fat), 45mg chol., 335mg sod., 24g carb. (4g sugars, 4g fiber), 9g pro. **Diabetic exchanges:** 1½ starch, 1 fat.

SPINACH FETA STRATA

This is a fairly new recipe for me. A friend shared it with me, and my family loved it the first time I made it, so it'll be a regular.
—Pat Lane, Pullman, WA

Prep: 10 min. + chilling • **Bake:** 40 min.
Makes: 12 servings

10	slices French bread (1 in. thick) or 6 croissants, split
6	large eggs, lightly beaten
1½	cups 2% milk
1	pkg. (10 oz.) frozen chopped spinach, thawed and squeezed dry
½	tsp. salt
¼	tsp. ground nutmeg
¼	tsp. pepper
1½	cups shredded Monterey Jack cheese
1	cup crumbled feta cheese

1. In a greased 3-qt. or 13x9-in. baking dish, arrange French bread or croissant halves with sides overlapping.
2. In a large bowl, combine the eggs, milk, spinach, salt, nutmeg and pepper; pour over bread. Sprinkle with cheeses. Cover and refrigerate for 8 hours or overnight.
3. Remove from refrigerator 30 minutes before baking. Bake, uncovered, at 350° until a knife inserted in the center comes out clean, 40-45 minutes. Let stand for 5 minutes before cutting. Serve warm.
1 serving: 190 cal., 10g fat (5g sat. fat), 128mg chol., 443mg sod., 13g carb. (2g sugars, 2g fiber), 12g pro.

SOUTHERN SCRAPPLE

Scrapple made from grits is a breakfast-time favorite in this area.
—Rusty Lovin, Greensboro, NC

Prep: 20 min. + chilling • **Cook:** 10 min.
Makes: 10 servings

- ½ lb. bulk pork sausage
- 4 cups water
- 1 cup grits
- 1 tsp. salt
- 1 tsp. pepper
   Dash cayenne pepper
- ¼ cup butter, cubed
- 1 cup shredded cheddar cheese
   Additional butter
   Maple syrup

1. In a large skillet, cook the sausage over medium heat until no longer pink; drain and set aside. In a large saucepan, bring water to a boil. Gradually add the grits, salt, pepper and cayenne, stirring constantly until thickened. Stir in butter and cheese until melted. Stir in sausage.
2. Press into a greased 9x5-in. loaf pan. Cover and refrigerate mixture for 1 hour or until cool.
3. Remove scrapple from the pan; cut into ½-in. slices. In a skillet, cook scrapple in butter until browned on both sides, adding more butter as needed. Serve warm with maple syrup.
1 slice: 141 cal., 12g fat (7g sat. fat), 32mg chol., 497mg sod., 4g carb. (0 sugars, 0 fiber), 4g pro.

BACON SWISS SQUARES

This savory breakfast-inspired pizza comes together easily, but it's the irresistible combination of eggs, bacon and Swiss cheese that keeps everyone coming back for more.
—Agarita Vaughan, Fairbury, IL

Takes: 30 min. • **Makes:** 12 servings

- 2 cups biscuit/baking mix
- ½ cup cold water
- 8 oz. sliced Swiss cheese
- 1 lb. sliced bacon, cooked and crumbled
- 4 large eggs, lightly beaten
- ¼ cup milk
- ½ tsp. onion powder

1. In a large bowl, combine the biscuit mix and water. Turn onto a floured surface; knead 10 times. Roll biscuit dough into a 14x10-in. rectangle.
2. Place on the bottom and ½ in. up the sides of a greased 13x9-in. baking dish. Arrange cheese over dough. Sprinkle with bacon. In a large bowl, whisk eggs, milk and onion powder; pour over bacon.
3. Bake at 425° until a knife inserted in the center comes out clean, 15-18 minutes. Cut into 12 squares; serve immediately.
1 piece: 246 cal., 15g fat (6g sat. fat), 91mg chol., 470mg sod., 15g carb. (1g sugars, 1g fiber), 13g pro.

COCONUT PECAN ROLLS

You're never too busy for fresh-baked sweet rolls when you have this recipe in your morning rotation.
—Theresa Gingry, Blue Springs, NE

Prep: 20 min. • **Bake:** 25 min.
Makes: 8 rolls

1   Tbsp. sugar
½   tsp. ground cinnamon
1   tube (11 oz.) refrigerated breadsticks
⅔   cup coconut pecan frosting
⅓   cup chopped pecans

1. In a small bowl, combine the sugar and cinnamon. Remove breadstick dough from tube (do not unroll); cut into 8 slices with a serrated knife. Dip both sides of each slice in cinnamon-sugar.
2. Place in a greased 9-in. round baking pan. Spread with frosting; sprinkle with pecans. Bake at 350° until golden brown, 25-30 minutes. Serve warm.
1 roll: 257 cal., 12g fat (3g sat. fat), 0 chol., 330mg sod., 33g carb. (13g sugars, 2g fiber), 3g pro.

MAKE AHEAD

PEACH FRENCH TOAST

Let the heavenly aroma of baked peaches, brown sugar and cinnamon wake up your houseful of sleepyheads. When you serve the tender slices of French toast, be sure to scoop up plenty of that sweet golden syrup in the bottom of the pan, and drizzle it liberally on top of each of the pieces. It's the best part.
—Geraldine Casey, Anderson, IN

Prep: 20 min. + chilling • **Bake:** 45 min.
Makes: 6 servings

1   cup packed brown sugar
½   cup butter, cubed
2   Tbsp. water
1   can (29 oz.) sliced peaches, drained
12   slices day-old French bread (¾ in. thick)
5   large eggs
1½   cups whole milk
1   Tbsp. vanilla extract
     Ground cinnamon

1. In a small saucepan, bring the brown sugar, butter and water to a boil. Reduce heat; simmer for 10 minutes, stirring frequently. Pour into a greased 13x9-in. baking dish; top with peaches. Arrange bread over peaches.
2. In a large bowl, whisk the eggs, milk and vanilla; slowly pour over bread. Cover and refrigerate for 8 hours or overnight.
3. Preheat oven to 350°. Remove the dish from the refrigerator 30 minutes before baking. Sprinkle with cinnamon. Cover and bake at for 20 minutes. Uncover; bake until a knife inserted in the center of the French toast comes out clean, for 25-30 minutes longer. Serve with a spoon.
2 pieces: 547 cal., 22g fat (12g sat. fat), 202mg chol., 438mg sod., 75g carb. (56g sugars, 2g fiber), 10g pro.

Taco Cornbread
Casserole
page 78

Main Dishes

The inspiration for your next event is just pages away when you flip through this chapter of hearty main dishes. From simple ready-to-grill chicken and ribs to perennial-favorite casseroles, chilis and subs, you'll find just the entree here.

CLASSIC BEEF STEW

Here's a good old-fashioned stew with lots of veggies in a rich beef gravy. It's the perfect dish for a blustery winter day.
—Alberta McKay, Bartlesville, OK

Prep: 15 min. • **Bake:** 2½ hours
Makes: 8 servings (2 qt.)

- 2 lbs. beef stew meat, cut into 1-in. cubes
- 1 to 2 Tbsp. canola oil
- 1½ cups chopped onions
- 1 can (14½ oz.) diced tomatoes, undrained
- 1 can (10½ oz.) condensed beef broth, undiluted
- 3 Tbsp. quick-cooking tapioca
- 1 garlic clove, minced
- 1 Tbsp. dried parsley flakes
- 1 tsp. salt
- ¼ tsp. pepper
- 1 bay leaf
- 6 medium carrots, cut into 2-in. pieces
- 3 medium potatoes, peeled and cut into 2-in. pieces
- 1 cup sliced celery (1-in. lengths)

1. In an oven-safe Dutch oven, brown beef in batches in oil; drain. Return all meat to the pan. Add onions, tomatoes, broth, tapioca, garlic, parsley, salt, pepper and bay leaf. Bring to a boil.
2. Cover stew and bake at 350° for 1 hour. Stir in carrots, potatoes and celery. Bake, covered, 1 hour longer or until meat and vegetables are tender. Discard bay leaf.
1 cup: 245 cal., 10g fat (3g sat. fat), 71mg chol., 751mg sod., 14g carb. (6g sugars, 3g fiber), 24g pro.

BACON-CHICKEN CRESCENT RING

This ring is really very easy to put together. It's so good that people always ask for the recipe.
—Michele McWhorter, Jacksonville, NC

Prep: 25 min. • **Bake:** 20 min.
Makes: 8 servings

- 2 tubes (8 oz. each) refrigerated crescent rolls
- 1 can (10 oz.) chunk white chicken, drained and flaked
- 1½ cups shredded Swiss cheese
- ¾ cup mayonnaise
- ½ cup finely chopped sweet red pepper
- ¼ cup finely chopped onion
- 6 bacon strips, cooked and crumbled
- 2 Tbsp. Dijon mustard
- 1 Tbsp. Italian salad dressing mix

1. Grease a 14-in. pizza pan. Unroll crescent roll dough; separate into 16 triangles. Place wide end of one triangle 3 in. from edge of prepared pan with point overhanging edge of pan. Repeat with remaining triangles along outer edge of pan, overlapping the wide ends (dough will look like a sun when complete). Lightly press wide ends together.
2. In a small bowl, combine the remaining ingredients. Spoon over wide ends of dough. Fold points of triangles over filling and tuck under wide ends (filling will be visible). Bake at 375° until golden brown, 20-25 minutes.
1 serving: 502 cal., 34g fat (7g sat. fat), 42mg chol., 1002mg sod., 26g carb. (7g sugars, 0 fiber), 21g pro.

GRILLED PICNIC CHICKEN

This tasty chicken marinates overnight. The next day, I just pop it on the grill for dinner in no time.
—Cindy DeRoos, Iroquois, ON

Prep: 5 min. + marinating • **Grill:** 40 min.
Makes: 12 servings

- 1½ cups white vinegar
- ¾ cup canola oil
- 6 Tbsp. water
- 4½ tsp. salt
- 1½ tsp. poultry seasoning
- ¾ tsp. garlic powder
- ¾ tsp. pepper
- 3 broiler/fryer chickens (3 to 4 lbs. each), cut up

1. In a bowl, combine the first 7 ingredients. Remove 1 cup for basting; cover and refrigerate. Pour the remaining marinade into a large shallow dish; add chicken. Turn to coat; refrigerate for 4 hours or overnight, turning once or twice.

2. Drain chicken, discarding marinade in bag. Grill chicken, uncovered, over medium heat for 15 minutes on each side. Baste with the reserved marinade.

3. Grill the chicken 10-20 minutes longer or until the juices run clear, turning and basting several times.

7 oz cooked chicken: 522 cal., 34g fat (8g sat. fat), 157mg chol., 725mg sod., 0 carb. (0 sugars, 0 fiber), 50g pro.

TACO CORNBREAD CASSEROLE

Green chiles add fire to this cornbread casserole. For less heat, you can use just part of the can to your taste.
—Lisa Paul, Terre Haute, IN

Prep: 25 min. • **Bake:** 1 hour
Makes: 8 servings

- 2 lbs. ground beef
- 2 envelopes taco seasoning
- 2 cans (14½ oz. each) diced tomatoes, drained
- 1 cup water
- 1 cup cooked rice
- 1 can (4 oz.) chopped green chiles
- 2 pkg. (8½ oz. each) cornbread/muffin mix
- 1 can (8¾ oz.) whole kernel corn, drained
- 1 cup sour cream
- 2 cups corn chips
- 2 cups shredded Mexican cheese blend or cheddar cheese, divided
- 1 can (2¼ oz.) sliced ripe olives, drained
  Optional: Shredded lettuce, chopped tomatoes and chopped red onion

1. Preheat oven to 400°. In a Dutch oven, cook beef over medium heat until no longer pink, breaking into crumbles, 8-10 minutes; drain. Stir in taco seasoning. Add diced tomatoes, water, rice and green chiles; heat through, stirring occasionally.

2. Meanwhile, prepare the cornbread mix according to package directions; stir in corn. Pour half of the batter into a greased 13x9-in. baking dish. Layer with half of meat mixture, all the sour cream, half of the corn chips and 1 cup cheese. Top with the remaining batter, remaining meat mixture, olives and remaining corn chips.

3. Bake, uncovered, until cornbread is cooked through, 55-60 minutes. Sprinkle with the remaining cheese; bake until cheese is melted, 3-5 minutes longer. If desired, serve with lettuce, tomatoes and red onion.

1½ cups: 817 cal., 40g fat (17g sat. fat), 183mg chol., 1982mg sod., 74g carb. (20g sugars, 4g fiber), 36g pro.

BEEF & NOODLE CASSEROLE

When I was working on the local election board in the '50s, one of my co-workers gave me this recipe. It has been a family favorite ever since. It's quick to make for unexpected company or easily doubled for a potluck.
—Mary Hinman, Escondido, CA

Prep: 20 min. • **Bake:** 45 min.
Makes: 8 servings

- 1½ lbs. ground beef
- 1 Tbsp. butter
- 1 large onion, chopped
- 1 cup chopped green pepper
- 1 Tbsp. Worcestershire sauce
- 6¼ cups uncooked wide egg noodles, cooked and drained
- 2 cans (10¾ oz. each) condensed tomato soup, undiluted
- 1 can (10¾ oz.) condensed cream of mushroom soup, undiluted
- 1 cup shredded cheddar cheese

1. In a large skillet, cook beef over medium heat until no longer pink; drain. In the same skillet, melt butter over medium-high heat. Saute onion and pepper until tender. Stir in the beef, Worcestershire sauce, egg noodles and soups.

2. Transfer to a greased 3-qt. baking dish; top with cheese. Bake, uncovered, at 350° for 45-50 minutes or until heated through.

1 cup: 445 cal., 20g fat (9g sat. fat), 112mg chol., 747mg sod., 39g carb. (7g sugars, 2g fiber), 27g pro.

RICE-STUFFED PEPPERS

My mother used to fix this dish when we had guests. The cheese sauce sets these irresistible peppers apart.
—Lisa Easley, Longview, TX

Prep: 40 min. • **Bake:** 1 hour
Makes: 8 servings

- 2 lbs. ground beef
- 1 medium onion, chopped
- 1 small green pepper, chopped
- 2 garlic cloves, minced
- 1 tsp. salt
- ½ tsp. pepper
- 3¾ cup water
- 1 can (14½ oz.) diced tomatoes, undrained
- 1 can (10 oz.) diced tomatoes and green chiles, undrained
- 1 can (15 oz.) tomato sauce
- 1 Tbsp. ground cumin
- 3 cups uncooked instant rice
- 4 medium green peppers

CHEESE SAUCE
- 1½ lbs. process American cheese, cubed
- 1 can (10 oz.) diced tomatoes and green chiles, undrained

1. In a Dutch oven, cook beef, onion, chopped green pepper, garlic, salt and pepper over medium heat until the beef is no longer pink; drain. Add the water, tomatoes, tomato sauce and cumin. Bring to a boil. Reduce the heat; simmer, uncovered, for 10 minutes.

2. Stir in the rice; simmer, uncovered, for 5 minutes. Remove from the heat; cover and let stand for 5 minutes.

3. Remove tops and seeds from the peppers; cut in half widthwise. Place in a large pan of boiling water; boil for 4 minutes.

4. Drain peppers and stuff with meat mixture. Place remaining meat mixture in an ungreased 13x9-in. baking dish; top with stuffed peppers, pressing down gently. Cover and bake at 350° for 1 hour. In a saucepan, heat the sauce ingredients until cheese is melted. Serve over stuffed peppers.

1 stuffed pepper: 662 cal., 33g fat (17g sat. fat), 139mg chol., 1964mg sod., 51g carb. (12g sugars, 5g fiber), 40g pro.

To use frozen casserole: Thaw in refrigerator 8 hours. Preheat oven to 375°. Remove from refrigerator 30 minutes before baking. Cover and bake, increasing time as necessary to heat through and for a thermometer inserted in center to read 165°, 20-25 minutes.

Note: Wear disposable gloves when cutting hot peppers; the oils can burn skin. Avoid touching your face.

1 cup: 321 cal., 15g fat (7g sat. fat), 64mg chol., 673mg sod., 23g carb. (5g sugars, 4g fiber), 24g pro.

BREADED RANCH CHICKEN

A crunchy coating of cornflakes and Parmesan cheese adds delectable flavor to zesty ranch chicken. This golden, crispy chicken is a mainstay dish I can always count on.

—Launa Shoemaker, Landrum, SC

Prep: 10 min. • **Bake:** 45 min.
Makes: 8 servings

- ¼ cup unsalted butter, melted
- ¾ cup crushed cornflakes
- ¾ cup grated Parmesan cheese
- 1 envelope ranch salad dressing mix
- 8 boneless skinless chicken breast halves (4 oz. each)

1. Place butter in a shallow bowl. In another shallow bowl, combine the cornflakes, cheese and salad dressing mix. Dip the chicken in butter, then roll in cornflake mixture to coat.
2. Place in a greased 13x9-in. baking dish. Bake, uncovered, at 350° until a thermometer reads 170°, about 45 minutes.

1 chicken breast half: 254 cal., 10g fat (5g sat. fat), 84mg chol., 959mg sod., 13g carb. (1g sugars, 0 fiber), 26g pro.

MAKE AHEAD

SOUTHWESTERN CASSEROLE

I've been making this mild family-pleasing casserole for years. It tastes wonderful, fits nicely into our budget and, best of all, makes a second dish to freeze and enjoy some other day.

—Joan Hallford, North Richland Hills, TX

Prep: 25 min. • **Bake:** 40 min.
Makes: 2 casseroles (6 servings each)

- 2 cups (8 oz.) uncooked elbow macaroni
- 2 lbs. ground beef
- 1 large onion, chopped
- 2 garlic cloves, minced
- 2 cans (14½ oz. each) diced tomatoes, undrained
- 1 can (16 oz.) kidney beans, rinsed and drained
- 1 can (6 oz.) tomato paste
- 1 can (4 oz.) chopped green chiles, drained
- 1½ tsp. salt
- 1 tsp. chili powder
- ½ tsp. ground cumin
- ½ tsp. pepper
- 2 cups shredded Monterey Jack cheese
- 2 jalapeno peppers, seeded and chopped

1. Cook macaroni according to package directions. Meanwhile, in a large saucepan, cook beef and onion over medium heat, crumbling beef, until meat is no longer pink. Add garlic; cook 1 minute longer. Drain. Stir in next 8 ingredients. Bring to a boil. Reduce heat; simmer, uncovered, for 10 minutes. Drain macaroni; stir into beef mixture.
2. Preheat oven to 375°. Transfer macaroni mixture to 2 greased 2-qt. baking dishes. Top with cheese and jalapenos. Cover and bake at 375° for 30 minutes. Uncover; bake until bubbly and heated through, about 10 minutes longer. Serve one casserole. Cool the second casserole; cover casserole and freeze for up to 3 months.

MAKE AHEAD

NEW ENGLAND LAMB BAKE

This dish is hearty and perfect for warming up on a chilly winter evening. The aroma is almost as delightful as the dish itself.
—Frank Grady, Fort Kent, ME

Prep: 25 min. • **Bake:** 1½ hours
Makes: 8 servings

- 1 Tbsp. canola oil
- 2 lbs. boneless leg of lamb, cut into 1-in. cubes
- 1 large onion, chopped
- ¼ cup all-purpose flour
- 3 cups chicken broth
- 2 large leeks (white portion only), cut into ½-in. slices
- 2 large carrots, sliced
- 2 Tbsp. minced fresh parsley, divided
- ½ tsp. dried rosemary, crushed
- ½ tsp. salt
- ¼ tsp. pepper
- ¼ tsp. dried thyme
- 3 large potatoes, peeled and sliced
- 3 Tbsp. butter, melted and divided

1. Preheat oven to 375°. In a Dutch oven, heat oil over medium heat. Add lamb and onion; cook and stir until meat is no longer pink. Stir in the flour until blended. Gradually add the broth. Bring to a boil; cook until thickened, 1-2 minutes, stirring to loosen browned bits from pan. Add the leeks, carrots, 1 Tbsp. parsley, rosemary, salt, pepper and thyme.

2. Spoon into a greased 13x9-in. or 3-qt. baking dish. Cover with potato slices; brush with 2 Tbsp. melted butter. Bake 1 hour; brush potatoes with remaining butter. Return to oven; bake until meat is tender and potatoes are golden, 30 minutes to 1 hour longer. Cool briefly; sprinkle with remaining parsley.

Freeze option: Remove baking dish from oven; cool completely. Before adding the remaining parsley, cover dish and freeze. Freeze parsley separately. To use, partially thaw lamb bake in refrigerator overnight. Remove from refrigerator 30 minutes before baking; thaw remaining parsley. Preheat oven to 350°. Reheat, covered, until a thermometer reads 165°, about 1 hour. Sprinkle with remaining minced parsley.

1 piece: 356 cal., 13g fat (5g sat. fat), 82mg chol., 631mg sod., 34g carb. (4g sugars, 4g fiber), 25g pro. **Diabetic exchanges:** 3 starch, 3 lean meat, 1½ fat.

MEAT LOAF MINIATURES

I don't usually like meat loaf, but my family and I can't get enough of these little muffins topped with a sweet ketchup sauce. It's quick and so easy to make a double batch.
—Joyce Wegmann, Burlington, IA

....

Prep: 20 min. • **Bake:** 30 min.
Makes: 1½ dozen

- 1 **cup ketchup**
- 3 **to 4 Tbsp. packed brown sugar**
- 1 **tsp. ground mustard**
- 2 **large eggs, lightly beaten**
- 4 **tsp. Worcestershire sauce**
- 3 **cups Crispix cereal, crushed**
- 3 **tsp. onion powder**
- ½ **to 1 tsp. seasoned salt**
- ½ **tsp. garlic powder**
- ½ **tsp. pepper**
- 3 **lbs. lean ground beef (90% lean)**

1. In a large bowl, combine the ketchup, brown sugar and mustard. Remove ½ cup for topping; set aside. Add the eggs, Worcestershire sauce, cereal and seasonings to remaining ketchup mixture. Let stand for 5 minutes. Crumble beef over cereal mixture and mix well.

2. Press meat mixture into 18 muffin cups (about ⅓ cup each). Bake at 375° for 18-20 minutes. Drizzle with reserved ketchup mixture; bake 10 minutes longer or until meat is no longer pink and a thermometer reads 160°.

3. Serve desired number of meat loaves. Cool remaining loaves. Transfer to freezer container; close and freeze for up to 3 months.

To use frozen meat loaves: Completely thaw in the refrigerator. Place loaves in a greased baking dish. Bake at 350° for 30 minutes or until heated through, or cover and microwave on high for 1 minute or until heated through.

1 serving: 165 cal., 6g fat (2g sat. fat), 61mg chol., 305mg sod., 11g carb. (4g sugars, 0 fiber), 16g pro.

MAKE AHEAD

ITALIAN STUFFED SHELLS

A dear friend first brought over this casserole. Now I take it to other friends' homes and to potlucks, because it's always such a hit!
—Beverly Austin, Fulton, MO

....

Prep: 50 min. • **Bake:** 35 min.
Makes: 8 servings

1	lb. ground beef
1	cup chopped onion
1	garlic clove, minced
2	cups hot water
1	can (12 oz.) tomato paste
1	Tbsp. beef bouillon granules
1½	tsp. dried oregano
1	large egg, lightly beaten
2	cups 4% cottage cheese
2	cups shredded part-skim mozzarella cheese, divided
½	cup grated Parmesan cheese
24	jumbo pasta shells, cooked and drained

1. In a large skillet, cook beef, onion and garlic over medium heat, crumbling beef, until meat is no longer pink; drain. Stir in water, tomato paste, bouillon and oregano. Reduce heat; simmer, uncovered, for 30 minutes.

2. Meanwhile, combine egg, cottage cheese, 1 cup mozzarella and Parmesan cheese. Stuff shells with cheese mixture.

3. Preheat oven to 350°. Arrange shells in a greased 13x9-in. or 3-qt. baking dish. Pour meat sauce over the shells. Cover; bake for 30 minutes. Uncover; sprinkle with remaining mozzarella cheese. Bake until the cheese is melted, about 5 minutes longer.

Freeze option: After assembling, cover and freeze. To use, partially thaw in refrigerator overnight. Remove 30 minutes before baking. Preheat oven to 350°. Bake as directed, adding the remaining 1 cup mozzarella cheese after 30-40 minutes and increasing the time as necessary for a thermometer inserted in the center to read 165°.

3 stuffed shells and sauce: 430 cal., 17g fat (8g sat. fat), 94mg chol., 866mg sod., 37g carb. (9g sugars, 3g fiber), 32g pro.

BRUSCHETTA CHICKEN

We enjoy serving this tasty chicken to both family and to company. It just might become your new favorite way to use up summer tomatoes and basil.
—Carolin Cattoi-Demkiw, Lethbridge, AB

Prep: 10 min. • **Bake:** 30 min.
Makes: 4 servings

- ½ cup all-purpose flour
- ½ cup egg substitute
- 4 boneless skinless chicken breast halves (4 oz. each)
- ¼ cup grated Parmesan cheese
- ¼ cup dry bread crumbs
- 1 Tbsp. butter, melted
- 2 large tomatoes, seeded and chopped
- 3 Tbsp. minced fresh basil
- 1 Tbsp. olive oil
- 2 garlic cloves, minced
- ½ tsp. salt
- ¼ tsp. pepper

1. Preheat oven to 375°. Place flour and egg substitute in separate shallow bowls. Dip the chicken in flour, then in egg substitute; place in a greased 13x9-in. baking dish. In a small bowl, mix cheese, bread crumbs and butter; sprinkle over chicken.

2. Loosely cover baking dish with foil. Bake 20 minutes. Uncover; bake 5-10 minutes longer or until a thermometer reads 165°.

3. Meanwhile, in a small bowl, toss the tomatoes with the remaining ingredients. Spoon over chicken; bake 3-5 minutes or until tomato mixture is heated through.

1 serving: 316 cal., 11g fat (4g sat. fat), 75mg chol., 563mg sod., 22g carb. (4g sugars, 2g fiber), 31g pro. **Diabetic exchanges:** 3 lean meat, 1½ fat, 1 starch, 1 vegetable.

SIMPLE CHICKEN ENCHILADAS

This recipe is so quick and easy, and I always receive a ton of compliments. It quickly becomes a favorite of friends whenever I share it. Modify the spiciness with the intensity of the salsa and the green chiles to suit your taste.
—Kristi Black, Harrison Township, MI

Prep: 20 min. • **Bake:** 25 min.
Makes: 5 servings

- 1 can (10 oz.) enchilada sauce, divided
- 4 oz. cream cheese, cubed
- 1½ cups salsa
- 2 cups cubed cooked chicken
- 1 can (15 oz.) pinto beans, rinsed and drained
- 1 can (4 oz.) chopped green chiles
- 10 flour tortillas (6 in.)
- 1 cup shredded Mexican cheese blend
  Optional: Shredded lettuce, chopped tomato, sour cream and sliced ripe olives

1. Spoon ½ cup enchilada sauce into a greased 13x9-in. baking dish. In a large saucepan, cook and stir the cream cheese and salsa over medium heat for 2-3 minutes or until blended. Stir in the chicken, beans and green chiles.

2. Place about ⅓ cup of chicken mixture down the center of each tortilla. Roll up and place seam side down over sauce. Top with the remaining enchilada sauce; sprinkle with Mexican cheese blend.

3. Cover and bake at 350° for 25-30 minutes or until heated through. Serve with lettuce, tomato, sour cream and olives if desired.

2 enchiladas: 468 cal., 13g fat (6g sat. fat), 75mg chol., 1394mg sod., 51g carb. (6g sugars, 8g fiber), 34g pro.

HEARTY PENNE BEEF

This is comfort food at its finest! The best of everything is found here—it's tasty, easy and a great way to sneak some spinach in for extra nutrition.
—*Taste of Home* Test Kitchen

Takes: 30 min. • **Makes:** 4 servings

- 1¾ cups uncooked penne pasta
- 1 lb. ground beef
- 1 tsp. minced garlic
- 1 can (15 oz.) tomato puree
- 1 can (14½ oz.) beef broth
- 1½ tsp. Italian seasoning
- 1 tsp. Worcestershire sauce
- ¼ tsp. salt
- ¼ tsp. pepper
- 2 cups chopped fresh spinach
- 2 cups shredded part-skim mozzarella cheese

1. Cook the pasta according to package directions. Meanwhile, in a Dutch oven, cook beef over medium heat until no longer pink. Add garlic; cook 1 minute longer. Drain. Stir in the tomato puree, broth, Italian seasoning, Worcestershire sauce, salt and pepper.

2. Bring to a boil. Reduce heat; simmer, uncovered, for 10-15 minutes or until slightly thickened. Add spinach; cook for 1-2 minutes or until wilted.

3. Drain pasta; stir into beef mixture. Sprinkle with cheese; cover and cook for 3-4 minutes or until cheese is melted.

Freeze option: Freeze cooled pasta mixture in freezer containers. To use, partially thaw in refrigerator overnight. Heat through in a saucepan, stirring occasionally; add broth or water if necessary.

1½ cups: 482 cal., 20g fat (10g sat. fat), 88mg chol., 1001mg sod., 33g carb. (5g sugars, 2g fiber), 41g pro.

BACON CHEESEBURGER SLOPPY JOES

My family doesn't even like sloppy joes. But we are big fans of this recipe. Win!
—Janine Smith, Columbia, SC

Takes: 25 min. • **Makes:** 8 servings

- 1½ lbs. ground turkey
- 1 large red onion, finely chopped
- 12 bacon strips, cooked and crumbled
- 2 medium tomatoes, chopped
- ¾ cup ketchup
- ½ cup chopped dill pickle
- 2 Tbsp. yellow mustard
- 1½ cups shredded cheddar cheese
- 8 hamburger buns, split

1. In a large skillet, cook and crumble turkey with onion over medium heat until turkey is no longer pink, 6-8 minutes. Stir in bacon, tomatoes, ketchup, dill pickle and mustard; heat through.

2. Stir in cheese until melted. Spoon meat mixture onto bun bottoms. Replace tops.

1 sandwich: 431 cal., 20g fat (8g sat. fat), 90mg chol., 1022mg sod., 32g carb. (11g sugars, 2g fiber), 31g pro.

DEBRA'S CAVATINI

I love this recipe because it makes two hearty casseroles. I add a little something different every time I make it, such as extra garlic, to give it an added boost of flavor.
—Debra Lynn Butcher, Decatur, IN

....

Prep: 45 min. • **Bake:** 35 min.
Makes: 2 casseroles (6 servings each)

- 1 pkg. (16 oz.) penne pasta
- 1 lb. ground beef
- 1 lb. bulk Italian pork sausage
- 1¾ cups sliced fresh mushrooms
- 1 medium onion, chopped
- 1 medium green pepper, chopped
- 2 cans (14½ oz. each) Italian diced tomatoes
- 1 jar (23½ oz.) Italian sausage and garlic spaghetti sauce
- 1 jar (16 oz.) chunky mild salsa
- 1 pkg. (8 oz.) sliced pepperoni, chopped
- 1 cup shredded Swiss cheese, divided
- 4 cups shredded part-skim mozzarella cheese, divided
- 1½ cups shredded Parmesan cheese, divided
- 1 jar (24 oz.) 3-cheese spaghetti sauce

1. Cook the pasta according to package directions. Meanwhile, in a Dutch oven, cook beef, sausage, mushrooms, onion and green pepper over medium heat until meat is no longer pink; drain.

2. Drain pasta; add to the meat mixture. Stir in the tomatoes, sausage and garlic spaghetti sauce, salsa and pepperoni.

3. Preheat oven to 350°. Divide half the pasta mixture between 2 greased 13x9-in. baking dishes. Sprinkle each with ¼ cup Swiss cheese, 1 cup mozzarella cheese and ⅓ cup Parmesan cheese. Spread ¾ cup 3-cheese spaghetti sauce over each. Top with remaining pasta mixture and the 3-cheese spaghetti sauce. Sprinkle with remaining cheeses.

4. Cover and bake until bubbly, about 25 minutes. Uncover; bake until cheese is melted, about 10 minutes longer.

Freeze option: Cover unbaked casserole and freeze up to 3 months. To use, thaw in refrigerator overnight. Remove from refrigerator 30 minutes before baking. Preheat oven to 350°. Bake the casserole, covered, 45 minutes. Uncover; bake for 10 minutes or until cheese is melted.

1 serving: 669 cal., 34g fat (15g sat. fat), 90mg chol., 1825mg sod., 54g carb. (20g sugars, 5g fiber), 37g pro.

GRILLED LEMON CHICKEN

The secret behind this summer-sensational chicken? It's lemonade concentrate!
—Linda Nilsen, Anoka, MN

Prep: 5 min. • **Grill:** 40 min.
Makes: 12 servings

- ¾ cup thawed lemonade concentrate
- ⅓ cup soy sauce
- 1 garlic clove, minced
- 1 tsp. seasoned salt
- ½ tsp. celery salt
- ⅛ tsp. garlic powder
- 2 broiler/fryer chickens
  (3 to 3½ lbs. each), cut up

1. In a bowl, whisk the first 6 ingredients until combined. Pour half into a shallow glass dish. Cover and refrigerate remaining sauce.
2. Dip chicken on both sides into sauce; discard sauce. Grill the chicken, covered, over medium heat for 30 minutes, turning occasionally. Brush with reserved sauce. Grill 10-20 minutes longer, brushing frequently with sauce, until a thermometer reads 165°.
5 oz. cooked chicken: 320 cal., 17g fat (5g sat. fat), 104mg chol., 504mg sod., 6g carb. (5g sugars, 0 fiber), 34g pro.

MEXICAN CARNITAS

Ever hear of carnitas? They're easy-to-make pork crisps that are popular in Mexico. The secret to this recipe is the quick frying and the kiss of citrus. Be sure the meat is well drained before it's placed in oil or it will spatter and pop.
—Patricia Collins, Imbler, OR

Prep: 40 min. • **Bake:** 2 hours
Makes: 12 servings

- 1 **boneless pork shoulder butt roast (3 to 4 lbs.), cut into 1-in. cubes**
- 6 **large garlic cloves, minced**
- ½ **cup fresh cilantro leaves, chopped**
- 1 **tsp. salt**
  Pepper to taste
- 3 **large oranges, divided**
- 1 **large lemon**
  Oil for frying
- 12 **flour tortillas (8 in.), warmed**
  Optional toppings: Chopped tomatoes, shredded cheddar cheese, sliced green onions, sour cream and avocado slices

1. Place meat in a medium-size roasting pan. Sprinkle with garlic and cilantro. Season with salt and pepper. Squeeze the juice from one orange and the lemon over the meat. Slice the remaining oranges and place over the meat.

2. Cover and bake at 350° for about 2 hours or until meat is tender. With a slotted spoon, remove meat and drain well on paper towels. Heat a small amount of oil in a skillet and fry meat in batches until browned and crispy.

3. Serve warm in tortillas with toppings of your choice.

Freeze option: Freeze cooled pork mixture in freezer containers. To use, partially thaw in the refrigerator overnight. Fry the meat in batches as directed until crispy and brown. Serve as directed.

1 serving: 468 cal., 26g fat (6g sat. fat), 67mg chol., 501mg sod., 34g carb. (4g sugars, 3g fiber), 24g pro.

CHICKEN & DUMPLING CASSEROLE

This savory casserole is one of my husband's favorites. He loves the fluffy dumplings with plenty of gravy poured over them.
—Sue Mackey, Jackson, WI

Prep: 30 min. • **Bake:** 40 min.
Makes: 8 servings

- ½ cup chopped onion
- ½ cup chopped celery
- ¼ cup butter, cubed
- 2 garlic cloves, minced
- ½ cup all-purpose flour
- 2 tsp. sugar
- 1 tsp. salt
- 1 tsp. dried basil
- ½ tsp. pepper
- 4 cups chicken broth
- 1 pkg. (10 oz.) frozen green peas
- 4 cups cubed cooked chicken

DUMPLINGS
- 2 cups biscuit/baking mix
- 2 tsp. dried basil
- ⅔ cup 2% milk

1. Preheat oven to 350°. In a large saucepan, saute onion and celery in butter until tender. Add garlic; cook 1 minute longer. Stir in flour, sugar, salt, basil and pepper until blended. Gradually add broth; bring to a boil. Cook and stir 1 minute or until thickened; reduce heat. Add peas and cook for 5 minutes, stirring constantly. Stir in chicken. Pour into a greased 13x9-in. baking dish.

2. For dumplings, in a small bowl, combine the baking mix and basil. Stir in milk with a fork until moistened. Drop by tablespoonfuls into mounds over chicken mixture.

3. Bake, uncovered, 30 minutes. Cover and bake 10 minutes longer or until a toothpick inserted in a dumpling comes out clean.

1 serving: 393 cal., 17g fat (7g sat. fat), 80mg chol., 1313mg sod., 33g carb. (6g sugars, 3g fiber), 27g pro.

NIKKI'S PERFECT PASTITSIO

My mother used to work so hard in the kitchen to make this classic Greek dish, and the results were always well worth her effort. My recipe is easier, a bit lighter and every bit as great as Mom's.
—Nikki Tsangaris, Westfield, IN

Prep: 45 min. • **Bake:** 50 min.
Makes: 12 servings

- 2½ cups uncooked penne pasta
- 2 Tbsp. butter, melted
- 1 cup grated Parmesan cheese
- 1½ lbs. ground sirloin
- 1 medium onion, chopped
- 2 garlic cloves, minced
- 1 can (15 oz.) tomato sauce
- ½ tsp. salt
- ½ tsp. ground cinnamon
- 1 cup shredded Parmesan cheese, divided

BECHAMEL SAUCE
- ½ cup butter, cubed
- ⅔ cup all-purpose flour
- ½ tsp. salt
- ¼ tsp. pepper
- 4 cups 2% milk
- 2 large eggs, beaten

1. Cook the pasta according to package directions; drain. Toss with butter; add grated Parmesan cheese. Transfer to a greased 13x9-in. baking dish.
2. Preheat oven to 350°. In a large skillet, cook beef and onion over medium heat 8-10 minutes or until beef is no longer pink, breaking beef into crumbles; drain. Add garlic; cook 2 minutes longer. Stir in tomato sauce, salt and cinnamon; heat through. Spoon over pasta. Sprinkle with ½ cup shredded Parmesan cheese.
3. In a large saucepan, melt butter for sauce. Stir in flour, salt and pepper until smooth; gradually add milk. Bring to a boil; cook and stir until thickened, 1-2 minutes.
4. Whisk a small amount of hot mixture into eggs; return all to pan, whisking constantly. Bring to a gentle boil; cook and stir 2 minutes. Pour over the beef mixture. Sprinkle with the remaining cheese.
5. Bake, covered, 20 minutes. Uncover; bake 30-40 minutes longer or until golden brown.
1 piece: 332 cal., 18g fat (10g sat. fat), 98mg chol., 718mg sod., 24g carb. (6g sugars, 1g fiber), 20g pro.

COBB SALAD SUB

When we need a quick meal to share, we turn Cobb salad into a sandwich masterpiece. Sometimes I substitute flour tortillas for the bread and make wraps instead.
—Kimberly Grusendorf, Medina, OH

Takes: 15 min. • **Makes:** 12 servings

- 1 loaf (1 lb.) unsliced Italian bread
- ½ cup balsamic vinaigrette or dressing of your choice
- 5 oz. fresh baby spinach (about 6 cups)
- 1½ lbs. sliced deli ham
- 4 hard-boiled large eggs, finely chopped
- 8 bacon strips, cooked and crumbled
- ½ cup crumbled Gorgonzola cheese
- 1 cup cherry tomatoes, chopped

Cut loaf of bread in half lengthwise; hollow out top and bottom, leaving a ¾-in. shell (discard removed bread or save for another use). Brush vinaigrette over bread halves. Layer spinach, ham, eggs, bacon, cheese and tomatoes on bread bottom. Replace top. Cut loaf in half lengthwise from top to bottom; cut crosswise 5 times to make 12 pieces.

1 slice: 233 cal., 10g fat (3g sat. fat), 97mg chol., 982mg sod., 17g carb. (3g sugars, 1g fiber), 18g pro.

TRADITIONAL LASAGNA

My family tasted this rich lasagna at a friend's house, and it became a tradition for our family gatherings. My sister's Italian in-laws request it often.
—Lorri Foockle, Granville, IL

Prep: 30 min. + simmering
Bake: 70 min. + standing
Makes: 12 servings

- 1 lb. ground beef
- ¾ lb. bulk pork sausage
- 3 cans (8 oz. each) tomato sauce
- 2 cans (6 oz. each) tomato paste
- 2 garlic cloves, minced
- 2 tsp. sugar
- 1 tsp. Italian seasoning
- ½ to 1 tsp. salt
- ¼ to ½ tsp. pepper
- 3 large eggs
- 3 Tbsp. minced fresh parsley
- 3 cups 4% small-curd cottage cheese
- 1 cup ricotta cheese
- ½ cup grated Parmesan cheese
- 9 lasagna noodles, cooked and drained
- 6 slices provolone cheese (about 6 oz.)
- 3 cups shredded part-skim mozzarella cheese, divided

1. In a large skillet over medium heat, cook and crumble beef and sausage until no longer pink; drain. Add next 7 ingredients. Bring to a boil. Reduce heat; simmer, uncovered, 1 hour, stirring occasionally. Adjust seasoning with additional salt and pepper, if desired.

2. Meanwhile, in a large bowl, lightly beat eggs. Add parsley; stir in cottage cheese, ricotta and Parmesan cheese.

3. Preheat oven to 375°. Spread 1 cup meat sauce in an ungreased 13x9-in. baking dish. Layer with three lasagna noodles, provolone cheese, 2 cups cottage cheese mixture, 1 cup mozzarella, three noodles, 2 cups meat sauce, remaining cottage cheese mixture and 1 cup mozzarella. Top with remaining noodles, meat sauce and mozzarella (dish will be full).

4. Cover; bake 50 minutes. Uncover; bake until heated through, about 20 minutes. Let stand 15 minutes before cutting.

1 piece: 503 cal., 27g fat (13g sat. fat), 136mg chol., 1208mg sod., 30g carb. (9g sugars, 2g fiber), 36g pro.

TURKEY TETRAZZINI

This recipe comes from a cookbook our church compiled. After the holidays, we use leftover turkey to prepare this dish for university students. They clean their plates every time!
—Gladys Waldrop, Clavert City, KY

Prep: 15 min. • **Bake:** 40 min.
Makes: 8 servings

- 1 pkg. (7 oz.) spaghetti, broken into 2-in. pieces
- 2 cups cubed cooked turkey
- 1 cup shredded cheddar cheese
- 1 can (10¾ oz.) condensed cream of mushroom soup, undiluted
- 1 medium onion, chopped
- 2 cans (4 oz. each) sliced mushrooms, drained
- ⅓ cup 2% milk
- ¼ cup chopped green pepper
- 1 jar (2 oz.) chopped pimientos, drained
- ¼ tsp. salt
- ⅛ tsp. pepper
  Additional shredded cheddar cheese, optional

1. Cook spaghetti according to package directions; drain. Transfer to a large bowl; add the next 10 ingredients.
2. Spoon into a greased 2½-qt. casserole; sprinkle with additional cheese if desired. Bake, uncovered, at 375° for 40-45 minutes or until heated through.
1 serving: 252 cal., 8g fat (4g sat. fat), 45mg chol., 519mg sod., 26g carb. (3g sugars, 2g fiber), 18g pro.

MAKE AHEAD

CHICKEN & SWISS STUFFING BAKE

I love to cook but just don't have much time. This casserole is both comforting and fast, which makes it my favorite kind of recipe. I serve it with a green salad.
—Jena Coffey, Sunset Hills, MO

Prep: 20 min. • **Bake:** 25 min.
Makes: 8 servings

- 1 can (10¾ oz.) condensed cream of mushroom soup, undiluted
- 1 cup whole milk
- 1 pkg. (6 oz.) stuffing mix
- 2 cups cubed cooked chicken breast
- 2 cups fresh broccoli florets, cooked
- 2 celery ribs, finely chopped
- 1½ cups shredded Swiss cheese, divided

1. In a large bowl, combine soup and milk until blended. Add the stuffing mix with contents of seasoning packet, chicken, broccoli, celery and 1 cup cheese. Transfer to a greased 13x9-in. baking dish.
2. Bake, uncovered, at 375° for 20 minutes or until heated through. Sprinkle with remaining cheese; bake 5 minutes longer or until cheese is melted.
Freeze option: Sprinkle remaining cheese over unbaked casserole. Cover and freeze. To use, partially thaw in refrigerator overnight. Remove from refrigerator 30 minutes before baking. Preheat oven to 375°. Bake casserole as directed, increasing time as necessary to heat through and for a thermometer inserted in center to read 165°.
1 cup: 247 cal., 7g fat (4g sat. fat), 42mg chol., 658mg sod., 24g carb. (0 sugars, 3g fiber), 22g pro.

WHITE CHEDDAR & HAM SCALLOPED POTATOES

This recipe has evolved over the past eight years. After I added the thyme, ham and sour cream, my husband declared, "This is it!" I like to serve this rich, saucy entree with a salad and homemade French bread.
—Hope Toole, Muscle Shoals, AL

Prep: 40 min. • **Bake:** 70 min.
Makes: 10 servings

- ¼ cup butter
- 1 medium onion, finely chopped
- ¼ cup all-purpose flour
- 1 tsp. salt
- 1 tsp. dried parsley flakes
- ½ tsp. dried thyme
- ½ tsp. pepper
- 3 cups 2% milk
- 1 can (10¾ oz.) condensed cream of mushroom soup, undiluted
- 1 cup sour cream
- 8 cups thinly sliced peeled potatoes
- 3½ cups cubed fully cooked ham
- 2 cups shredded sharp white cheddar cheese

1. Preheat oven to 375°. In a large saucepan, heat butter over medium-high heat. Add onion; cook and stir until tender. Stir in flour and seasonings until blended; gradually whisk in milk. Bring to a boil, stirring constantly; cook and stir 2 minutes or until thickened. Stir in soup. Remove from heat; stir in sour cream.
2. In a greased 13x9-in. baking dish, layer half of each of the following: potatoes, cubed ham, cheese and sauce. Repeat layers.
3. Bake, covered, 30 minutes. Bake, uncovered, 40-50 minutes longer or until potatoes are tender.
1 serving: 417 cal., 20g fat (12g sat. fat), 88mg chol., 1267mg sod., 37g carb. (7g sugars, 3g fiber), 22g pro.

SAUCY GRILLED BABY BACK RIBS

The root beer in the sauce adds a subtle sweetness to this savory rib recipe.
—Terri Kandell, Addison, MI

Prep: 2 hours • **Grill:** 15 min.
Makes: 8 servings

- 2 cups ketchup
- 2 cups cider vinegar
- 1 cup corn syrup
- ¼ cup packed brown sugar
- ¼ cup root beer
- ½ tsp. salt
- ½ tsp. garlic powder
- ½ tsp. onion powder
- ½ tsp. hot pepper sauce
- 4 lbs. pork baby back ribs

1. In a large saucepan, combine the first 9 ingredients. Bring to a boil. Reduce heat; simmer, uncovered, 20-25 minutes or until slightly thickened, stirring occasionally.
2. Meanwhile, preheat oven to 325°. Set aside 3 cups of sauce for basting and serving.
3. Brush remaining sauce over ribs. Place bone side down on a rack in a large shallow roasting pan. Cover tightly with foil and bake until tender, 1½-2 hours. On a greased grill, cook the ribs, covered, over medium heat until browned, 15-25 minutes, turning and brushing occasionally with some of the reserved sauce. Cut into serving-size pieces; serve with sauce.
Note: If you are attending an off-site cookout, prepare ribs as directed, wrap in foil and place in an insulated container to keep warm. Just before serving, reheat theribs on a medium-hot grill.
1 serving: 603 cal., 31g fat (11g sat. fat), 122mg chol., 1046mg sod., 56g carb. (35g sugars, 0 fiber), 25g pro.

MAKE AHEAD

PIZZA PASTA CASSEROLE

Kids will line up for this zippy pizza-flavored dish. The recipe makes two casseroles, so you can serve one to your family right away and keep the other in the freezer for another night.
—Nancy Scarlett, Graham, NC

....

Prep: 20 min. • **Bake:** 25 min.
Makes: 2 casseroles (10 servings each)

- 2 lbs. ground beef
- 1 large onion, chopped
- 3½ cups spaghetti sauce
- 1 pkg. (16 oz.) spiral or cavatappi pasta, cooked and drained
- 4 cups shredded part-skim mozzarella cheese
- 8 oz. sliced pepperoni

1. Preheat oven to 350°. In a large skillet, cook beef and onion over medium heat until meat is no longer pink; drain. Stir in spaghetti sauce and pasta.
2. Transfer to 2 greased 13x9-in. baking dishes. Sprinkle with cheese. Arrange the pepperoni over the top.
3. Bake, uncovered, 25-30 minutes or until heated through.
Freeze option: Cool unbaked casseroles; cover and freeze up to 3 months. To use, partially thaw in the refrigerator overnight. Remove from refrigerator 30 minutes before baking. Preheat oven to 350°. Bake as directed, increasing time to 35-40 minutes or until the casserole is heated through and a thermometer reads 165°.
1 serving: 301 cal., 15g fat (6g sat. fat), 46mg chol., 545mg sod., 22g carb. (4g sugars, 1g fiber), 19g pro.

PENNE GORGONZOLA WITH CHICKEN

Having an easy recipe like this in your back pocket will come in handy if you're hosting a dinner party. The simple combination of wine, broth, cream and cheese makes a full-flavored sauce that nicely coats the pasta.
—Imelda Schroeder, Port Murray, NJ

Takes: 30 min. • **Makes:** 8 servings

- 1 pkg. (16 oz.) penne pasta
- 1 lb. boneless skinless chicken breasts, cut into ½-in. pieces
- 1 Tbsp. olive oil
- 1 large garlic clove, minced
- ¼ cup white wine
- 1 cup heavy whipping cream
- ¼ cup chicken broth
- 2 cups crumbled Gorgonzola cheese
- 6 to 8 fresh sage leaves, thinly sliced
  Salt and pepper to taste
  Grated Parmigiano-Reggiano cheese and minced fresh parsley

1. Cook pasta according to package directions. Meanwhile, in a large skillet over medium heat, brown chicken in oil on all sides. Add the garlic; cook 1 minute longer. Add wine, stirring to loosen browned bits from pan.

2. Add cream and broth; cook until sauce is slightly thickened and chicken is no longer pink. Stir in the Gorgonzola cheese, sage, salt and pepper; cook just until the cheese is melted.

3. Drain pasta; toss with sauce. Sprinkle with Parmigiano-Reggiano cheese and minced fresh parsley.

1¼ cups: 489 cal., 23g fat (14g sat. fat), 97mg chol., 453mg sod., 43g carb. (2g sugars, 3g fiber), 26g pro.

CRISPY FRIED CHICKEN

This fried chicken can be served hot or pulled out of the fridge the next day as leftovers. Either way, folks love it.
—Jeanne Schnitzler, Lima, MT

Prep: 15 min. • **Cook:** 15 min./batch
Makes: 12 servings

- 4 cups all-purpose flour, divided
- 2 Tbsp. garlic salt
- 1 Tbsp. paprika
- 3 tsp. pepper, divided
- 2½ tsp. poultry seasoning
- 2 large eggs
- 1½ cups water
- 1 tsp. salt
- 2 broiler/fryer chickens (3½ to 4 lbs. each), cut up
  Oil for frying

1. In a large shallow dish, combine 2⅔ cups flour, 2 Tbsp. garlic salt, 1 Tbsp. paprika, 2½ tsp. pepper and 2½ tsp. poultry seasoning. In another shallow dish, beat eggs and 1½ cups water; add 1 tsp. salt and the remaining 1⅓ cup flour and ½ tsp. pepper. Dip chicken in egg mixture, then place in the flour mixture, a few pieces at a time. Turn chicken to coat.

2. In a deep-fat fryer, heat oil to 375°. Working in batches, fry chicken, several pieces at a time, until golden brown and a thermometer inserted into chicken reads 165°, about 7-8 minutes on each side. Drain on paper towels.

5 oz. cooked chicken: 543 cal., 33g fat (7g sat. fat), 137mg chol., 798mg sod., 17g carb. (0 sugars, 1g fiber), 41g pro.

MAKE AHEAD

WHITE CHICKEN CHILI

Folks will enjoy a change from the traditional when they spoon into this flavorful blend of chicken, white beans and green chile pepper.
—*Taste of Home* Test Kitchen

Prep: 15 min. • **Cook:** 25 min.
Makes: 10 servings (2½ qt.)

- 1 lb. boneless skinless chicken breasts, chopped
- 1 medium onion, chopped
- 1 Tbsp. olive oil
- 2 garlic cloves, minced
- 2 cans (14 oz. each) chicken broth
- 1 can (4 oz.) chopped green chiles
- 2 tsp. ground cumin
- 2 tsp. dried oregano
- 1½ tsp. cayenne pepper
- 3 cans (14½ oz. each) great northern beans, drained, divided
- 1 cup shredded Monterey Jack cheese
  Sliced jalapeno pepper, optional

1. In a Dutch oven over medium heat, cook chicken and onion in oil until lightly browned. Add garlic; cook 1 minute longer. Stir in the broth, chiles, cumin, oregano and cayenne; bring to a boil.

2. Reduce heat to low. With a potato masher, mash one can of beans until smooth. Add to saucepan. Add the remaining beans to the saucepan. Simmer for 20-30 minutes or until chicken is no longer pink and onion is tender.

3. Top each serving with Monterey Jack cheese and, if desired, jalapeno pepper.

Freeze option: Freeze cooled chili in freezer containers. To use, partially thaw in the refrigerator overnight. Heat through in a saucepan, stirring occasionally; add broth or water if necessary.

1 cup: 219 cal., 7g fat (3g sat. fat), 37mg chol., 644mg sod., 21g carb. (1g sugars, 7g fiber), 19g pro. **Diabetic exchanges:** 2 lean meat, 1½ starch, 1 fat.

STUFFED PASTA SHELLS

These savory shells never fail to make a big impression, even though the recipe is very easy. One or two of these stuffed shells makes a great individual serving at a potluck, so a single batch goes a long way.
—Jena Coffey, St. Louis, MO

Prep: 15 min. • **Bake:** 30 min.
Makes: 12 servings

  4 cups shredded mozzarella cheese
  1 carton (15 oz.) ricotta cheese
  1 pkg. (10 oz.) frozen chopped spinach, thawed and squeezed dry
  1 pkg. (12 oz.) jumbo pasta shells, cooked and drained
3½ cups spaghetti sauce
    Grated Parmesan cheese, optional

Preheat oven to 350°. Combine cheeses and spinach; stuff into shells. Arrange shells in a greased 13x9-in. baking dish. Pour spaghetti sauce over the shells. Cover and bake until heated through, about 30 minutes. Sprinkle with grated Parmesan cheese after baking if desired.

1 serving: 314 cal., 13g fat (7g sat. fat), 44mg chol., 576mg sod., 32g carb. (9g sugars, 3g fiber), 18g pro.

★ ★ ★ ★ ★ **READER REVIEW**

"This is really good. Great for potlucks as a choice for vegetarians. You will be asked to bring it again."
CLAIREMOTT TASTEOFHOME.COM

MAKE AHEAD

GOLDEN CHICKEN POTPIE

The golden crust and creamy sauce make these veggie-packed pies a sure hit. The family-favorite recipe makes two mild and comforting pies.
—*Taste of Home* Test Kitchen

Prep: 20 min. • **Bake:** 35 min.
Makes: 2 potpies (6 servings each)

  4 cups cubed cooked chicken
  4 cups frozen cubed hash brown potatoes, thawed
  1 pkg. (16 oz.) frozen mixed vegetables, thawed and drained
  1 can (10½ oz.) condensed cream of chicken soup, undiluted
  1 can (10½ oz.) condensed cream of onion soup, undiluted
  1 cup whole milk
  1 cup sour cream
  2 Tbsp. all-purpose flour
 ½ tsp. salt
 ½ tsp. pepper
 ¼ tsp. garlic powder
  2 sheets refrigerated pie crust

1. Preheat oven to 400°. Combine the first 11 ingredients. Divide between two 9-in. deep-dish pie plates.
2. Roll out crusts to fit top of each pie. Place over filling; trim, seal and flute edges. Cut slits in the top. Bake until golden brown, 35-40 minutes.

Freeze option: Cover and freeze unbaked pies up to 3 months. To use, remove from freezer 30 minutes before baking (do not thaw). Preheat oven to 425°. Place pie on a baking sheet; cover edges loosely with foil. Bake for 30 minutes. Reduce heat to 350°. Remove foil and bake until golden brown or until heated through and a thermometer inserted in center reads 165°, 50-55 minutes longer.

1 serving: 415 cal., 19g fat (8g sat. fat), 69mg chol., 706mg sod., 39g carb. (5g sugars, 3g fiber), 20g pro.

FOURTH OF JULY BEAN CASSEROLE

The outstanding barbecue taste of these beans makes them a favorite for cookouts all summer and into the fall. It's a popular dish, even with kids. The beef makes it so much better than plain pork and beans.
—Donna Fancher, Lawrence, IN

Prep: 20 min. • **Bake:** 1 hour
Makes: 12 servings

½ lb. bacon strips, diced
½ lb. ground beef
1 cup chopped onion
1 can (28 oz.) pork and beans
1 can (16 oz.) kidney beans, rinsed and drained
1 can (15¼ oz.) lima beans, rinsed and drained
½ cup barbecue sauce
½ cup ketchup
½ cup sugar
½ cup packed brown sugar
2 Tbsp. prepared mustard
2 Tbsp. molasses
1 tsp. salt
½ tsp. chili powder

1. In a large skillet over medium heat, cook bacon, beef and onion until meat is no longer pink; drain.
2. Transfer to a greased 2½-qt. baking dish; add all beans and mix well. In a small bowl, combine the remaining ingredients; stir into beef and bean mixture.
3. Cover and bake at 350° for 45 minutes. Uncover; bake 15 minutes longer.
1 cup: 278 cal., 6g fat (2g sat. fat), 15mg chol., 933mg sod., 47g carb. (26g sugars, 7g fiber), 12g pro.

REUBEN STRATA

Sure, you could turn leftover corned beef into a Reuben sandwich, but strata is more fun—and just as simple.
—Patterson Watkins, Philadelphia, PA

Prep: 15 min. • **Bake:** 45 min. + standing •
Makes: 12 servings

1 loaf (1 lb.) day-old pumpernickel bread, cubed
3 lbs. corned beef brisket, cubed
1¾ cups sauerkraut, rinsed and well drained
8 large eggs, beaten
3 cups heavy whipping cream
½ cup Thousand Island salad dressing
1 cup shredded Swiss cheese

1. In a large bowl, combine the bread, corned beef and sauerkraut. In another bowl, whisk the eggs, cream and salad dressing; pour over bread mixture and toss to coat. Transfer to a greased 13x9-in. baking dish. Let stand 5 minutes.
2. Cover and bake at 375° for 40 minutes. Uncover; sprinkle with cheese and bake 5-10 minutes longer or until a knife inserted in the center comes out clean. Let strata stand for 10 minutes before cutting.
1 piece: 639 cal., 47g fat (22g sat. fat), 312mg chol., 1488mg sod., 27g carb. (6g sugars, 3g fiber), 26g pro.

TACORITOS

This mild and meaty southwestern dish combines the delicious flavor of tacos with the heartiness of burritos. Your family's going to love these!
—Monica Flatford, Knoxville, TN

Prep: 40 min. • **Bake:** 20 min.
Makes: 8 servings

- ¼ cup butter, cubed
- ¼ cup all-purpose flour
- 4 cups water
- 3 Tbsp. chili powder
- 1 tsp. garlic salt
- 1 lb. ground beef
- 1 lb. bulk pork sausage
- ¼ cup chopped onion
- 1 cup refried beans
- 8 flour tortillas (8 in.), warmed
- 3 cups shredded Monterey Jack cheese
  Optional toppings: Shredded lettuce, chopped tomatoes, sliced ripe olives and sour cream

1. In a large saucepan, melt butter. Stir in flour until smooth; gradually add water. Bring to a boil; cook and stir for 1 minute or until thickened. Stir in chili powder and garlic salt. Bring to a boil. Reduce heat; simmer, uncovered, for 10 minutes.
2. In a large skillet over medium heat, cook the beef, sausage and onion until meat is no longer pink; drain. Stir in refried beans; heat through.
3. Spread ¼ cup sauce in a greased 13x9-in. baking dish. Spread 1 Tbsp. sauce over each tortilla; place ⅔ cup meat mixture down the center of each. Top each with ¼ cup cheese. Roll up and place seam side down in baking dish. Pour the remaining sauce over the top; sprinkle with the remaining cheese.
4. Bake, uncovered, at 350° for 18-22 minutes or until bubbly and cheese is melted. Serve with optional toppings as desired.
1 tacorito: 627 cal., 40g fat (19g sat. fat), 111mg chol., 1131mg sod., 36g carb. (2g sugars, 3g fiber), 31g pro.

SPIEDIS

This is our favorite cookout dish. The recipe originated here in my hometown in the 1930s. Our meat preference for spiedis is venison, but we use others when it's not available.
—Gertrude Skinner, Binghamton, NY

Prep: 10 min. + marinating • **Grill:** 10 min.
Makes: 8 servings

- 1 cup canola oil
- ⅔ cup cider vinegar
- 2 Tbsp. Worcestershire sauce
- ½ medium onion, finely chopped
- ½ tsp. salt
- ½ tsp. sugar
- ½ tsp. dried basil
- ½ tsp. dried marjoram
- ½ tsp. dried rosemary, crushed
- 2½ lbs. boneless lean pork, beef, lamb, venison, chicken or turkey, cut into 1½- to 2-in. cubes
  Italian rolls or hot dog buns

1. In a glass or plastic bowl, combine the first 9 ingredients. Add the meat and toss to coat. Cover and let marinate for 24 hours, stirring occasionally.
2. Drain and discard marinade. Thread meat on metal or soaked wooden skewers. Grill over medium heat until meat reaches desired doneness, 10-15 minutes, turning occasionally. Remove meat from skewers and serve on Italian rolls or hot dog buns.
4 oz. cooked meat: 205 cal., 12g fat (0 sat. fat), 42mg chol., 104mg sod., 1g carb. (0 sugars, 0 fiber), 22g pro. **Diabetic exchanges:** 2 lean meat, 1 fat.

CHICKEN CORDON BLEU BAKE

A friend shared this awesome hot dish recipe with me. I freeze several pans to share with neighbors or for days when I'm scrambling at mealtime.
—Rea Newell, Decatur, IL

....

Prep: 20 min. • **Bake:** 40 min.
Makes: 2 casseroles (6 servings each)

- 2 pkg. (6 oz. each) reduced-sodium stuffing mix
- 1 can (10¾ oz.) condensed cream of chicken soup, undiluted
- 1 cup 2% milk
- 8 cups cubed cooked chicken
- ½ tsp. pepper
- ¾ lb. sliced deli ham, cut into 1-in. strips
- 1 cup shredded Swiss cheese
- 3 cups shredded cheddar cheese

1. Preheat oven to 350°. Prepare stuffing mixes according to package directions. Meanwhile, whisk together soup and milk.
2. Toss chicken with pepper; divide between 2 greased 13x9-in. baking dishes. Layer with the ham, Swiss cheese, 1 cup cheddar, soup mixture and stuffing. Sprinkle with remaining cheddar cheese.
3. Bake, covered, 30 minutes. Uncover; bake until cheese is melted, 10-15 minutes.
Freeze option: Cover and freeze unbaked casseroles. To use, partially thaw in refrigerator overnight. Remove from the refrigerator 30 minutes before baking. Preheat oven to 350°. Bake, covered, until heated through and a thermometer inserted in center reads 165°, about 45 minutes. Uncover; bake until cheese is melted, 10-15 minutes.
1 cup: 555 cal., 29g fat (15g sat. fat), 158mg chol., 1055mg sod., 26g carb. (5g sugars, 1g fiber), 46g pro.

MEXICAN CHICKEN ALFREDO

One family member likes Italian, another likes Mexican. They never have to argue when this rich and creamy sensation is on the menu!
—Tia Woodley, Stockbridge, GA

....

Prep: 25 min. • **Bake:** 30 min.
Makes: 2 casseroles (4 servings each)

- 1 pkg. (16 oz.) gemelli or spiral pasta
- 2 lbs. boneless skinless chicken breasts, cubed
- 1 medium onion, chopped
- ¼ tsp. salt
- ¼ tsp. pepper
- 1 Tbsp. canola oil
- 2 jars (15 oz. each) Alfredo sauce
- 1 cup grated Parmesan cheese
- 1 cup medium salsa
- ¼ cup 2% milk
- 2 tsp. taco seasoning

1. Preheat oven to 350°. Cook pasta according to package directions.
2. Meanwhile, in a large skillet over medium heat, cook chicken, onion, salt and pepper in oil until chicken is no longer pink. Stir in Alfredo sauce; bring to a boil. Stir in cheese, salsa, milk and taco seasoning.
3. Drain pasta; toss with chicken mixture. Divide between 2 greased 8-in. square baking dishes. Cover and bake until bubbly, 30-35 minutes.
Freeze option: Cover and freeze unbaked casserole up to 3 months. To use, thaw in the refrigerator overnight. Remove from refrigerator 30 minutes before baking. Preheat oven to 350°. Bake casserole, covered, until bubbly, 50-60 minutes.
1½ cups: 559 cal., 20g fat (11g sat. fat), 102mg chol., 899mg sod., 55g carb. (4g sugars, 3g fiber), 40g pro.

THREE-BEAN TACO CHILI

This hearty chili is filling, nourishing and tastes like it simmered all day long. Leftover chili freezes well for a later time, so why not make a double recipe?
—Wanda Lee, Hemet, CA

Takes: 30 min. • **Makes:** 9 servings

- 2 lbs. ground beef
- 2 cups water
- 1 can (16 oz.) refried beans
- 1 can (16 oz.) kidney beans, rinsed and drained
- 1 can (16 oz.) chili beans, undrained
- 1 can (15¼ oz.) whole kernel corn, drained
- 1 can (14½ oz.) stewed tomatoes
- 1 can (8 oz.) tomato sauce
- 1 cup chunky salsa
- 1 envelope taco seasoning
- 1 can (2¼ oz.) sliced ripe olives, drained
- 1 cup shredded cheddar cheese

1. In a Dutch oven, cook beef over medium heat until no longer pink; drain. Stir in the water, beans, corn, tomatoes, tomato sauce, salsa, taco seasoning and olives.

2. Bring to a boil. Reduce heat; simmer, uncovered, for 10 minutes. Garnish with cheddar cheese.

1½ cups: 446 cal., 18g fat (8g sat. fat), 80mg chol., 1360mg sod., 41g carb. (7g sugars, 9g fiber), 31g pro.

★ ★ ★ ★ ★ **READER REVIEW**

"This was great! I'm happy with how much it made too! I sprinkled broken chips on top to give each spoonful a little crunch. Yum!"

OOH! TASTEOFHOME.COM

ENCHILADA CASSER-OLE!

My husband loves this casserole, and it never lasts long. Packed with black beans, cheese, tomatoes and Southwest flavor, it's an impressive-looking entree that's as simple as it is simply delicious.
—Marsha Wills, Homosassa, FL

Prep: 25 min. • **Bake:** 30 min.
Makes: 8 servings

- 1   lb. lean ground beef (90% lean)
- 1   large onion, chopped
- 2   cups salsa
- 1   can (15 oz.) black beans, rinsed and drained
- ¼   cup reduced-fat Italian salad dressing
- 2   Tbsp. reduced-sodium taco seasoning
- ¼   tsp. ground cumin
- 6   flour tortillas (8 in.)
- ¾   cup reduced-fat sour cream
- 1   cup shredded reduced-fat Mexican cheese blend
- 1   cup shredded lettuce
- 1   medium tomato, chopped
- ¼   cup minced fresh cilantro

1. In a large skillet, cook beef and onion over medium heat until meat is no longer pink; drain. Stir in the salsa, beans, dressing, taco seasoning and cumin. Place 3 tortillas in an 11x7-in. baking dish coated with cooking spray. Layer with half of the meat mixture, sour cream and cheese. Repeat layers.
2. Cover and bake at 400° for 25 minutes. Uncover and bake until heated through, 5-10 minutes longer. Let stand 5 minutes; top with lettuce, tomato and cilantro.
1 piece: 357 cal., 12g fat (5g sat. fat), 45mg chol., 864mg sod., 37g carb. (6g sugars, 3g fiber), 23g pro. **Diabetic exchanges:** 3 lean meat, 2 starch, 1 vegetable, 1 fat.

TANGY & SWEET MEATBALLS

When we entertain friends for Sunday dinner, I frequently serve these tangy meatballs. Everyone loves the distinctive sauce, but they're often surprised to learn it is made with gingersnaps.
—Melody Mellinger, Myerstown, PA

Prep: 30 min. • **Bake:** 40 min.
Makes: 8 servings

- 3 **large eggs**
- 1 **medium onion, chopped**
- 1½ **cups dry bread crumbs**
- 1 **tsp. salt**
- 2 **lbs. ground beef**
- 2 **Tbsp. canola oil**

SAUCE
- 3½ **cups tomato juice**
- 1 **cup packed brown sugar**
- 10 **gingersnaps, finely crushed**
- ¼ **cup white vinegar**
- 1 **tsp. onion salt**

1. In a large bowl, combine the eggs, onion, bread crumbs and salt. Crumble beef over mixture and mix well. Shape into 1½-in. balls.

2. In a large skillet, brown the meatballs in batches in oil. Transfer to a greased 13x9-in. baking dish.

3. In a large saucepan, combine the sauce ingredients. Bring to a boil over medium heat, stirring until the cookie crumbs are dissolved. Pour over meatballs.

4. Bake, uncovered, at 350° until meat is no longer pink, 40-45 minutes.

1 serving: 526 cal., 21g fat (7g sat. fat), 155mg chol., 1226mg sod., 55g carb. (35g sugars, 1g fiber), 29g pro.

Sweet Corn &
Tomato Salad
page 121

Sides & Salads

Never underestimate the power of a stellar side dish, the kind that keeps folks coming back for more. They'll be asking for your recipe for these great choices, and they'll request you bring them time and again.

COTTAGE POTATOES

I often make this crunchy and colorful potato dish for our family reunions. It's my cousin's recipe. I always know we won't have to worry about leftovers.
—Mary Sholtis, Ashtabula, OH

Prep: 20 min. • **Bake:** 55 min.
Makes: 14 servings

12	large potatoes, peeled and diced
8	oz. process cheese (Velveeta), cubed
1	large onion, finely chopped
1	large green pepper, chopped
1	jar (2 oz.) diced pimientos, drained
1	slice bread, torn into crumbs
3	Tbsp. minced fresh parsley, divided
½	tsp. salt
½	cup milk
½	cup butter, melted
1½	cups cornflakes, crushed

1. Place the potatoes in a large saucepan or Dutch oven and cover with water. Bring to a boil; reduce heat to medium. Cover and cook until tender, for 5-7 minutes; drain. In a bowl, combine the cheese, onion, green pepper, pimientos, bread, 2 Tbsp. parsley and salt.
2. In a greased shallow 4-qt. baking dish, layer a third of the potatoes and a third of the cheese mixture. Repeat layers twice. Pour milk and butter over all; sprinkle with cornflake crumbs.
3. Cover and bake at 350° for 45 minutes. Uncover; bake until bubbly and the top is golden, 10-15 minutes longer. Sprinkle with remaining parsley.
1 cup: 389 cal., 11g fat (7g sat. fat), 31mg chol., 393mg sod., 64g carb. (8g sugars, 6g fiber), 10g pro.

ARTICHOKE CAPRESE PLATTER

I dressed up the classic Italian trio of mozzarella, tomatoes and basil with marinated artichokes. It looks so yummy on a pretty platter set out on a buffet. Using softer fresh mozzarella is the key to the best taste and variety of textures.
—Margaret Wilson, San Bernardino, CA

Takes: 15 min. • **Makes:** 12 servings

2	jars (7½ oz. each) marinated artichoke hearts
2	Tbsp. red wine vinegar
2	Tbsp. olive oil
6	plum tomatoes, sliced
1	lb. fresh mozzarella cheese, sliced
2	cups loosely packed fresh basil leaves
	Coarsely ground pepper, optional

1. Drain artichoke hearts, reserving ½ cup of the marinade. In a small bowl, whisk the vinegar, oil and reserved marinade.
2. On a large serving platter, arrange the artichokes, tomatoes, mozzarella cheese and fresh basil. Drizzle with vinaigrette. If desired, sprinkle with pepper.
Note: Fresh mozzarella can be found in the deli section of most grocery stores.
½ cup: 192 cal., 16g fat (7g sat. fat), 30mg chol., 179mg sod., 5g carb. (2g sugars, 1g fiber), 7g pro.

SUMMER ORZO

I'm always looking for fun ways to use the fresh veggies that come in my Community Supported Agriculture box, and this salad is one of my favorite creations. I like to improvise with whatever I have on hand—feel free to do the same here.
—Shayna Marmar, Philadelphia, PA

- -

Prep: 30 min. + chilling
Makes: 16 servings

1	**pkg. (16 oz.) orzo pasta**
¼	**cup water**
1½	**cups fresh or frozen corn**
24	**cherry tomatoes, halved**
2	**cups (8 oz.) crumbled feta cheese**
1	**medium cucumber, seeded and chopped**
1	**small red onion, finely chopped**
¼	**cup minced fresh mint**
2	**Tbsp. capers, drained and chopped, optional**
½	**cup olive oil**
¼	**cup lemon juice**
1	**Tbsp. grated lemon zest**
1½	**tsp. salt**
1	**tsp. pepper**
1	**cup sliced almonds, toasted**

1. Cook orzo according to the package directions for al dente. Drain orzo; rinse with cold water and drain well. Transfer to a large bowl.

2. In a large nonstick skillet, heat water over medium heat. Add corn; cook and stir until crisp-tender, 3-4 minutes. Add to orzo; stir in the tomatoes, feta cheese, cucumber, onion, mint and, if desired, capers. In a small bowl, whisk oil, lemon juice, lemon zest, salt and pepper until blended. Pour over orzo mixture; toss to coat. Refrigerate 30 minutes.

3. Just before serving, stir in almonds.

¾ cup: 291 cal., 15g fat (4g sat. fat), 15mg chol., 501mg sod., 28g carb. (3g sugars, 3g fiber), 11g pro.

★ ★ ★ ★ ★ **READER REVIEW**

"Really enjoyed this salad. I was asked to bring one that could sit out for a while. I already was a fan of orzo but never thought of putting it in a salad like this. The dressing was good, but I added about a half-cup of extra lemon juice (for a double batch) to get the light, lemony taste I wanted."

PAT TASTEOFHOME.COM

SQUASH DRESSING

I got this recipe from my husband's cousin. She always made the luscious dressing for her mother at Thanksgiving.
—Anna Mayer, Fort Branch, IN

- -

Prep: 30 min. + cooling • **Bake:** 40 min.
Makes: 8 servings

- 1 pkg. (8½ oz.) cornbread/ muffin mix
- ½ cup water
- 4 cups chopped yellow summer squash
- ½ cup butter
- ½ cup each chopped onion, celery and green pepper
- 1 can (10¾ oz.) condensed cream of chicken soup, undiluted
- 1 cup whole milk
- 1 tsp. salt
- ½ tsp. pepper

1. Prepare cornbread according to the package directions. Cool and crumble into a large bowl; set aside.
2. In a large saucepan, bring ½ in. of water to a boil. Add squash; cook, covered, until crisp-tender, for 3-5 minutes. Drain. Meanwhile, in a large skillet, melt butter. Add the onion, celery and green pepper; saute until tender.
3. Add vegetable mixture and squash to the cornbread. In a small bowl, combine the soup, milk, salt and pepper; add to the cornbread and stir until blended. Transfer to a greased 11x7-in. baking dish.
4. Bake, uncovered, at 350° until golden brown, 40-45 minutes.
¾ cup: 311 cal., 19g fat (10g sat. fat), 70mg chol., 930mg sod., 31g carb. (9g sugars, 2g fiber), 6g pro.

HERBED BREAD TWISTS

My family loves these simple breadsticks. They eat them as fast as I can get them out of the oven.
—Deb Stapert, Comstock Park, MI

- -

Prep: 30 min. + rising • **Bake:** 10 min.
Makes: 2 dozen

- ¼ cup butter, softened
- ¼ tsp. garlic powder
- ¼ tsp. each dried basil, marjoram and oregano
- 1 loaf (1 lb.) frozen bread dough, thawed
- ¾ cup shredded part-skim mozzarella cheese
- 1 large egg
- 1 Tbsp. water
- 4 tsp. sesame seeds

1. Combine butter and seasonings. On a lightly floured surface, roll dough into a 12-in. square. Spread butter mixture to within ½ in. of edges; sprinkle with cheese.
2. Fold dough into thirds. Cut widthwise into 24 strips. Twist each strip twice; pinch ends to seal. Place 2 in. apart on greased baking sheets. Cover and let rise in a warm place until doubled, about 40 minutes.
3. Beat egg and water; brush over dough. Sprinkle with sesame seeds. Bake at 375° until light golden brown, 10-12 minutes. Remove from pans to wire racks.
1 twist: 84 cal., 4g fat (2g sat. fat), 17mg chol., 140mg sod., 10g carb. (1g sugars, 1g fiber), 3g pro.

SPICY ANTIPASTO SALAD

Packed with inviting ingredients and fabulous flavors, this salad is a favorite at all of our family picnics. Dried herbs can be used in a pinch.
—Jennifer Banahan, Lexington, KY

Prep: 30 min. + chilling
Makes: 16 servings

- 2 large tomatoes, seeded and chopped
- 1 can (14 oz.) water-packed artichoke hearts, rinsed, drained and quartered
- 12 pepperoncini
- 1½ cups cubed part-skim mozzarella cheese
- 1 cup cubed salami
- 1 cup chopped fresh parsley
- 1 cup pitted Greek olives, sliced
- 1 small red onion, thinly sliced
- ½ cup sliced pepperoni
- ½ cup capers, drained
- ¾ cup olive oil
- ¼ cup white balsamic vinegar
- 2 Tbsp. minced fresh basil
- 2 Tbsp. minced fresh oregano
- 2 tsp. crushed red pepper flakes
- 1 tsp. salt
- 1 tsp. pepper

In a large bowl, combine the first 10 ingredients. Whisk the oil, vinegar, basil, oregano, pepper flakes, salt and pepper; pour over salad and toss to coat. Cover and refrigerate for at least 1 hour to allow flavors to blend.
½ cup: 218 cal., 19g fat (5g sat. fat), 15mg chol., 843mg sod., 5g carb. (1g sugars, 1g fiber), 7g pro.

BRUSSELS SPROUTS & KALE SAUTE

This colorful side dish is filled with healthy greens. It pairs well with turkey, potatoes and other holiday staples. The surprising crispy sauteed salami is my kid's favorite ingredient, and it makes the dish over-the-top delicious.
—Jennifer McNabb, Brentwood, TN

Takes: 30 min.
Makes: 12 servings

- ¼ lb. thinly sliced hard salami, cut into ¼-in. strips
- 1½ tsp. olive oil
- 2 Tbsp. butter
- 2 lbs. fresh Brussels sprouts, thinly sliced
- 2 cups shredded fresh kale
- 1 large onion, finely chopped
- ½ tsp. kosher salt
- ⅛ tsp. cayenne pepper
- ¼ tsp. coarsely ground pepper
- 1 garlic clove, minced
- ½ cup chicken broth
- ½ cup chopped walnuts
- 1 Tbsp. balsamic vinegar

1. In a Dutch oven, cook and stir salami in oil over medium-high heat for 3-5 minutes or until crisp. Remove to paper towels with a slotted spoon; reserve drippings in pan.
2. Add butter to the drippings; heat over medium-high heat. Add Brussels sprouts, kale, onion, salt, cayenne and black pepper; cook and stir until the vegetables are crisp-tender. Add garlic; cook mixture 1 minute longer.
3. Stir in the broth; bring to a boil. Reduce heat; cover and cook until Brussels sprouts are tender, for 4-5 minutes. Stir in walnuts and vinegar. Top with salami.
½ cup: 126 cal., 9g fat (3g sat. fat), 14mg chol., 341mg sod., 9g carb. (3g sugars, 3g fiber), 6g pro. **Diabetic exchanges:** 2 fat, 1 vegetable.

SAUSAGE SPINACH BAKE

A friend gave me this delicious recipe, which uses packaged stuffing mix, years ago. Your favorite salad is all you'll need to add for a satisfying lunch or dinner. It's versatile, and it's become a regular at our brunches.
—Kathleen Grant, Swan Lake, MT

Prep: 20 min. • **Bake:** 40 min.
Makes: 12 servings

1	pkg. (6 oz.) savory herb-flavored stuffing mix
½	lb. bulk pork sausage
¼	cup chopped green onions
½	tsp. minced garlic
1	pkg. (10 oz.) frozen chopped spinach, thawed and squeezed dry
1½	cups shredded Monterey Jack cheese
1½	cups half-and-half cream
3	large eggs
2	Tbsp. grated Parmesan cheese

1. Prepare stuffing according to package directions. Meanwhile, crumble sausage into a large skillet. Add onions; cook over medium heat until meat is no longer pink. Add garlic; cook 1 minute longer. Drain.
2. In a large bowl, combine the stuffing, sausage mixture and spinach. Transfer to a greased 11x7-in. baking dish; sprinkle with Monterey Jack cheese. In a small bowl, combine the cream and eggs; pour over sausage mixture.
3. Bake at 400° until a thermometer reads 160°, 35-40 minutes. Sprinkle with the Parmesan cheese and bake until bubbly, about 5 minutes longer.
1 serving: 258 cal., 17g fat (9g sat. fat), 95mg chol., 494mg sod., 14g carb. (2g sugars, 2g fiber), 11g pro.

SOUR CREAM CUCUMBERS

It's been a tradition at our house to serve this dish with the other Hungarian specialties my mom learned to make from the women at church. It can't be beat during the hot summer, made with freshly picked garden cucumbers.
—Pamela Eaton, Monclova, OH

- -

Prep: 15 min. + chilling • **Makes:** 8 servings

- ½ cup sour cream
- 3 Tbsp. white vinegar
- 1 Tbsp. sugar
  Pepper to taste
- 4 medium cucumbers, peeled if desired and thinly sliced
- 1 small sweet onion, thinly sliced and separated into rings

In a bowl, whisk sour cream, vinegar, sugar and pepper until blended. Add cucumbers and onion; toss to coat. Refrigerate, covered, at least 4 hours. Serve with a slotted spoon.

¾ cup: 62 cal., 3g fat (2g sat. fat), 10mg chol., 5mg sod., 7g carb. (5g sugars, 2g fiber), 2g pro. **Diabetic exchanges:** 1 vegetable, ½ fat.

TEST KITCHEN TIP
Many grocery store cucumbers are coated with wax to prolong freshness. They should be peeled before eating. But there's no need to peel English cucumbers that are wrapped in plastic instead. Ditto for cucumbers from the farmers market or your own garden. Whether or not to peel these cukes is just a taste preference.

BACON MACARONI SALAD

This pleasing pasta salad is like a BLT in a bowl. Chock-full of crispy crumbled bacon, chopped tomato, and crunchy celery and green onion, the salad is a real crowd-pleaser!
—Norene Wright, Manilla, IN

- -

Prep: 20 min. + chilling
Makes: 12 servings

      2 cups uncooked elbow macaroni
      1 large tomato, finely chopped
      2 celery ribs, finely chopped
      5 green onions, finely chopped
    1¼ cups mayonnaise
      5 tsp. white vinegar
      ¼ tsp. salt
      ⅛ to ¼ tsp. pepper
      1 lb. bacon strips, cooked
         and crumbled

1. Cook macaroni according to package directions; drain and rinse in cold water. Transfer to a large bowl; stir in tomato, celery and green onions.
2. Whisk mayonnaise, vinegar, salt and pepper. Pour over macaroni mixture and toss to coat. Refrigerate, covered, at least 2 hours. Just before serving, stir in bacon.
¾ cup: 290 cal., 25g fat (5g sat. fat), 19mg chol., 387mg sod., 11g carb. (1g sugars, 1g fiber), 6g pro.

★ ★ ★ ★ ★ **READER REVIEW**

"I will never use store-bought again. Made it for a reunion. Everyone raved. My only change was to add more mayo for creaminess and more salt to taste."

AMYKEPLER TASTEOFHOME.COM

COLOR IT RUBY SALAD

Just looking at this bright red salad cheers me up—and then I get to taste it! Garnish with a sprinkle of fresh green chives and mild white cheese.
—Lorraine Caland, Shuniah, ON

- -

Takes: 20 min. • **Makes:** 12 servings

    2 Tbsp. red wine vinegar
    1 Tbsp. Dijon mustard
    ½ tsp. kosher salt
    ¼ tsp. pepper
    ⅓ cup extra virgin olive oil
    1 lb. small tomatoes, quartered
    ¾ lb. cherry tomatoes, halved
    ¾ lb. fresh strawberries,
       hulled and sliced
    2 cans (15 oz. each) beets,
       drained and chopped

Mix vinegar, mustard, salt and pepper; gradually whisk in oil until blended. Toss with tomatoes, strawberries and beets. Serve immediately.
1 cup: 98 cal., 6g fat (1g sat. fat), 0 chol., 251mg sod., 10g carb. (7g sugars, 3g fiber), 1g pro. **Diabetic exchanges:** 1 fat, ½ starch.

GARDEN BOUNTY PANZANELLA SALAD

When my sister gave me fresh tomatoes and basil, I made this traditional bread salad. The longer it sits, the more the bread soaks up the seasonings.
—Jannine Fisk, Malden, MA

Prep: 15 min. • **Cook:** 20 min.
Makes: 16 servings

- ¼ cup olive oil
- 12 oz. French or ciabatta bread, cut into 1-in. cubes (about 12 cups)
- 4 large tomatoes, coarsely chopped
- 1 English cucumber, coarsely chopped
- 1 medium green pepper, cut into 1-in. pieces
- 1 medium sweet yellow pepper, cut into 1-in. pieces
- 1 small red onion, halved and thinly sliced
- ½ cup coarsely chopped fresh basil
- ¼ cup grated Parmesan cheese
- ¾ tsp. kosher salt
- ¼ tsp. coarsely ground pepper
- ½ cup Italian salad dressing

1. In a large skillet, heat 2 Tbsp. oil over medium heat. Add half of the bread cubes; cook and stir until toasted, 8 minutes. Remove from pan. Repeat with remaining oil and bread cubes.
2. Combine the bread cubes, tomatoes, cucumber, peppers, onion, basil, cheese, salt and pepper. Toss with dressing.
1 cup: 131 cal., 6g fat (1g sat. fat), 1mg chol., 310mg sod., 18g carb. (3g sugars, 2g fiber), 3g pro. **Diabetic exchanges:** 1 starch, 1 vegetable, 1 fat.

SWEET CORN & POTATO GRATIN

Two popular vegetables come together in this down-home side. The garlic and onion flavors appeal to adults, while the crispy topping has kids looking for second helpings.
—Jennifer Olson, Pleasanton, CA

Prep: 30 min. • **Bake:** 45 min. + standing
Makes: 8 servings

- 1 medium onion, thinly sliced
- 2 Tbsp. butter
- 2 Tbsp. all-purpose flour
- 2 garlic cloves, minced
- 1 tsp. salt
- ½ tsp. pepper
- 1 cup whole milk
- 2 lbs. medium Yukon Gold potatoes, peeled and cut into ⅛-in. slices
- 2 cups fresh or frozen corn
- 1 can (8¼ oz.) cream-style corn
- ¾ cup panko (Japanese) bread crumbs
- 1 Tbsp. butter, melted

1. Preheat oven to 350°. In a saucepan, saute onion in butter until tender. Stir in flour, garlic, salt and pepper until blended; gradually add milk. Stir in potatoes. Bring to a boil. Reduce heat; cook and stir until potatoes are crisp-tender, 8-10 minutes.
2. Stir in the corn and cream-style corn. Transfer to an 8-in. square baking dish coated with cooking spray.
3. In a small bowl, combine bread crumbs and butter; sprinkle over potatoes. Bake until golden brown and the potatoes are tender, 45-50 minutes. Let gratin stand for 10 minutes before serving.
¾ cup: 213 cal., 6g fat (3g sat. fat), 14mg chol., 452mg sod., 37g carb. (6g sugars, 3g fiber), 5g pro.

CHERRY BAKED BEANS

Here's a perfect dish to take to a family reunion or any get-together. It's fast and easy to prepare. But don't count on taking home any leftovers...because there won't be any.
—Margaret Smith, Superior, WI

Prep: 20 min. • **Bake:** 40 min.
Makes: 12 servings

- 1 lb. lean ground beef (90% lean)
- 2 cans (15 oz. each) pork and beans
- 2 cups frozen pitted tart cherries, thawed
- 1 can (16 oz.) kidney beans, rinsed and drained
- 1 cup ketchup
- ½ cup water
- 1 envelope onion soup mix
- 2 Tbsp. prepared mustard
- 2 tsp. cider vinegar

1. In a large skillet, cook beef over medium heat until no longer pink; drain. In a large bowl, combine the remaining ingredients; stir in beef.
2. Transfer to an ungreased 2½ qt. baking dish. Bake beans, uncovered, at 400° until heated through, stirring occasionally, for 40-45 minutes.
⅔ cup: 189 cal., 4g fat (1g sat. fat), 19mg chol., 800mg sod., 28g carb. (12g sugars, 6g fiber), 13g pro.

PICKLED BELL PEPPERS

Well received at potlucks, this colorful, tasty dish adds zest to the menu. I also make it as a salad to accompany lunch or dinner at home.
—Heather Prendergast, Sundre, AB

Prep: 20 min. + chilling • **Makes:** 4 cups

- 2 each medium green, sweet red and yellow peppers, cut into 1-in. pieces
- 1 large red onion, halved and thinly sliced
- 2 tsp. mixed pickling spices
- ½ tsp. celery seed
- 1 cup sugar
- 1 cup cider vinegar
- ⅓ cup water

1. In a large glass bowl, combine peppers and onion. Place pickling spices and celery seed on a double thickness of cheesecloth. Gather corners of the cloth to enclose the seasonings; tie securely with string.
2. In a saucepan, combine sugar, vinegar, water and spice bag. Bring to a boil; boil 1 minute. Transfer spice bag to pepper mixture. Pour vinegar mixture over top. Cool to room temperature. Refrigerate, covered, 24 hours, stirring occasionally.
3. Discard spice bag. Refrigerate pickled peppers up to 1 month.
¼ cup: 67 cal., 0 fat (0 sat. fat), 0 chol., 2mg sod., 17g carb. (15g sugars, 1g fiber), 1g pro.

LEMON ROASTED FINGERLINGS & BRUSSELS SPROUTS

I've tried this recipe with other combinations of veggies, too. The trick is choosing ones that take about the same amount of time to roast. Try skinny green beans and thinly sliced onions, cauliflower florets and baby carrots, or okra and cherry tomatoes.

—Courtney Gaylord, Columbus, IN

Prep: 15 min. • **Bake:** 20 min.
Makes: 8 servings

1 lb. fingerling potatoes, halved
1 lb. Brussels sprouts, halved
6 Tbsp. olive oil, divided
¾ tsp. salt, divided
¼ tsp. pepper
3 Tbsp. lemon juice
1 garlic clove, minced
1 tsp. Dijon mustard
1 tsp. honey

1. Preheat oven to 425°. Place potatoes and Brussels sprouts in a greased 15x10x1-in. baking pan. Drizzle vegetables with 2 Tbsp. of oil; sprinkle with ½ tsp. salt and the pepper. Toss to coat. Roast until tender, 20-25 minutes, stirring once.

2. In a small bowl, whisk lemon juice, garlic, mustard, honey and remaining oil and salt until blended. Transfer vegetables to a large bowl; drizzle with vinaigrette and toss to coat. Serve warm.

¾ cup: 167 cal., 10g fat (1g sat. fat), 0 chol., 256mg sod., 17g carb. (3g sugars, 3g fiber), 3g pro. **Diabetic exchanges:** 2 fat, 1 starch, 1 vegetable.

MELON WITH SERRANO-MINT SYRUP

I created several recipes to take advantage of the mint I grow, and this is one. The serrano pepper contrasts nicely with the sweetness of the syrup and fruit.
—Jennifer Fisher, Austin, TX

Takes: 30 min. + chilling
Makes: 12 servings

- ⅓ cup sugar
- ⅓ cup water
- ¼ cup lemon juice
- 3 Tbsp. honey
- ½ tsp. minced serrano pepper
- ¼ cup minced fresh mint
- 1 Tbsp. grated lemon zest
- 4 cups each cubed watermelon, cantaloupe and honeydew

1. In a small saucepan, bring sugar, water, lemon juice, honey and serrano pepper to a boil; cook 3-5 minutes or until slightly thickened. Remove from heat; stir in mint and lemon zest. Cool completely.
2. Strain syrup; discard pepper, mint and lemon zest. In a large bowl, combine the melons. Add syrup; gently toss to coat. Refrigerate, covered, for at least 2 hours, stirring several times.
Note: Wear disposable gloves when cutting hot peppers; the oils can burn skin. Avoid touching your face.
1 cup: 92 cal., 0 fat (0 sat. fat), 0 chol., 13mg sod., 25g carb. (23g sugars, 1g fiber), 1g pro.
Diabetic exchanges: 1 fruit, ½ starch.

WHITE BALSAMIC BLUEBERRY, CORN, & FETA SALAD

 I'm not typically a huge fan of summer corn, but when it comes to this sweet, salty, refreshing salad, I can't put my fork down. I find that grilling the corn inside of the husk makes it easier to remove all the corn silk from each cob.
—Colleen Delawder, Herndon, VA

- -

Prep: 30 min. + soaking • **Grill:** 20 min.
Makes: 10 servings

8	medium ears sweet corn
3	Tbsp. olive oil
3	Tbsp. white balsamic vinegar
1	Tbsp. minced fresh chives, plus more for garnish
¾	tsp. kosher salt
¼	tsp. pepper
1	cup fresh blueberries
½	cup crumbled feta cheese

1. Carefully peel back corn husks to within 1 in. of bottoms; remove silk. Rewrap corn in husks; secure with kitchen string. Place in a stockpot; cover with cold water. Soak 20 minutes; drain.

2. Grill corn, covered, over medium heat about 20 minutes or until tender, turning often. Cut string and peel back husks. Cool slightly. Cut corn from cobs; transfer to a large bowl.

3. In a small bowl, whisk the oil, vinegar, chives, salt and pepper. Pour over corn; toss to coat. Gently fold in blueberries and feta. Garnish with additional chives as desired.

¾ cup: 133 cal., 6g fat (1g sat. fat), 3mg chol., 210mg sod., 19g carb. (8g sugars, 2g fiber), 4g pro. **Diabetic exchanges:** 1 starch, 1 fat.

TEST KITCHEN TIP
If you don't have white balsamic vinegar, you can use traditional balsamic vinegar instead. The corn and feta will take on some of its darker color.

CRUNCHY RAMEN SALAD

For potlucks and picnics, this salad's a knockout. I tote the veggies in a bowl, dressing in a jar and noodles in a bag. Then I shake them up together when it's time to eat.

—L.J. Porter, Bauxite, AR

Takes: 25 min. • **Makes:** 16 servings

- 1 Tbsp. plus ½ cup olive oil, divided
- ½ cup slivered almonds
- ½ cup sunflower kernels
- 2 pkg. (14 oz. each) coleslaw mix
- 12 green onions, chopped (about 1½ cups)
- 1 medium sweet red pepper, chopped
- ⅓ cup cider vinegar
- ¼ cup sugar
- ⅛ tsp. pepper
- 2 pkg. (3 oz. each) chicken ramen noodles

1. In a large skillet, heat 1 Tbsp. oil over medium heat. Add the almonds and sunflower kernels; cook until toasted, about 4 minutes. Cool.

2. In a large bowl, combine coleslaw mix, onions and red pepper. In a small bowl, whisk vinegar, sugar, pepper, contents of ramen seasoning packets and remaining oil. Pour over salad; toss to coat.

3. Refrigerate until serving. Break noodles into small pieces. Just before serving the salad, stir in ramen noodles, almonds and sunflower kernels.

¾ cup: 189 cal., 13g fat (2g sat. fat), 0 chol., 250mg sod., 16g carb. (6g sugars, 3g fiber), 4g pro.

MAKE AHEAD

CREAMY HASH BROWN CASSEROLE

Not much is better than the steaks and other meats we grill, but this versatile dish is a welcome sidekick. With a creamy cheese sauce and crunchy topping, the casserole is always the right choice for family dinners and potlucks.

—Teresa Stutzman, Adair, OK

Prep: 10 min. • **Bake:** 50 min.
Makes: 8 servings

- 1 pkg. (32 oz.) frozen cubed hash brown potatoes, thawed
- 1 lb. process cheese (Velveeta), cubed
- 2 cups sour cream
- 1 can (10 ¾ oz.) condensed cream of chicken soup, undiluted
- ¾ cup butter, melted, divided
- 3 Tbsp. chopped onion
- ¼ tsp. paprika
- 2 cups cornflakes, lightly crushed
  Fresh savory, optional

In a large bowl, combine the hash browns, cheese, sour cream, soup, ½ cup butter and onion. Spread into a greased 13x9-in. baking dish. Sprinkle with paprika. Combine cornflakes and remaining butter; sprinkle on top. Bake, covered, at 350° until heated through, 40-50 minutes. Uncover; bake until top is golden brown, 10 minutes longer. If desired, garnish with savory.

Freeze option: Cover and freeze unbaked casserole. To use, partially thaw in refrigerator overnight. Remove from refrigerator 30 minutes before baking. Preheat the oven to 350°. Bake the casserole as directed, increasing the time as necessary to heat through and for a thermometer inserted in center to read 165°.

¾ cup: 663 cal., 43g fat (27g sat. fat), 125mg chol., 1359mg sod., 49g carb. (9g sugars, 3g fiber), 19g pro.

THREE-BEAN BAKED BEANS

I got this recipe from an aunt and made a couple of changes to suit my family's tastes. With ground beef and bacon mixed in, these hearty, satisfying beans are a big hit at backyard barbecues and church picnics. Friends always ask me to bring my special beans.
—Julie Currington, Gahanna, OH

Prep: 20 min. • **Bake:** 1 hour
Makes: 12 servings

½ lb. ground beef
5 bacon strips, diced
½ cup chopped onion
⅓ cup packed brown sugar
¼ cup sugar
¼ cup ketchup
¼ cup barbecue sauce
2 Tbsp. molasses
2 Tbsp. prepared mustard
½ tsp. chili powder
½ tsp. salt
2 cans (16 oz. each) pork and beans, undrained
1 can (16 oz.) butter beans, rinsed and drained
1 can (16 oz.) kidney beans, rinsed and drained

1. Preheat oven to 350°. In a large skillet, cook and crumble beef with bacon and onion over medium heat until beef is no longer pink; drain.
2. Stir in sugars, ketchup, barbecue sauce, molasses, mustard, chili powder and salt until blended. Stir in beans. Transfer to a greased 2½-qt. baking dish. Bake, covered, until beans reach the desired thickness, about 1 hour.
Freeze option: Freeze cooled beans in freezer containers. To use, partially thaw in refrigerator overnight. Heat through in a saucepan, stirring occasionally and adding water if necessary.

¾ cup: 269 cal., 8g fat (2g sat. fat), 19mg chol., 708mg sod., 42g carb. (21g sugars, 7g fiber), 13g pro.

GARLIC ROASTED BRUSSELS SPROUTS

My roommate and I used to make garlicky Brussels sprouts at least twice a week. Now I make them as a healthy side whenever I get a chance, for all sorts of occasions.
—Katherine Moore-Colasurd, Cincinnati, OH

Prep/Total: 30 min.
Makes: 12 servings

2 lbs. fresh Brussels sprouts, trimmed and halved
2 medium red onions, cut into 1-in. pieces
3 Tbsp. olive oil
7 garlic cloves, finely chopped
1 tsp. salt
½ tsp. pepper

1. Preheat oven to 425°. Divide Brussels sprouts and onions between two foil-lined 15x10x1-in. baking pans.
2. In a small bowl, mix oil, garlic, salt and pepper; drizzle half of the mixture over each pan and toss to coat. Roast until tender, 20-25 minutes, stirring mixture occasionally and switching position of pans halfway.
½ cup: 69 cal., 4g fat (1g sat. fat), 0 chol., 215mg sod., 8g carb. (2g sugars, 3g fiber), 3g pro. **Diabetic exchanges:** 1 vegetable, ½ fat.

TORTELLINI BAKE

Summer in New Hampshire brings plenty of fresh zucchini and other squash...one year I had so much that I was searching for different ways to prepare it, and that's when I came up with this baked pasta recipe. Serve it as a side dish or on its own as a light meal.
—Donald Roberts, Amherst, NH

- -

Prep: 20 min. • **Bake:** 20 min.
Makes: 8 servings

- 1 pkg. (10 oz.) refrigerated cheese tortellini
- 1 Tbsp. olive oil
- 1 small zucchini, diced
- 1 yellow squash, diced
- 1 onion, diced
- 1 sweet red pepper, diced
- 1 tsp. dried basil
- ½ tsp. pepper
- ½ tsp. salt
- 1 cup shredded part-skim mozzarella cheese
- 1 cup half-and-half cream

1. Cook tortellini according to package directions. Meanwhile, heat oil in a skillet; cook zucchini, yellow squash, onion, red pepper and seasonings until vegetables are crisp-tender.
2. Drain tortellini; combine with vegetable mixture, mozzarella and cream in a 1½-qt. baking dish.
3. Bake, uncovered, at 375° until heated through, about 20 minutes.
Freeze option: Cool unbaked casserole; cover and freeze. To use, partially thaw in refrigerator overnight. Remove casserole from refrigerator 30 minutes before baking. Preheat the oven to 375°. Bake casserole as directed, increasing time as necessary for a thermometer inserted in center to read 165°.
¾ cup: 219 cal., 10g fat (5g sat. fat), 38mg chol., 362mg sod., 22g carb. (5g sugars, 2g fiber), 10g pro.

SWEET CORN & TOMATO SALAD

I always make this for family events. It reminds me of all the fun BBQs and picnics over the years.
—Jessica Kleinbaum, Plant City, FL

- -

Prep: 15 min. • **Cook:** 10 min. + chilling
Makes: 10 servings

- 8 medium ears sweet corn, husks removed
- 1 large sweet red pepper, chopped
- 2 cups cherry tomatoes, halved
- 1 small red onion, finely chopped
- ¼ cup coarsely chopped fresh basil
DRESSING
- ½ cup canola oil
- ¼ cup rice vinegar
- 2 Tbsp. lime juice
- 1¼ tsp. salt
- ½ to 1 tsp. hot pepper sauce
- ½ tsp. garlic powder
- ½ tsp. grated lime zest
- ¼ tsp. pepper

1. Place corn in a large stock pot; add water to cover. Bring to a boil. Cook, covered, until crisp-tender, 6-8 minutes; drain. Cool slightly. Cut corn from cobs and place in a large bowl. Stir in the red pepper, tomatoes and onion.
2. Combine dressing ingredients. Pour over the corn mixture; toss to coat. Refrigerate, covered, at least 1 hour.
¾ cup: 192 cal., 12g fat (1g sat. fat), 0 chol., 407mg sod., 21g carb. (9g sugars, 3g fiber), 3g pro. **Diabetic exchanges:** 2 fat, 1 starch, 1 vegetable.

GREEN ONION ROLLS

Better double the batch—these savory, elegant rolls will disappear fast.
—Jane Kroeger, Key Largo, FL

- -

Prep: 30 min. + rising • **Bake:** 20 min.
Makes: 1 dozen

1	Tbsp. butter
1½	cups chopped green onions
½	tsp. pepper
¾	tsp. garlic salt, optional
1	loaf (1 lb.) frozen bread dough, thawed
½	cup shredded part-skim mozzarella cheese
⅓	cup grated Parmesan cheese

1. Preheat oven to 375°. In a large skillet, heat butter over medium-high heat; saute green onions until tender. Stir in pepper and, if desired, garlic salt. Remove skillet from heat.
2. On a lightly floured surface, roll dough into a 12x8-in. rectangle. Spread with onion mixture. Sprinkle with cheeses.
3. Roll up jelly-roll style, starting with a long side; pinch seam to seal. Cut into 12 slices; place in greased muffin cups. Cover with greased plastic wrap; let rise in a warm place until doubled, about 30 minutes. Preheat oven to 375°.
4. Bake until golden brown, 18-20 minutes. Remove from pan to a wire rack. Serve warm.
1 roll: 142 cal., 4g fat (1g sat. fat), 7mg chol., 415mg sod., 20g carb. (2g sugars, 2g fiber), 6g pro.

BACON PEA SALAD

My husband absolutely loves peas. My middle son isn't the biggest fan, but he loves bacon. And so I decided to combine the two, and it was perfect! This salad makes an awesome side dish, especially for a backyard barbecue.

—Angela Lively, Conroe, TX

Prep: 10 min. + chilling • **Makes:** 6 servings

4 cups frozen peas (about 16 oz.), thawed
½ cup shredded sharp cheddar cheese
½ cup ranch salad dressing
⅓ cup chopped red onion
¼ tsp. salt
¼ tsp. pepper
4 bacon strips, cooked and crumbled

Combine the first 6 ingredients; toss to coat. Refrigerate, covered, at least 30 minutes. Stir in bacon before serving.

¾ cup: 218 cal., 14g fat (4g sat. fat), 17mg chol., 547mg sod., 14g carb. (6g sugars, 4g fiber), 9g pro.

CARROT & KALE VEGETABLE SAUTE

Thanks to fresh veggie dishes like this one, I almost forget I'm eating wheat- and gluten-free. This gorgeous side dish with bacon is awesome.
—Darla Andrews, Schertz, TX

Prep: 15 min. • **Cook:** 20 min.
Makes: 8 servings

- 8 bacon strips, coarsely chopped
- 4 large carrots, sliced
- 2 cups peeled cubed butternut squash (½-in. pieces)
- 1 poblano pepper, seeded and chopped
- ½ cup finely chopped red onion
- 1 tsp. smoked paprika
- ¼ tsp. salt
- ¼ tsp. pepper
- 2 plum tomatoes, chopped
- 2 cups chopped fresh kale

1. In a large skillet, cook bacon over medium heat until crisp, stirring occasionally. Using a slotted spoon, remove bacon to paper towels. Pour off all but 1 Tbsp. drippings.

2. Add carrots and squash to drippings; cook, covered, over medium heat for 5 minutes. Add poblano pepper and onion; cook until vegetables are tender, about 5 minutes, stirring occasionally. Stir in seasonings. Add tomatoes and kale; cook, covered, until kale is wilted, 2-3 minutes. Top with bacon.

¾ cup: 101 cal., 5g fat (2g sat. fat), 10mg chol., 251mg sod., 11g carb. (4g sugars, 3g fiber), 4g pro. **Diabetic exchanges:** 1 vegetable, 1 fat, ½ starch.

COMPANY FRUIT SALAD

We first tried a salad like this at a local deli. Since I couldn't get that recipe, I started mixing up different dressings until I hit on this one. Now I make this refreshing salad for nearly every picnic and get-together. It can be a snack, side dish or even dessert.

—Connie Osterhout, Napoleon, OH

- -

Takes: 20 min. • **Makes:** 20 servings

- 4 medium **Golden Delicious apples**, diced
- 4 medium **Red Delicious apples**, diced
- 2 cups **seedless green grapes**, halved
- 2 cups **seedless red grapes**, halved
- 1 can (20 oz.) **pineapple chunks**, drained
- 1 can (11 oz.) **mandarin oranges**, drained

DRESSING
- 3 oz. **cream cheese**, softened
- ½ cup **sour cream**
- ½ cup **mayonnaise**
- ½ cup **sugar**

In a bowl, combine the first 6 ingredients. In a small bowl, beat dressing ingredients until smooth. Pour over fruit; toss gently to coat.

¾ cup: 161 cal., 7g fat (2g sat. fat), 11mg chol., 48mg sod., 25g carb. (22g sugars, 2g fiber), 1g pro.

LAYERED FRESH FRUIT SALAD

Fresh fruit flavor shines in this medley. It's got a little zing from citrus zest and cinnamon—and is just sweet enough to feel like dessert.
—Page Alexander, Baldwin City, KS

- -

Prep: 20 min. + chilling
Cook: 10 min.
Makes: 12 servings

- ½ tsp. grated orange zest
- ⅔ cup orange juice
- ½ tsp. grated lemon zest
- ⅓ cup lemon juice
- ⅓ cup packed light brown sugar
- 1 cinnamon stick

FRUIT SALAD
- 2 cups cubed fresh pineapple
- 2 cups sliced fresh strawberries
- 2 medium kiwifruit, peeled and sliced
- 3 medium bananas, sliced
- 2 medium oranges, peeled and sectioned
- 1 medium red grapefruit, peeled and sectioned
- 1 cup seedless red grapes

1. Place first 6 ingredients in a saucepan; bring to a boil. Reduce heat; simmer, uncovered, 5 minutes. Cool completely. Remove cinnamon stick.
2. Layer fruit in a large glass bowl. Pour juice mixture over the top. Refrigerate, covered, several hours.
1 serving: 110 cal., 0 fat (0 sat. fat), 0 chol., 5mg sod., 28g carb. (21g sugars, 2g fiber), 1g pro. **Diabetic exchanges:** 1 starch, 1 fruit.

PECAN RICE PILAF

This is one of my standby side dishes, which can complement most meat and meatless entrees. It's special enough for company, quick enough for weeknights.
—Jacqueline Oglesby, Spruce Pine, NC

- -

Prep: 15 min. • **Cook:** 20 min.
Makes: 9 servings

- 1 cup chopped pecans
- 5 Tbsp. butter, divided
- 1 small onion, chopped
- 2 cups uncooked long grain rice
- 1 carton (32 oz.) chicken broth
- 3 Tbsp. minced fresh parsley, divided
- ½ tsp. salt
- ¼ tsp. dried thyme
- ⅛ tsp. pepper
- 1 cup shredded carrots

1. In a large saucepan, saute the pecans in 2 Tbsp. butter until toasted; remove from the pan and set aside.
2. In the same pan, saute onion in remaining butter until tender. Add rice; cook and stir until rice is lightly browned, 3-4 minutes. Stir in the broth, 2 Tbsp. parsley, salt, thyme and pepper. Bring to a boil. Reduce heat; cover and simmer for 10 minutes.
3. Add carrots; simmer until rice is tender, 3-5 minutes longer. Stir in toasted pecans and remaining parsley. Fluff with a fork.
Freeze option: Reserving pecans for later, freeze cooled pilaf in a freezer container. To use, partially thaw in the refrigerator overnight. Microwave, covered, on high in a microwave-safe dish, adding 2-3 Tbsp. water to moisten, until heated through. Toast pecans; add to pilaf.
¾ cup: 313 cal., 16g fat (5g sat. fat), 19mg chol., 623mg sod., 37g carb. (2g sugars, 2g fiber), 5g pro.

GERMAN PASTA SALAD

I took this salad to a neighbor's party that included a houseful of teachers. The dish was graded an A+! It's a standout for Oktoberfest, too.
—Nichole Fischer, Las Vegas, NV

Takes: 30 min.
Makes: 16 servings

    4   cups uncooked egg noodles
    ⅓   cup packed brown sugar
    ¼   cup olive oil
    ¼   cup Dijon mustard
    2   Tbsp. cider vinegar
    1½ tsp. caraway seeds
    6   cups coleslaw mix
    8   oz. sliced deli corned
        beef, cut into strips
    ¼   cup shredded Swiss cheese

1. In a large saucepan, cook the noodles according to package directions.
2. Meanwhile, in a small saucepan over low heat, combine brown sugar, oil, mustard, vinegar and caraway seeds. Cook and stir until heated through, 3-5 minutes.
3. Drain noodles. In a large bowl, combine the coleslaw mix, noodles, corned beef and warm dressing; toss to coat. Sprinkle with the cheese. Serve warm or at room temperature. Refrigerate leftovers.
¾ cup: 131 cal., 5g fat (1g sat. fat), 21mg chol., 267mg sod., 16g carb. (5g sugars, 1g fiber), 5g pro.

TARRAGON ASPARAGUS

I grow purple asparagus, so I'm always looking for new ways to prepare it. Recently, my husband and I discovered how wonderful any color of asparagus tastes when it's grilled. Here's a simple and elegant way to try it.
—Sue Gronholz, Beaver Dam, WI

Takes: 15 min. • **Makes:** 8 servings

    2   lbs. fresh asparagus, trimmed
    2   Tbsp. olive oil
    1   tsp. salt
    ½   tsp. pepper
    ¼   cup honey
    2   to 4 Tbsp. minced fresh tarragon

On a large plate, toss asparagus with oil, salt and pepper. Grill, covered, over medium heat until crisp-tender, about 6-8 minutes, turning occasionally and basting frequently with honey during the last 3 minutes. Sprinkle with tarragon.
1 serving: 76 cal., 4g fat (1g sat. fat), 0 chol., 302mg sod., 11g carb. (10g sugars, 1g fiber), 2g pro. **Diabetic exchanges:** 1 vegetable, ½ starch, ½ fat.

YOU'RE-BACON-ME-CRAZY POTATO SALAD

My kids and I always want potato salad when we grill or barbecue, but we don't like the store-bought versions. I toyed with many combinations and then finally developed this one—now it's their top side-dish request.
—Paul Cogswell, League City, TX

- -

Prep: 10 min.
Cook: 25 min. + chilling
Makes: 12 servings

2½ lbs. small red potatoes,
   cut into 1-in. pieces
3 tsp. salt
1 lb. bacon strips, finely chopped
1 large onion, chopped
3 celery ribs, finely chopped
2 cups mayonnaise
2 Tbsp. Dijon or yellow mustard
¾ tsp. dill weed
½ tsp. celery salt
¼ tsp. celery seed

1. Place potatoes in a 6-qt. stockpot; add water to cover. Add salt; bring to a boil. Reduce heat; cook, uncovered, until potatoes are tender, 12-15 minutes.
2. Meanwhile, in a large skillet, cook bacon over medium heat until crisp, stirring occasionally. Remove with a slotted spoon and drain on paper towels; reserve 4 Tbsp. bacon drippings. Cook and stir onion in reserved drippings until browned, about 6-8 minutes.
3. Reserve ¼ cup of the cooked bacon for topping. Add onion, drippings, celery and remaining bacon to potatoes.
4. In a bowl, mix mayonnaise, mustard and seasonings. Pour over potato mixture; toss to coat. Refrigerate, covered, until chilled, about 1 hour. Just before serving, sprinkle with reserved bacon.

¾ cup: 424 cal., 36g fat (7g sat. fat), 20mg chol., 1147mg sod., 17g carb. (2g sugars, 2g fiber), 7g pro.

CHILLED SHRIMP PASTA SALAD

This chilled salad is just the right thing for lunch on a hot summer day. It also makes a nice side dish for sharing anytime.
—Mary Price, Youngstown, OH

- -

Takes: 30 min.
Makes: 12 servings

- 3 cups uncooked small pasta shells
- ½ cup sour cream
- ½ cup mayonnaise
- ¼ cup horseradish sauce
- 2 Tbsp. grated onion
- 1½ tsp. seasoned salt
- ¾ tsp. pepper
- 1 lb. peeled and deveined cooked small shrimp
- 1 large cucumber, seeded and chopped
- 3 celery ribs, thinly sliced
  Red lettuce leaves, optional

1. Cook pasta according to the package directions. Drain; rinse with cold water.
2. In a large bowl, mix the sour cream, mayonnaise, horseradish sauce, onion, seasoned salt and pepper. Stir in shrimp, cucumber, celery and pasta. Refrigerate until serving. If desired, serve on lettuce.
¾ cup: 239 cal., 12g fat (2g sat. fat), 72mg chol., 344mg sod., 20g carb. (3g sugars, 1g fiber), 11g pro. **Diabetic exchanges:** 2 fat, 1 starch, 1 lean meat.

CRANBERRY PECAN STUFFING

I love stuffing, but my family wasn't that fond of it—that is, until I found this recipe. I added a few extras and now they gobble it up. I think the cranberries give it that something special.
—Robin Lang, Muskegon, MI

- -

Prep: 30 min. • **Bake:** 40 min.
Makes: 13 servings

- 1 cup orange juice
- ½ cup dried cranberries
- ½ lb. bulk pork sausage
- ¼ cup butter, cubed
- 3 celery ribs, chopped
- 1 large onion, chopped
- 1 tsp. poultry seasoning
- 6 cups seasoned stuffing cubes
- 1 medium tart apple, peeled and finely chopped
- ½ cup chopped pecans
- ¼ tsp. salt
- ⅛ tsp. pepper
- ¾ to 1 cup chicken broth

1. In a small saucepan, bring orange juice and cranberries to a boil. Remove from the heat; let stand 5 minutes. Meanwhile, in a large skillet, cook sausage until no longer pink; drain. Transfer to a large bowl.
2. In the same skillet, melt butter. Add the celery and onion; saute until tender. Stir in poultry seasoning.
3. Add to the sausage mixture. Stir in the stuffing cubes, orange juice mixture, apple, pecans, salt, pepper and enough broth to reach desired moistness.
4. Transfer to a greased 13x9-in. baking dish. Cover stuffing and bake at 325° for 30 minutes. Uncover; bake until lightly browned, 10-15 minutes longer.
¾ cup: 219 cal., 11g fat (4g sat. fat), 16mg chol., 532mg sod., 27g carb. (8g sugars, 2g fiber), 4g pro.

TEST KITCHEN TIP
Pecans have higher fat content than other nuts, so they're more prone to becoming rancid. They'll stay fresh twice as long in the freezer as they would at room temperature.

GRANDMOTHER'S CORN PUDDING

My grandmother always served this pudding for family reunions and other big gatherings. It's a popular side dish on Maryland's Eastern Shore.
—Susan Brown Langenstein, Salisbury, MD

Prep: 10 min. • **Bake:** 50 min.
Makes: 9 servings

- 4 **large eggs**
- 1 **cup whole milk**
- 1 **can (15 oz.) cream-style corn**
- ½ **cup sugar**
- 5 **slices day-old bread, crusts removed**
- 1 **Tbsp. butter, softened**

In a bowl, beat eggs and milk. Add corn and sugar; mix well. Cut bread into ½-in. cubes and place in a greased 9-in. square baking dish. Pour egg mixture over bread. Dot with butter. Bake, uncovered, at 350° until a knife inserted in the center comes out clean, 50-60 minutes.

1 serving: 175 cal., 5g fat (2g sat. fat), 102mg chol., 264mg sod., 28g carb. (14g sugars, 1g fiber), 6g pro.

★ ★ ☆ ☆ ☆ **READER REVIEW**

"This is something I make several times a year. It's delicious and the grandkids eat it up every Thanksgiving. I do cut the sugar a little; otherwise, it's a perfect side dish."

JELLYBUG TASTEOFHOME.COM

NUTTY BROCCOLI SLAW

My daughter gave me this delightful salad recipe. The sweet dressing nicely coats a crisp blend of broccoli coleslaw mix, onions, almonds and sunflower kernels. Crushed ramen noodles provide even more crunch. It has been a smash hit wherever I take it.
—Dora Mae Clapsaddle, Kensington, OH

- -

Takes: 15 min. • **Makes:** 16 servings

1	pkg. (3 oz.) chicken ramen noodles
1	pkg. (16 oz.) broccoli coleslaw mix
2	cups sliced green onions (about 2 bunches)
1½	cups broccoli florets
1	can (6 oz.) ripe olives, drained and halved
1	cup sunflower kernels, toasted
½	cup slivered almonds, toasted
½	cup sugar
½	cup cider vinegar
½	cup olive oil

1. Set aside the noodle seasoning packet; crush the noodles and place in a large bowl. Add the slaw mix, onions, broccoli, olives, sunflower kernels and almonds.

2. In a jar with a tight-fitting lid, combine the sugar, vinegar, oil and contents of seasoning packet; shake well. Drizzle over salad and toss to coat. Serve immediately.

¾ cup: 206 cal., 15g fat (2g sat. fat), 0 chol., 248mg sod., 16g carb. (9g sugars, 3g fiber), 4g pro.

TEST KITCHEN TIP
Shave a few calories from this recipe by reducing the vinegar and oil from ½ cup each to ⅓ cup.

VEGGIE MACARONI & CHEESE

This creamy mac 'n' cheese definitely doesn't come from a box! Fresh veggies add crunch and color and will leave everyone saying, "More, please!"
—Marsha Morril, Harrisburg, OR

- -

Prep: 30 min. • **Bake:** 15 min.
Makes: 12 servings

- 1½ cups uncooked elbow macaroni
- 3 cups fresh broccoli florets
- 2 cups fresh cauliflowerets
- 3 large carrots, halved lengthwise and thinly sliced
- 2 celery ribs, sliced
- 1 Tbsp. butter
- 1 medium onion, chopped
- ¼ cup all-purpose flour
- 1 cup 2% milk
- 1 cup chicken broth
- 3 cups shredded sharp cheddar cheese
- 1 Tbsp. Dijon mustard
- ¼ tsp. salt
- ⅛ tsp. pepper
- ¼ tsp. paprika

1. Preheat oven to 350°. In a 6-qt. stockpot, cook macaroni according to package directions, adding broccoli, cauliflower, carrots and celery during the last 6 minutes of cooking. Drain; transfer to a greased 13x9-in. baking dish.
2. Meanwhile, in a large saucepan, heat butter over medium-high heat; saute onion until tender. Stir in flour until blended. Gradually stir in milk and broth; bring to a boil. Cook and stir until sauce is thickened, about 2 minutes; stir in cheese, mustard, salt and pepper.
3. Add to macaroni mixture, stirring to coat; sprinkle with paprika. Bake the casserole, uncovered, until heated through, 15-20 minutes.

1 cup: 200 cal., 11g fat (6g sat. fat), 33mg chol., 391mg sod., 15g carb. (3g sugars, 2g fiber), 10g pro.

White Velvet Cutouts
page 163

Big Batch Dishes

Big celebrations call for a nice, big spread of tasty foods . Here, you'll find the crowd-sized recipes you need to serve 20 hungry guests or more!

3. Bake, covered, 30 minutes. Uncover and bake stuffing until lightly browned and a thermometer reads 165°, 12-18 minutes longer. If desired, top the stuffing with chopped fresh parsley.

Note: If using this recipe to stuff poultry, replace the eggs with 3/4 cup egg substitute. Bake until a thermometer in thick part of poultry thigh reads 170° to 175° and in stuffing, 165°. Allow 3/4 cup stuffing per pound of turkey. Bake remaining stuffing as directed in the recipe.

¾ cup: 202 cal., 6g fat (2g sat. fat), 37mg chol., 572mg sod., 28g carb. (3g sugars, 2g fiber), 9g pro. **Diabetic exchanges:** 2 starch, 1 fat.

CREAMY CARAMEL DIP

Because I feed my husband, a member of the Royal Canadian Mounted Police, and our two boys, I love satisfying snacks that are easy to make. We all appreciate this cool, light fruit dip.
—Karen Laubman, Spruce Grove, AB

Prep: 10 min. + chilling • **Makes:** 3½ cups

- 1 pkg. (8 oz.) cream cheese, softened
- ¾ cup packed brown sugar
- 1 cup sour cream
- 2 tsp. vanilla extract
- 2 tsp. lemon juice
- 1 cup cold milk
- 1 pkg. (3.4 oz.) instant vanilla pudding mix
  Assorted fresh fruit

1. In a bowl, beat cream cheese and brown sugar until smooth. Add the sour cream, vanilla, lemon juice, milk and pudding mix, beating well after each addition.
2. Cover and chill for at least 1 hour. Serve as a dip for fruit.

2 Tbsp. dip: 87 cal., 5g fat (3g sat. fat), 16mg chol., 83mg sod., 10g carb. (9g sugars, 0 fiber), 1g pro.

TRADITIONAL HOLIDAY STUFFING

Sausage and sage add a gourmet taste to this stuffing. The recipe makes quite a big batch, so it's perfect for large holiday gatherings. There's a reason it's a timeless classic.
—Lorraine Brauckhoff, Zolfo Springs, FL

Prep: 35 min. • **Bake:** 45 min.
Makes: 24 servings (¾ cup each)

- 1 pkg. (12 oz.) reduced-fat bulk pork sausage or breakfast turkey sausage links, casings removed
- 3 celery ribs, chopped
- 1 large onion, chopped
- 2 Tbsp. reduced-fat mayonnaise
- 2 Tbsp. prepared mustard
- 4 tsp. rubbed sage
- 1 Tbsp. poultry seasoning
- 2 loaves (16 oz. each) day-old white bread, cubed
- 1 loaf (16 oz.) day-old whole wheat bread, cubed
- 3 large eggs, lightly beaten
- 2 cans (14½ oz. each) reduced-sodium chicken broth
  Chopped fresh parsley, optional

1. Preheat oven to 350°. In a large nonstick skillet cook sausage, celery and onion over medium heat until meat is no longer pink, breaking up sausage into crumbles; drain. Remove from heat; stir in mayonnaise, mustard, sage and poultry seasoning.
2. Place bread cubes in a large bowl; add sausage mixture and toss. In a small bowl, whisk eggs and broth; pour over bread cubes and stir gently to combine. Transfer to two 3-qt. baking dishes coated with cooking spray.

BIG BATCH DISHES | 145

SEASONED TURKEY SANDWICHES

Make these homemade turkey sandwiches for a great casual dinner. This recipe steals the show at any potluck or family reunion, and it's been a huge hit at all of our graduation parties, football dinners and more. I like to add some lettuce and tomato for crunch and color; serve with the condiments you like!
—LaVonne Hegland, St. Michael, MN

Prep: 45 min. + rising
Grill: 2½ hours + standing
Makes: 2 dozen

HOMEMADE SANDWICH BUNS
- 2 pkg. (¼ oz. each) active dry yeast
- 2 cups warm water (110° to 115°), divided
- ½ cup sugar
- 1 large egg, room temperature
- 3 Tbsp. shortening
- 1 tsp. salt
- 6½ to 7 cups all-purpose flour
- 3 Tbsp. butter, softened

GRILLED TURKEY
- 2 tsp. salt
- 2 tsp. garlic powder
- 2 tsp. pepper
- 1 turkey (14 to 16 lbs.)
- ½ cup butter, cubed

1. In a large bowl, dissolve yeast in ½ cup of warm water. Add the sugar, egg, shortening, salt, remaining water and 2 cups flour. Beat until smooth. Stir in enough remaining flour to form a soft dough (dough will be sticky).

2. Turn onto a floured surface; knead until smooth and elastic, about 6-8 minutes. Place in a greased bowl, turning once to grease top. Cover and let rise in a warm place until doubled, about 1 hour.

3. Punch dough down. Turn onto a lightly floured surface; divide in half. Divide each portion into 12 pieces. Shape each into a ball. Place 3 in. apart on greased baking sheets. Brush with butter. Cover and let rise until doubled, about 30 minutes.

4. Bake at 400° for 8-10 minutes or until golden brown. Remove the buns to wire racks to cool.

5. Meanwhile, combine the salt, garlic powder and pepper; rub over turkey. Place butter inside turkey cavity; tie drumsticks together. Prepare grill for indirect medium heat. Tuck wings under turkey and place with breast side up in a disposable roasting pan; place on grill rack.

6. Grill turkey, covered, for 1 hour. If using a charcoal grill, add 10 briquettes to coals. Baste with pan drippings. Cover and grill until a thermometer reads 180°, about 1½ to 2 hours longer, adding 10 briquettes to maintain the heat and brushing turkey with the pan drippings every 30 minutes. (Cover loosely with foil if turkey browns too quickly.)

7. Cover and let stand for 20 minutes before carving. Split buns in half; fill with sliced turkey.

6 oz. cooked turkey with bun: 513 cal., 21g fat (8g sat. fat), 166mg chol., 452mg sod., 31g carb. (5g sugars, 1g fiber), 46g pro.

MAKE AHEAD

ORANGE BANANA NUT BREAD

I like this recipe because orange juice gives the banana bread such a bright flavor. The loaf stays tender even after it's been frozen.

—Barbara Roethlisberger, Shepherd, MI

Prep: 15 min. • **Bake:** 50 min. + cooling
Makes: 2 loaves (12 slices each)

- 1½ cups sugar
- 3 Tbsp. canola oil
- 2 large eggs, room temperature
- 3 medium ripe bananas, mashed (about 1¼ cups)
- ¾ cup orange juice
- 3 cups all-purpose flour
- 1½ tsp. baking powder
- 1½ tsp. baking soda
- ½ tsp. salt
- 1 cup chopped walnuts

1. In a bowl, combine the sugar, oil and eggs; mix well. Stir in bananas and orange juice. Combine the dry ingredients; add to the banana mixture, beating just until moistened. Stir in walnuts. Pour batter into 2 greased 8x4-in. loaf pans.
2. Bake bread at 325° until a toothpick inserted in the center comes out clean, 50-60 minutes. Cool for 10 minutes; remove loaves from pans to a wire rack to cool completely.
Freeze option: Securely wrap cooled loaves in plastic and foil; freeze. To use, thaw at room temperature.
1 slice: 131 cal., 4g fat (0 sat. fat), 13mg chol., 119mg sod., 22g carb. (12g sugars, 1g fiber), 3g pro.

...HERRY PASTRY CUPS

...own and flaky, these bite-sized ...es with creamy Brie and sweet ...eserves could easily double as a ...us dessert.

—Marilyn McSween, Mentor, OH

- -

Takes: 30 min. • **Makes:** 3 dozen

1	**sheet frozen puff pastry, thawed**
½	**cup cherry preserves**
4	**oz. Brie cheese, cut into** **½-in. cubes**
¼	**cup chopped pecans or walnuts**
2	**Tbsp. minced chives**

1. Unfold puff pastry; cut into 36 squares. Gently press squares onto the bottoms of 36 greased miniature muffin cups.

2. Bake at 375° for 10 minutes. Using the end of a wooden spoon handle, make a ½-in.-deep indentation in the center of each. Bake 6-8 minutes longer or until golden brown. With spoon handle, press squares down again.

3. Spoon a rounded ½ tsp. of preserves into each cup. Top with cheese; sprinkle with nuts and chives. Bake until cheese is melted, 3-5 minutes.

1 appetizer: 61 cal., 3g fat (1g sat. fat), 3mg chol., 42mg sod., 7g carb. (3g sugars, 1g fiber), 1g pro.

★★★★☆ **READER REVIEW**

"Outstanding! It's tempting to eat several after tasting them. I made them exactly like the recipe said and will make them for special occasions. A little pricey for all the ingredients, but it is worth it."

R_UTH TASTEOFHOME.COM

DIPPED GINGERSNAPS

I get a great deal of satisfaction making and giving time-tested treats like these soft, chewy cookies. Dipping them into the white chocolate makes these great gingersnaps even more special.
—Laura Kimball, West Jordan, UT

Prep: 20 min.
Bake: 10 min./batch + cooling
Makes: 14½ dozen

2	**cups sugar**
1½	**cups canola oil**
2	**large eggs, room temperature**
½	**cup molasses**
4	**cups all-purpose flour**
4	**tsp. baking soda**
3	**tsp. ground ginger**
2	**tsp. ground cinnamon**
1	**tsp. salt**
	Additional sugar
2	**pkg. (10 to 12 oz. each) white baking chips**
¼	**cup shortening**

1. In a large bowl, combine sugar and oil. Beat in eggs. Stir in molasses. Combine the flour, baking soda, ginger, cinnamon and salt; gradually add to the creamed mixture and mix well.

2. Shape into ¾-in. balls and roll in sugar. Place 2 in. apart on ungreased baking sheets. Bake at 350° until cookies spring back when touched lightly, 10-12 minutes. Remove to wire racks to cool.

3. In a microwave, melt the chips and shortening; stir until smooth. Dip cookies halfway into the melted chips or drizzle with mixture; allow excess to drip off. Place on waxed paper; let stand until set.

1 cookie: 47 cal., 2g fat (0 sat. fat), 2mg chol., 44mg sod., 6g carb. (4g sugars, 0 fiber), 0 pro.

BLACK FOREST HAM ROLL-UPS

We love to entertain at home and the office. Ham and cheese rolled in tortillas make a quick and easy appetizer that's easy to transport.

—Susan Zugehoer, Hebron, KY

- -

Prep: 25 min. + chilling
Makes: about 6½ dozen

- 1 pkg. (8 oz.) cream cheese, softened
- 2 tsp. minced fresh parsley
- 2 tsp. dried celery flakes
- 2 tsp. Dijon mustard
- 1 tsp. lemon juice
- ⅛ tsp. salt
- ⅛ tsp. pepper
- ½ cup dried cranberries, chopped
- 2 green onions, chopped
- 5 flour tortillas (10 in.), room temperature
- ½ lb. thinly sliced Black Forest deli ham
- ½ lb. thinly sliced Swiss cheese

1. In a bowl, mix the first 7 ingredients until blended. Stir in cranberries and green onions; spread over tortillas. Layer with ham and cheese. Roll up tightly; wrap in plastic. Refrigerate at least 1 hour.

2. Just before serving, unwrap and cut each tortilla crosswise into 16 slices.

1 appetizer: 42 cal., 2g fat (1g sat. fat), 7mg chol., 83mg sod., 3g carb. (1g sugars, 0g fiber), 2g pro.

MAKE AHEAD
MOCHA TRUFFLES

Nothing compares to the melt-in-your-mouth flavor of these truffles...or to the simplicity of the recipe. Whenever I make them my family and friends devour them quickly. No one has to know how easy they are to prepare.
—Stacy Abell, Olathe, KS

- -

Prep: 25 min. + chilling
Makes: 5½ dozen

2 pkg. (12 oz. each) semisweet chocolate chips
1 pkg. (8 oz.) cream cheese, softened
3 Tbsp. instant coffee granules
2 tsp. water
1 lb. dark chocolate candy coating, coarsely chopped
   White candy coating, optional

1. In a microwave, melt chocolate chips; stir until smooth. Beat in cream cheese. Dissolve coffee in water; add to cream cheese and beat until smooth.

2. Chill until firm enough to shape. Shape into 1-in. balls and place on waxed paper-lined baking sheets. Chill until firm, 1-2 hours.

3. In a microwave, melt chocolate coating; stir until smooth. Dip balls in chocolate; allow excess to drip off. Place on waxed paper; let stand until set. If desired, melt white coating and drizzle over truffles.

Note: Candy coating, the product used for dipping chocolate, is found in the baking section of most grocery stores. Sometimes labeled almond bark or confectionery coating, it is sold in bulk packages (1 to 1½ pounds). A substitute for 6 oz. chocolate coating would be 1 cup (6 oz.) semisweet, dark or white chocolate chips and 1 Tbsp. shortening melted together.

Freeze option: Truffles can be frozen for several months before dipping in chocolate. Thaw in the refrigerator before dipping.

1 truffle: 73 cal., 5g fat (3g sat. fat), 4mg chol., 11mg sod., 8g carb. (7g sugars, 0 fiber), 1g pro.

MAKE AHEAD
BUTTERHORNS

Mom loved to make these rolls. They're beautiful and impressive, and their wonderful taste carries with it the memories of home.
—Bernice Morris, Marshfield, MO

- -

Prep: 30 min. + freezing • **Bake:** 15 min.
Makes: 32 rolls

2 pkg. (¼ oz. each) active dry yeast
⅓ cup warm water (110° to 115°)
2 cups warm 2% milk (110° to 115°)
1 cup shortening
1 cup sugar
6 large eggs, room temperature
2 tsp. salt
9 cups all-purpose flour, divided
3 to 4 Tbsp. butter, melted

1. In a large bowl, dissolve yeast in water. Add milk, shortening, sugar, eggs, salt and 4 cups flour; beat until smooth. Add enough of remaining flour to form a soft dough.

2. Turn onto a floured surface; knead lightly. Place in a greased bowl, turning once to grease top. Cover and let rise in a warm place until doubled, about 2 hours.

3. Punch the dough down; divide into 4 equal parts. Roll each into a 9-in. circle; brush with butter. Cut each circle into 8 pie-slice shaped wedges; roll up each wedge from wide edge to tip of dough and pinch to seal.

4. Place rolls with tip down on baking sheets; freeze. Place frozen rolls in freezer bags and seal. Store in freezer for up to 4 weeks.

To use frozen rolls: Arrange frozen rolls 2 in. apart on greased baking sheets. Cover with lightly greased plastic wrap; thaw in refrigerator overnight. Let rolls rise in a warm place until doubled, about 1 hour. Bake at 375° until golden brown, 12-15 minutes. Serve warm.

1 roll: 239 cal., 9g fat (3g sat. fat), 39mg chol., 178mg sod., 34g carb. (7g sugars, 1g fiber), 6g pro.

FRUIT SALAD WITH APRICOT DRESSING

Whenever I serve this lovely, refreshing salad for picnics, potlucks and holidays, the bowl empties in a hurry!
—Carol Lambert, El Dorado, AR

Takes: 30 min. • **Makes:** 26 servings

- 1 cup sugar
- 1 Tbsp. cornstarch
- 2 cans (5½ oz. each) apricot nectar
- 1 tsp. vanilla extract
- 6 large red apples, coarsely chopped
- 8 medium firm bananas, sliced
- 1 medium fresh pineapple, peeled and cut into chunks (about 5 cups)
- 1 qt. fresh strawberries, quartered
- 2 cups green grapes

1. In a microwave-safe bowl, stir the sugar, cornstarch and apricot nectar until smooth. Microwave, uncovered, on high until slightly thickened, for 4-6 minutes, stirring every 2 minutes. Stir in the vanilla. Refrigerate mixture.
2. In a bowl, combine the fruit. Drizzle with dressing; gently toss to coat. Cover and refrigerate until serving.
1 cup: 125 cal., 1g fat (0 sat. fat), 0 chol., 2mg sod., 32g carb. (27g sugars, 3g fiber), 1g pro.

MARMALADE SOY WINGS

Whether I use drumettes or chicken wings, these savory bites are always popular. I keep the pretty glazed appetizers warm during parties by serving them in my slow cooker.
—Carole Nelson, Parkville, MO

Prep: 15 min. + marinating • **Bake:** 40 min.
Makes: 2½ dozen

- 3 lbs. chicken wings (about 15)
- 1 cup soy sauce
- 1 cup orange marmalade
- 3 garlic cloves, minced
- 1 tsp. ground ginger
- ¼ tsp. pepper

1. Cut the chicken wings into 3 sections; discard wing tip sections. In a small bowl, combine the soy sauce, marmalade, garlic, ginger and pepper. Cover and refrigerate ½ cup marinade for basting.
2. Place remaining marinade in a large shallow dish. Add wing sections and turn to coat evenly. Cover and refrigerate for 8 hours or overnight.
3. Drain and discard the marinade. Place chicken wings in a greased 15x10x1-in. baking pan. Bake wings, uncovered, at 350° for 15 minutes.
4. Baste with a third of the reserved marinade; bake 15 minutes longer. Baste with remaining marinade. Bake until chicken juices run clear, 10-20 minutes.
Note: Uncooked chicken wing sections (wingettes) may be substituted for whole chicken wings.
1 piece: 78 cal., 3g fat (1g sat. fat), 14mg chol., 451mg sod., 6g carb. (6g sugars, 0 fiber), 6g pro.

MAPLE-GINGERROOT VEGETABLES

My family loves a drizzling of golden maple syrup on these roasted root vegetables. I prefer to use dark maple syrup. Either way, it's an easy way to get kids (and adults) to eat their veggies.
—Kelli Ritz, Innisfail, AB

Prep: 35 min. • **Bake:** 45 min.
Makes: 24 servings

- 5 medium parsnips, peeled and sliced
- 5 small carrots, sliced
- 3 medium turnips, peeled and cubed
- 1 large sweet potato, peeled and cubed
- 1 small rutabaga, peeled and cubed
- 1 large sweet onion, cut into wedges
- 1 small red onion, cut into wedges
- 2 Tbsp. olive oil
- 1 Tbsp. minced fresh gingerroot
- 1 tsp. salt
- ½ tsp. pepper
- 1 cup maple syrup

1. Place the first 7 ingredients in a large resealable plastic bag; add the oil, ginger, salt and pepper. Seal bag and shake to coat. Arrange vegetables in a single layer in two 15x10x1-in. baking pans coated with cooking spray.
2. Bake at 425° for 25 minutes, stirring once. Drizzle with the syrup. Bake until vegetables are tender, 20-25 minutes longer, stirring once more.
¾ cup: 92 cal., 1g fat (0 sat. fat), 0 chol., 119mg sod., 20g carb. (13g sugars, 2g fiber), 1g pro. **Diabetic exchanges:** 1 starch.

CHEESY BEEF TACO DIP

For a warm, hearty snack with a bit of a kick, try this recipe. It's a hit with my family, and guests rave about it, too. Ideal for parties, it makes a big potful. All you'll need to add is a brimming bowl of tortilla chips.
—Carol Smith, Sanford, NC

Takes: 20 min. • **Makes:** 10 cups

- 2 lbs. ground beef
- 1 large onion, finely chopped
- 1 medium green pepper, finely chopped
- 1 lb. process cheese (Velveeta), cubed
- 1 lb. pepper jack cheese, cubed
- 1 jar (16 oz.) taco sauce
- 1 can (10 oz.) diced tomatoes and green chiles, drained
- 1 can (4 oz.) mushroom stems and pieces, drained and chopped
- 1 can (2¼ oz.) sliced ripe olives, drained
  Tortilla chips

In a large skillet, cook the beef, onion and green pepper over medium heat until meat is no longer pink; drain. Stir in the cheeses, taco sauce, tomatoes and chiles, mushrooms and olives. Cook and stir over low heat until the cheese is melted. Serve warm with tortilla chips.
¼ cup: 127 cal., 9g fat (5g sat. fat), 30mg chol., 332mg sod., 3g carb. (2g sugars, 0 fiber), 9g pro.

PINEAPPLE SMOKIES

With a tangy-sweet sauce, these little sausages are an excellent starter for holiday parties or any occasion. Plus they take just 15 minutes to prepare.
—Dorothy Anderson, Ottawa, KS

Takes: 15 min. • **Makes:** about 8 dozen

- 1 cup packed brown sugar
- 3 Tbsp. all-purpose flour
- 2 tsp. ground mustard
- 1 cup pineapple juice
- ½ cup white vinegar
- 1½ tsp. reduced-sodium soy sauce
- 2 lbs. miniature smoked sausages

In a large saucepan, combine sugar, flour and mustard. Gradually stir in pineapple juice, vinegar and soy sauce. Bring to a boil over medium heat; cook and stir until thickened, 2 minutes. Add the sausages; stir to coat. Cook until heated through, about 5 minutes longer. Serve warm.

1 sausage: 40 cal., 3g fat (1g sat. fat), 6mg chol., 100mg sod., 3g carb. (3g sugars, 0 fiber), 1g pro.

RASPBERRY-RHUBARB SLAB PIE

Slab pie is a pastry baked in a jelly-roll pan and cut in slabs like a bar cookie—or a pie bar, if you will. My grandfather was a professional baker and served pieces of slab pie to his customers back in the day.
—Jeanne Ambrose, Milwaukee, WI

Prep: 30 min. + chilling
Bake: 45 min.
Makes: 2 dozen

- 3¼ cups all-purpose flour
- 1 tsp. salt
- 1 cup butter
- ¾ cup plus 1 to 2 Tbsp. 2% milk
- 1 large egg yolk

- 2 cups sugar
- ⅓ cup cornstarch
- 5 cups fresh or frozen raspberries, thawed and drained
- 3 cups sliced fresh or frozen rhubarb, thawed and drained

VANILLA ICING
- 1¼ cups confectioners' sugar
- ½ tsp. vanilla extract
- 5 to 6 tsp. 2% milk

1. In a large bowl, combine flour and salt; cut in butter until crumbly. Whisk ¾ cup milk and egg yolk; gradually add to flour mixture, tossing with a fork until dough forms a ball. Add additional milk, 1 Tbsp. at a time, if necessary.

2. Divide dough in two portions so that one is slightly larger than the other; wrap each. Refrigerate the dough until easy to handle, 1 hour.

3. Preheat oven to 375°. Roll out larger portion of dough between two large sheets of lightly floured waxed paper into an 18x13-in. rectangle. Transfer to an ungreased 15x10x1-in. baking pan. Press onto the bottom and up sides of pan; trim pastry to edges of pan.

4. In a large bowl, combine the sugar and cornstarch. Add raspberries and rhubarb; toss to coat. Spoon into pastry.

5. Roll out remaining dough; place over filling. Fold bottom pastry over edge of top pastry; seal with a fork. Prick top with a fork.

6. Bake until golden brown, 45-55 minutes. Cool completely on a wire rack.

7. For icing, combine the confectioners' sugar, vanilla and enough milk to achieve a drizzling consistency; drizzle over pie. Cut pie into squares.

Note: If using frozen rhubarb, measure the rhubarb while it is still frozen, then thaw completely. Drain in a colander, but do not press liquid out.

1 piece: 247 cal., 8g fat (5g sat. fat), 29mg chol., 159mg sod., 42g carb. (25g sugars, 2g fiber), 3g pro.

SAUSAGE-STUFFED JALAPENOS

If you like foods that have a little heat, you'll love these zippy cheese-and-sausage-filled jalapenos. The recipe is one of my favorites for parties.
—Rachel Oswald, Greenville, MI

- -

Prep: 20 min. • **Bake:** 15 min.
Makes: 44 appetizers

- 1 **lb. bulk pork sausage**
- 1 **pkg. (8 oz.) cream cheese, softened**
- 1 **cup shredded Parmesan cheese**
- 22 **large jalapeno peppers, halved lengthwise and seeded**
  Ranch salad dressing, optional

1. In a large skillet, cook the sausage over medium heat until no longer pink; drain. In a small bowl, combine the cream cheese and Parmesan cheese; fold in cooked sausage.

2. Spoon about 1 tablespoonful into each jalapeno half. Place in two ungreased 13x9-in. baking dishes. Bake, uncovered, at 425° until filling is lightly browned and bubbly, 15-20 minutes. If desired, serve with ranch dressing.

Note: Wear disposable gloves when cutting hot peppers; the oils can burn your skin. Avoid touching your face.

1 appetizer: 56 cal., 5g fat (2g sat. fat), 13mg chol., 123mg sod., 1g carb. (0 sugars, 0 fiber), 2g pro.

ZESTY SLOPPY JOES

These sandwiches are always a hit at big family gatherings. I have never served them without getting recipe requests. Just the right blend of seasonings in a fantastic, hearty sandwich means that no one can eat just one.
—Sandy Abrams, Greenville, NY

- -

Prep: 20 min. • **Cook:** 65 min.
Makes: 25 servings

- 4 **lbs. ground beef**
- 1 **cup chopped onion**
- 1 **cup finely chopped green pepper**
- 2 **cans (10¾ oz. each) condensed tomato soup, undiluted**
- 1 **can (15 oz.) thick and zesty tomato sauce**
- 1 **can (8 oz.) tomato sauce**
- ¾ **cup packed brown sugar**
- ¼ **cup ketchup**
- 3 **Tbsp. Worcestershire sauce**
- 1 **Tbsp. prepared mustard**
- 1 **Tbsp. ground mustard**
- 1 **tsp. chili powder**
- 1 **tsp. garlic salt**
- 25 **hamburger buns**

In a Dutch oven, cook beef and onion over medium heat until meat is no longer pink. Add green pepper. Cook and stir for 5 minutes; drain. Add the next 10 ingredients; bring to a boil. Reduce heat; cover and simmer for 1 hour, stirring occasionally. Serve on buns.

1 sandwich: 263 cal., 8g fat (3g sat. fat), 36mg chol., 579mg sod., 29g carb. (11g sugars, 2g fiber), 17g pro.

BERRY CREAM MUFFINS

If you can't decide which berries to use in these muffins, you can't go wrong using half raspberries and half blueberries.
—Linda Gilmore, Hampstead, MD

Prep: 15 min. • **Bake:** 20 min.
Makes: about 2 dozen

  4   cups all-purpose flour
  2   cups sugar
1¼   tsp. baking powder
  1   tsp. baking soda
  1   tsp. salt
  3   cups fresh or frozen
       raspberries or blueberries
  4   large eggs, lightly beaten
  2   cups sour cream
  1   cup canola oil
  1   tsp. vanilla extract

1. In a bowl, combine the flour, sugar, baking powder, baking soda and salt; add fresh or frozen berries and toss. Combine eggs, sour cream, oil and vanilla; mix well. Stir into dry ingredients until moistened.

2. Fill greased muffin cups two-thirds full. Bake at 400° until a toothpick inserted in the center comes out clean, about 20-25 minutes. Cool muffins 5 minutes before removing from pans to a wire rack. Serve muffins warm.

1 muffin: 481 cal., 23g fat (6g sat. fat), 84mg chol., 330mg sod., 60g carb. (31g sugars, 3g fiber), 7g pro.

MAKE AHEAD
BREAKFAST SAUSAGE BREAD

Any time we take this savory, satisfying bread to a potluck, it goes over very well. We never bring any home. My husband usually makes it. He prides himself on the beautiful golden loaves.
—Shirley Caldwell, Northwood, OH

Prep: 25 min. + rising • **Bake:** 25 min.
Makes: 2 loaves (16 slices each)

  2   loaves (1 lb. each) frozen
       white bread dough, thawed
  ½   lb. mild pork sausage
  ½   lb. bulk spicy pork sausage
1½   cups diced fresh mushrooms
  ½   cup chopped onion
  3   large eggs, divided use
2½   cups shredded mozzarella cheese
  1   tsp. dried basil
  1   tsp. dried parsley flakes
  1   tsp. dried rosemary, crushed
  1   tsp. garlic powder

1. Cover dough and let rise in a warm place until doubled. Preheat oven to 350°. In a large skillet, cook sausage, mushrooms and onion over medium-high heat until sausage is no longer pink, breaking up the sausage into crumbles, 6-8 minutes. Drain. Transfer to a bowl; cool.

2. Stir in two eggs, cheese and seasonings. Roll each loaf of dough into a 16x12-in. rectangle. Spread half of the sausage mixture over each rectangle to within 1 in. of edges. Roll up jelly-roll style, starting with a short side; pinch the seams to seal. Place on a greased baking sheet.

3. In a small bowl, whisk remaining egg. Brush over tops. Bake until golden brown, 25-30 minutes. Serve warm.

Freeze option: Securely wrap and freeze cooled loaves in foil and place in resealable plastic freezer bags. To use, place foil-wrapped loaf on a baking sheet and reheat in a 450° oven until heated through, 10-15 minutes. Carefully remove the foil; return to oven a few minutes longer until crust is crisp.

1 slice: 102 cal., 6g fat (2g sat. fat), 32mg chol., 176mg sod., 8g carb. (1g sugars, 1g fiber), 5g pro.

BACON-WRAPPED SWEET POTATO BITES

After making the little bacon-wrapped sausages for years, I needed a change! I had an extra sweet potato and half a package of bacon on hand, so I put on my thinking cap and came up with this treat.
—Kelly Williams, Forked River, NJ

Prep: 25 min. • **Bake:** 40 min.
Makes: about 2½ dozen

- 2   **Tbsp. butter, melted**
- ½   **tsp. salt**
- ½   **tsp. cayenne pepper**
- ¼   **tsp. ground cinnamon**
- 2   **large sweet potatoes (about 1¾ lbs.), peeled and cut into 1-in. cubes**
- ¼   **cup packed brown sugar**
- 1   **lb. bacon strips, halved Maple syrup, warmed**

1. Preheat oven to 350°. In a large bowl, mix butter and seasonings. Add potatoes and toss to coat.

2. Wrap 1 piece of bacon around each sweet potato cube; secure with toothpick. Sprinkle with brown sugar. Place on a parchment-lined 15x10x1-in. baking pan.

3. Bake 40-45 minutes or until bacon is crisp and sweet potato is tender. Serve with maple syrup.

1 appetizer: 60 cal., 3g fat (1g sat. fat), 7mg chol., 136mg sod., 7g carb. (4g sugars, 1g fiber), 2g pro.

WHITE VELVET CUTOUTS

We make these cutouts every Christmas and Easter and give lots of them as gifts. Last year, we baked a batch a week for a month to be sure we'd have plenty for ourselves, too. These rich cookies melt in your mouth.

—Kim Hinkle, Wauseon, OH

- -

Prep: 25 min. + chilling
Bake: 10 min./batch + cooling
Makes: about 5½ dozen

- 2 cups butter, softened
- 1 pkg. (8 oz.) cream cheese, softened
- 2 cups sugar
- 2 large egg yolks, room temperature
- 1 tsp. vanilla extract
- 4½ cups all-purpose flour

FROSTING
- 3 Tbsp. butter, softened
- 1 Tbsp. shortening
- ½ tsp. vanilla extract
- 3½ cups confectioners' sugar
- 4 to 5 Tbsp. 2% milk
  Food coloring, optional

1. In a large bowl, cream butter, cream cheese and sugar until light and fluffy. Beat in egg yolks and vanilla. Gradually beat flour into creamed mixture. Divide dough in half. Shape each into a disk; wrap and refrigerate 2 hours or until firm enough to roll.

2. Preheat the oven to 350°. On a lightly floured surface, roll each portion of dough to ¼-in. thickness. Cut with floured 3-in. cookie cutters. Place cookies 1 in. apart on greased baking sheets. Bake until set (do not brown), 10-12 minutes. Cool on pans 5 minutes. Remove to wire racks to cool completely.

3. For frosting, in a bowl, beat the butter, shortening and vanilla until blended. Beat in the confectioners' sugar and enough milk to reach spreading consistency; beat until light and fluffy, 3 minutes. If desired, beat in food coloring. Frost the cookies. (Keep frosting covered with a damp towel to prevent it from drying out.)

1 cookie: 149 cal., 8g fat (5g sat. fat), 26mg chol., 62mg sod., 19g carb. (13g sugars, 0 fiber), 1g pro.

BREAD & BUTTER PICKLES

My mom always made these crisp pickles when we were kids, and she gave me the recipe. They are pleasantly sweet and tart, and so good.
—Karen Owen, Rising Sun, IN

Prep: 30 min. + standing • **Process:** 15 min.
Makes: 7 pints

- 4 lbs. cucumbers, sliced
- 8 small onions, sliced
- ½ cup canning salt
- 5 cups sugar
- 4 cups white vinegar
- 2 Tbsp. mustard seed
- 2 tsp. celery seed
- 1½ tsp. ground turmeric
- ½ tsp. ground cloves

1. In a large container, combine the cucumbers, onions and salt. Cover with crushed ice and mix well. Let stand for 3 hours. Drain; rinse and drain again.
2. In a Dutch oven, combine the sugar, vinegar and seasonings; bring to a boil. Add the cucumber mixture; return to a boil. Remove from the heat.
3. Carefully ladle hot mixture into hot pint jars, leaving ½-in. headspace. Remove air bubbles, wipe rims and adjust lids. Process for 15 minutes in a boiling-water canner.
Note: The processing time listed is for altitudes of 1,000 feet or less. For altitudes up to 3,000 feet, add 5 minutes; 6,000 feet, add 10 minutes; 8,000 feet, add 15 minutes; 10,000 feet, add 20 minutes.
¼ cup: 35 cal., 0 fat (0 sat. fat), 0 chol., 175mg sod., 8g carb. (7g sugars, 0 fiber), 0 pro.

TURKEY GRAVY

I can never have enough homemade gravy on hand for Thanksgiving dinner. The base for this flavorful gravy is prepared with turkey wings so you can make it a day or two ahead of time.
—Linda Fitzsimmons, Fort Edward, NY

Prep: 2¼ hours • **Cook:** 10 min.
Makes: 4¼ cups

- 2 turkey wings (1½ to 2 lbs.)
- 2 medium onions, quartered
- 2 cans (one 49 oz., one 14½ oz.) reduced-sodium chicken broth, divided
- 2 medium carrots, cut into 2-in. pieces
- 2 celery ribs with leaves, cut into 2-in. pieces
- 4 fresh thyme sprigs
- ½ cup plus 2 Tbsp. all-purpose flour
- 1 Tbsp. butter
- ¼ tsp. pepper

1. Place the wings and onions in a greased 13x9-in. baking dish. Bake, uncovered, at 400° for 1¼ hours, turning once.
2. Transfer wings and onions to a Dutch oven. Add the large can of broth, carrots, celery and thyme. Bring to a boil. Reduce heat; simmer, uncovered, for 45 minutes.
3. Strain; discard wings and vegetables. (Can be made ahead to this point and stored in the refrigerator for up to 2 days.) Skim fat from cooking liquid. Add enough remaining broth to measure 3½ cups; set strained liquid aside.
4. In a large saucepan, whisk flour and remaining broth until smooth. Gradually stir in cooking liquid. Bring to a boil; cook and stir for 2 minutes or until thickened. Stir in butter and pepper.
3 Tbsp. gravy: 61 cal., 2g fat (1g sat. fat), 12mg chol., 234mg sod., 5g carb. (1g sugars, 1g fiber), 5g pro.

HAM WITH PINEAPPLE SAUCE

My mom always finds ways to make good food taste even more special. An amazing example is ham served with sweet pineapple sauce.
—Debra Falkiner, St. Charles, MO

- -

Prep: 30 min. • **Bake:** 1¼ hours
Makes: 16 servings (3 cups sauce)

- 1 boneless fully cooked ham (4 to 6 lbs.)
- ¾ cup water, divided
- 1 cup packed brown sugar
- 4½ tsp. soy sauce
- 4½ tsp. ketchup
- 1½ tsp. ground mustard
- 1½ cups undrained crushed pineapple
- 2 Tbsp. plus 1 tsp. cornstarch

1. Place ham on a rack in a shallow roasting pan. Bake at 325° until a thermometer reads 140°, 1¼ to 2 hours.
2. In a saucepan, bring ¼ cup water, brown sugar, soy sauce, ketchup, mustard and pineapple to a boil. Reduce heat; cover and simmer 10 minutes. Combine cornstarch and remaining water until smooth; stir into pan. Cook until thickened. Serve with ham.
3 oz. cooked ham with 3 Tbsp. sauce: 199 cal., 4g fat (1g sat. fat), 58mg chol., 1285mg sod., 20g carb. (18g sugars, 0 fiber), 21g pro.

★ ★ ★ ★ ★ **READER REVIEW**
"I have been using this recipe for pineapple sauce a number of years. It is sweet and savory, and ham just isn't the same without it."
DONNALDAK TASTEOFHOME.COM

ALMOND TEA CAKES

When I have time, I love to bake. I make these tea cakes every Christmas season.
—Janet Fennema Ringelberg, Troy, ON

- -

Prep: 30 min. + chilling • **Bake:** 15 min.
Makes: 5 dozen

- 2 cups butter, softened
- ¾ cup sugar
- ¾ cup packed brown sugar
- 2 large eggs, room temperature
- 4 tsp. almond extract
- 4 cups all-purpose flour
- 1 tsp. baking powder

FILLING
- 1 large egg white
- ½ cup sugar
- ½ cup ground almonds
- ½ tsp. lemon juice
  Milk
  Sliced almonds

1. In a large bowl, cream butter and sugars until light and fluffy, about 5 minutes. Add eggs and extract; mix well. Add flour and baking powder (dough will be soft). Chill.
2. For filling, in a small bowl, stir egg white, sugar, almonds and lemon juice. Remove a portion of the dough at a time from the refrigerator. Place 1-in. balls of dough into miniature muffin cups, pressing slightly into sides and bottom. Place ½ tsp. filling into each. Cover with quarter-sized circles of dough.
3. Brush with a little milk and top with an almond. Bake at 350° until golden, for 14-16 minutes.

1 tea cake: 119 cal., 7g fat (4g sat. fat), 23mg chol., 73mg sod., 13g carb. (7g sugars, 0 fiber), 1g pro.

WAFFLE-FRY REUBEN BITES

I dearly love Reubens, so I turned the classic sammie into a fun and quick appetizer by putting all the classic fixings atop crispy waffle fries.
—Gloria Bradley, Naperville, IL

- -

Prep: 30 min. • **Bake:** 10 min./batch
Makes: about 4 dozen

- 1 **pkg. (22 oz.) frozen waffle-cut fries**
- 4 **oz. cream cheese, softened**
- 2 **cups shredded fontina cheese, divided**
- ⅓ **cup Thousand Island salad dressing**
- 3 **Tbsp. chopped sweet onion**
- 1½ **tsp. prepared horseradish**
- 12 **oz. sliced deli corned beef, coarsely chopped**
- 1 **cup sauerkraut, rinsed, well drained and chopped**
- 2 **Tbsp. minced fresh chives**

1. Prepare waffle fries according to the package directions for baking. Meanwhile, in a small bowl, beat cream cheese, 1 cup fontina cheese, salad dressing, onion and horseradish until blended.

2. Remove fries from oven; reduce oven setting to 400°. Top each waffle fry with about ¼ oz. corned beef and 1 tsp. each cream cheese mixture, sauerkraut and remaining fontina cheese. Bake until the cheese is melted, 8-10 minutes. Sprinkle with chives.

1 appetizer: 62 cal., 4g fat (2g sat. fat), 12mg chol., 168mg sod., 4g carb. (0 sugars, 0 fiber), 3g pro.

MAKE AHEAD

SUNFLOWER SEED & HONEY WHEAT BREAD

I've tried other bread recipes, but this one is a staple in our home. I won $50 in a baking contest with a loaf that I had stored in the freezer.
—Mickey Turner, Grants Pass, OR

- -

Prep: 40 min. + rising
Bake: 35 min.
Makes: 3 loaves (12 slices each)

- 2 pkg. (¼ oz. each) active dry yeast
- 3¼ cups warm water (110° to 115°)
- ¼ cup bread flour
- ⅓ cup canola oil
- ⅓ cup honey
- 3 tsp. salt
- 6½ to 7½ cups whole wheat flour
- ½ cup sunflower kernels
- 3 Tbsp. butter, melted

1. In a large bowl, dissolve yeast in warm water. Add the bread flour, oil, honey, salt and 4 cups whole wheat flour. Beat until smooth. Stir in sunflower kernels and enough of the remaining flour to form a firm dough.

2. Turn onto a floured surface; knead until smooth and elastic, 6-8 minutes. Place in a greased bowl, turning once to grease the top. Cover and let rise in a warm place until doubled, about 1 hour.

3. Punch dough down; divide into 3 equal portions. Shape into loaves; place dough in 3 greased 8x4-in. loaf pans. Cover and let rise until doubled, about 30 minutes.

4. Bake at 350° until golden brown, for 35-40 minutes. Brush with melted butter. Remove from pans to wire racks to cool.

Freeze option: Securely wrap and freeze cooled loaves in foil and place in resealable plastic freezer bags. To use, thaw at room temperature.

1 slice: 125 cal., 4g fat (1g sat. fat), 3mg chol., 212mg sod., 19g carb. (3g sugars, 3g fiber), 4g pro. **Diabetic exchanges:** 1 starch, 1 fat.

YUMMY CRACKER SNACKS

These treats are my family's favorite, and it seems no matter how many I make, they always disappear too soon.
—D. Weaver, Ephrata, PA

Prep: 1 hour + chilling • **Makes:** 4 dozen

> 96 **Ritz crackers**
> 1 **cup creamy peanut butter**
> 1 **cup marshmallow creme**
> 2 **lbs. milk chocolate candy coating, melted**
>   **Holiday sprinkles, optional**

1. Spread half of the crackers with peanut butter. Spread the remaining crackers with marshmallow creme; place the creme side down over peanut butter crackers to form a sandwich.
2. Dip the sandwiches in melted candy coating, allowing excess to drip off. Place on waxed paper-lined pans; refrigerate until set, about 15 minutes. If desired, drizzle with additional candy coating and decorate with sprinkles. Store snacks in an airtight container.
1 snack: 170 cal., 10g fat (6g sat. fat), 0 chol., 89mg sod., 19g carb. (14g sugars, 1g fiber), 2g pro.

BACON CHEESE WREATH

My grandmother makes this smoky bacon and Parmesan spread for parties and holiday get-togethers. For a pretty Yuletide presentation, accent the cream cheese wreath with parsley leaves and pimiento "berries."
—Lisa Carter, Warren, IN

Prep: 10 min. + chilling
Makes: about 3 cups

> 2 **pkg. (8 oz. each) cream cheese, softened**
> ½ **cup mayonnaise**
> ⅓ **cup grated Parmesan cheese**
> ¼ **cup sliced green onions, optional**
> 10 **bacon strips, cooked and crumbled**
>   **Parsley sprigs and diced pimientos, optional**
>   **Assorted crackers**

1. In a small bowl, beat the cream cheese, mayonnaise, Parmesan cheese and onions if desired. Stir in the bacon. Cover and refrigerate for 1-2 hours.
2. Invert a small bowl in the center of a serving platter. Drop the cream cheese mixture by rounded tablespoonfuls around edge of bowl. Remove the bowl. Smooth cream cheese mixture, forming a wreath. Garnish with the parsley and pimientos if desired. Serve with crackers.
2 Tbsp. spread: 87 cal., 9g fat (3g sat. fat), 15mg chol., 116mg sod., 0 carb. (0 sugars, 0 fiber), 2g pro.

CUBAN SLIDERS

Bake wonderful little rolls till they are lightly toasted and the cheese melts. Leftovers—if you have any, because just about everyone loves them—keep really well in the fridge and are just as good cold.
—Serene Herrera, Dallas, TX

Takes: 30 min. • **Makes:** 2 dozen

> 2 pkg. (12 oz. each) Hawaiian sweet rolls
> 1¼ lbs. thinly sliced deli ham
> 9 slices Swiss cheese (about 6 oz.)
> 24 dill pickle slices
> TOPPING
> ½ cup butter, cubed
> 2 Tbsp. finely chopped onion
> 2 Tbsp. Dijon mustard

1. Preheat the oven to 350°. Without separating rolls, cut each package of rolls in half horizontally; arrange bottom halves in a greased 13x9-in. baking pan. Layer with ham, cheese and pickles; replace top halves of rolls.
2. In a microwave, melt the butter; stir in the onion and mustard. Drizzle over rolls. Bake, covered, 10 minutes. Uncover; bake until golden brown and heated through, 5-10 minutes longer.
1 slider: 191 cal., 10g fat (5g sat. fat), 42mg chol., 532mg sod., 17g carb. (6g sugars, 1g fiber), 10g pro.

TEST KITCHEN TIP
Hawaiian sweet rolls are tender and slightly sweet. If they're not in your store, use egg or potato rolls, which are softer and richer than regular dinner rolls.

ICY HOLIDAY PUNCH

Pull out the punchbowl for this rosy thirst-quencher that dazzles at Christmas, the Fourth of July, and any other party. It's easy to prepare, and you can make the base ahead.
—Margaret Matson, Metamora, IL

Prep: 10 min. + freezing
Makes: 30 servings (about 5¾ qt.)

> 1 pkg. (6 oz.) cherry gelatin
> ¾ cup sugar
> 2 cups boiling water
> 1 can (46 oz.) unsweetened pineapple juice
> 6 cups cold water
> 2 liters ginger ale, chilled

In a 4-qt. freezer-proof container, dissolve gelatin and sugar in boiling water. Stir in pineapple juice and cold water. Cover and freeze overnight. Remove 2 hours before serving. Place mixture in a punch bowl; stir in ginger ale just before serving.
¾ cup: 89 cal., 0 fat (0 sat. fat), 0 chol., 19mg sod., 22g carb. (21g sugars, 0 fiber), 1g pro.

THREE-MEAT STROMBOLI

I made this hearty bread for a golf outing my husband attended and received many compliments. Several of the guys asked for the recipe, and they've told me they make it often. It's a good, hearty appetizer or sandwich for lunch.

—Lorelei Hull, Luling, LA

Prep: 20 min. • **Bake:** 35 min.
Makes: 2 loaves (16 slices each)

- 2 **loaves (1 lb. each) frozen bread dough, thawed**
- 2 **Tbsp. Dijon mustard**
- ½ **cup grated Parmesan cheese, divided**
- ¼ **lb. pastrami, finely chopped**
- ¼ **lb. pepperoni, finely chopped**
- ¼ **lb. hard salami, finely chopped**
- 1 **cup shredded Swiss cheese**
- 1 **large egg, beaten**

1. Roll each bread dough into a 12x7-in. rectangle. Spread mustard to within 1 in. of edges. Sprinkle each rectangle with 2 Tbsp. Parmesan cheese.
2. Combine meats and Swiss; sprinkle over dough. Top with the remaining Parmesan cheese. Brush edges of dough with egg. Roll up, jelly-roll style, beginning with a long side. Seal seam and ends.
3. Place seam side down on a greased baking sheet; cut 3 slits in the top of each loaf. Bake at 350° until golden brown, 35-40 minutes. Slice; serve warm.

1 slice: 135 cal., 6g fat (2g sat. fat), 18mg chol., 377mg sod., 15g carb. (1g sugars, 1g fiber), 7g pro.

Three-Cheese Meat Stromboli: Substitute ¼ lb. chopped fully cooked ham for the pastrami and omit the pepperoni. Use ¾ cup each of shredded mozzarella and cheddar cheeses instead of Swiss. Add ¼ cup chopped roasted red pepper to the meat-cheese mixture. Proceed as the recipe directs.

MAKE AHEAD

CHEESE CRISPIES

For years I've taken these crispy, crunchy snacks to work. They get high marks from everybody in the teachers lounge.

—Eileen Ball, Cornelius, NC

Prep: 15 min. + chilling
Bake: 15 min./batch
Makes: about 4½ dozen

- 1 **cup unsalted butter, softened**
- 2½ **cups shredded extra-sharp cheddar cheese**
- 2 **cups all-purpose flour**
- ¾ **tsp. salt**
- ½ **tsp. cayenne pepper**
- 2½ **cups Rice Krispies**
  Pecan halves, optional

1. Beat butter and cheese until blended. In another bowl, whisk flour, salt and cayenne; gradually beat into the cheese mixture. Stir in Rice Krispies. If necessary, turn onto a lightly floured surface and knead 4-6 times, forming a stiff dough.
2. Divide dough in half; shape each into a 7-in.-long roll. Wrap; refrigerate the dough 1 hour or overnight.
3. Preheat oven to 350°. Unwrap and cut dough crosswise into ¼-in. slices. Place 1 in. apart on parchment-lined baking sheets. If desired, top each slice with a pecan half. Bake until edges are golden brown, 14-16 minutes. Remove from pans to wire racks to cool.

Freeze option: Freeze wrapped logs in a resealable plastic freezer bag. To use, unwrap frozen logs and cut into slices. Bake as directed.
1 cracker: 73 cal., 5g fat (3g sat. fat), 15mg chol., 73mg sod., 5g carb. (0 sugars, 0 fiber), 2g pro.

PUMPKIN SWIRL BREAD

This combination of pumpkin, nuts and dates makes a delicious golden bread, plus there's a rich, creamy layer of cheesecake swirled inside each slice.
—Cindy May, Troy, MI

Prep: 25 min. • **Bake:** 65 min. + cooling
Makes: 3 loaves (16 slices each)

FILLING
- 2 pkg. (8 oz. each) cream cheese, softened
- ¼ cup sugar
- 1 large egg, room temperature
- 1 Tbsp. whole milk

BREAD
- 3 cups sugar
- 1 can (15 oz.) solid-pack pumpkin
- 4 large eggs, room temperature
- 1 cup canola oil
- 1 cup water

- 4 cups all-purpose flour
- 4 tsp. pumpkin pie spice
- 2 tsp. baking soda
- 1½ tsp. ground cinnamon
- 1 tsp. salt
- 1 tsp. baking powder
- 1 tsp. ground nutmeg
- ½ tsp. ground cloves
- 1 cup chopped walnuts
- 1 cup raisins
- ½ cup chopped dates

OPTIONAL TOPPINGS
- 1 cup confectioners' sugar
- ¼ tsp. vanilla extract
- 2 to 3 Tbsp. 2% milk
- Additional chopped walnuts

1. Preheat oven to 350°. Grease and flour three 8x4-in. loaf pans. In a small bowl, beat filling ingredients until smooth.
2. In a large bowl, beat sugar, pumpkin, eggs, oil and water until well blended. In another bowl, whisk flour, pie spice, soda, cinnamon, salt, baking powder, nutmeg and cloves; gradually beat into pumpkin mixture. Stir in walnuts, raisins and dates.
3. Pour half of the batter into prepared pans, dividing evenly. Spoon filling over the batter. Cover filling completely with remaining batter.
4. Bake until a toothpick inserted in bread portion comes out clean, 65-70 minutes. Cool for 10 minutes before removing loaves from pans to wire racks to cool completely. Wrap individually in foil; refrigerate until serving.
5. If desired, just before serving, in a small bowl, mix the confectioners' sugar, vanilla and enough of the milk to reach drizzling consistency. Drizzle over bread; sprinkle with walnuts.

1 slice: 189 cal., 8g fat (2g sat. fat), 27mg chol., 132mg sod., 27g carb. (17g sugars, 1g fiber), 3g pro.

COLORFUL CANDY BAR COOKIES

No one will guess these sweet treats with the candy bar center start with store-bought dough. Roll them in colored sugar—or just dip the tops for even faster assembly. Instead of using miniature candy bars, slice regular size Snickers candy bars into 1-inch pieces for the centers.
—*Taste of Home* Test Kitchen

Prep: 35 min. • **Bake:** 10 min./batch
Makes: about 3 dozen

  1 **tube (16½ oz.) refrigerated sugar cookie dough, softened**
  ⅔ **cup all-purpose flour**
 40 **miniature Snickers candy bars**
      Red and green colored sugar

1. Preheat oven to 350°. Beat cookie dough and flour until combined. Shape 2 teaspoonfuls of dough around each candy bar. Roll in colored sugar.
2. Place 2 in. apart on parchment -lined baking sheets. Bake until set, for about 9-11 minutes. Cool on pans 1 minute. Remove to wire racks to cool.

1 cookie: 93 cal., 4g fat (1g sat. fat), 4mg chol., 65mg sod., 13g carb. (7g sugars, 0 fiber), 1g pro.

MAC & CHEESE FOR A BUNCH

You'll delight many taste buds with this rich and comforting dish. Cover tender macaroni in a homemade cheese sauce, and then top with golden bread crumbs for a true crowd-pleaser.
—Dixie Terry, Goreville, IL

Prep: 30 min. • **Bake:** 35 min.
Makes: 36 servings (1 cup each)

- 3 pkg. (two 16 oz., one 7 oz.) elbow macaroni
- 1¼ cups butter, divided
- ¾ cup all-purpose flour
- 2 tsp. salt
- 3 qt. milk
- 3 lbs. sharp cheddar cheese, shredded
- 1½ cups dry bread crumbs

1. Cook macaroni according to package directions until almost tender.

2. Meanwhile, preheat oven to 350°. In a large stock pot, melt 1 cup butter. Stir in flour and salt until smooth. Gradually stir in the milk. Bring to a boil; cook and stir until thickened, 2 minutes. Reduce heat. Add cheese, stirring until melted. Drain macaroni; stir into sauce.

3. Transfer to 3 greased 13x9-in. baking dishes. Melt remaining butter; toss with bread crumbs. Sprinkle over casseroles.

4. Bake, uncovered, until golden brown, 35-40 minutes.

1 cup: 395 cal., 23g fat (14g sat. fat), 68mg chol., 510mg sod., 32g carb. (5g sugars, 1g fiber), 17g pro.

CHOCOLATE-PEANUT GRANOLA BARS

Nutella and peanut butter meet to make some amazing granola bars. Everyone thinks they're eating something naughty when I serve these, but they also are full of healthy oats and good fats.
—Brenda Caughell, Durham, NC

- -

Takes: 30 min. • **Makes:** 2 dozen

- 2½ **cups old-fashioned oats**
- ¾ **cup lightly salted dry roasted peanuts, coarsely chopped**
- ¾ **cup wheat germ**
- ¾ **cup sunflower kernels**
- ½ **cup honey**
- ¼ **cup packed brown sugar**
- 3 **Tbsp. butter**
- ⅓ **cup creamy peanut butter**
- ⅓ **cup Nutella**

1. Preheat oven to 400°. In an ungreased 15x10x1-in. baking pan, combine oats, peanuts, wheat germ and sunflower kernels. Bake, stirring occasionally, until toasted, 8-12 minutes. Cool in pan on a wire rack.

2. In a small saucepan, combine honey, brown sugar and butter. Cook and stir over medium heat until mixture comes to a boil; cook 2 minutes longer. Remove from heat; stir in the peanut butter and Nutella until blended.

3. Transfer oat mixture to a large bowl; add honey mixture and toss to coat. Press into a greased 13x9-in. pan. Cool. Cut into bars.

1 bar: 178 cal., 10g fat (2g sat. fat), 4mg chol., 75mg sod., 20g carb. (11g sugars, 2g fiber), 5g pro.

SPICY NACHO BAKE

I made this hearty southwestern casserole for a dinner meeting, and now I'm asked to bring it to every potluck. Our friends savor the beef and bean filling and crunchy, cheesy topping. The recipe makes two casseroles to feed a crowd, but you can easily halve it for a smaller guest list.
—Anita Wilson, Mansfield, OH

- -

Prep: 1 hour • **Bake:** 20 min.
Makes: 2 casseroles (15 servings each)

- 2 **lbs. ground beef**
- 2 **large onions, chopped**
- 2 **large green peppers, chopped**
- 2 **cans (28 oz. each) diced tomatoes, undrained**
- 2 **cans (16 oz. each) hot chili beans, undrained**
- 2 **cans (15 oz. each) black beans, rinsed and drained**
- 2 **cans (11 oz. each) whole kernel corn, drained**
- 2 **cans (8 oz. each) tomato sauce**
- 2 **envelopes taco seasoning**
- 2 **pkg. (13 oz. each) spicy nacho-flavored tortilla chips**
- 4 **cups shredded cheddar cheese**

1. In a Dutch oven, cook the beef, onions and green peppers over medium heat until meat is no longer pink; drain. Stir in the tomatoes, beans, corn, tomato sauce and taco seasoning. Bring to a boil. Reduce heat; simmer, uncovered, for 30 minutes (mixture will be thin).

2. In each of two greased 13x9-in. baking dishes, layer 5 cups of chips and 4⅔ cups of meat mixture. Repeat layers. Top each with 4 cups of chips and 2 cups of cheese.

3. Bake, uncovered, at 350° until golden brown, 20-25 minutes.

⅔ cup: 314 cal., 13g fat (6g sat. fat), 31mg chol., 845mg sod., 33g carb. (5g sugars, 5g fiber), 14g pro.

5. Place 2 in. apart on greased baking sheets. Brush with the remaining egg mixture. Bake at 400° until golden brown, 9-12 minutes.

6. Meanwhile, in a small saucepan, bring cream to a boil. Reduce heat; simmer, uncovered, until slightly thickened, for 5-7 minutes or stirring occasionally. Add the blue cheese; cook and stir 2 minutes longer or until cheese is melted and sauce thickens. Serve with empanadas.

To Make Ahead: Unbaked empanadas may be frozen for up to 2 months. Bake as directed for 12-16 minutes.

1 empanada with ½ tsp. sauce: 81 cal., 5g fat (2g sat. fat), 16mg chol., 120mg sod., 6g carb. (1g sugars, 0 fiber), 3g pro.

BLT DIP

Fans of bacon, lettuce and tomato sandwiches will fall for this creamy dip. It's easy to transport too, and always draws recipe requests.
—Emalee Payne, Eau Claire, WI

- -

Takes: 10 min. • **Makes:** 6 cups

2	cups sour cream
2	cups mayonnaise
2	lbs. sliced bacon, cooked and crumbled
6	plum tomatoes, chopped
3	green onions, chopped
	Additional crumbled cooked bacon and chopped green onions, optional
	Assorted crackers or chips

In a large bowl, combine the sour cream, mayonnaise, bacon, tomatoes and onions. Refrigerate until serving. Garnish with bacon and onions if desired. Serve with crackers or chips.

¼ cup: 123 cal., 12g fat (3g sat. fat), 15mg chol., 155mg sod., 1g carb. (1g sugars, 0 fiber), 2g pro.

BUFFALO CHICKEN EMPANADAS WITH BLUE CHEESE SAUCE

These little handheld pies feature the popular taste of Buffalo chicken wings and are fun to eat. Using a rotisserie chicken and refrigerated pie crust really speeds up the preparation.
—Melissa Millwood, Lyman, SC

- -

Prep: 35 min. • **Bake:** 10 min./batch
Makes: 8 dozen (1 cup sauce)

1	small onion, chopped
1	small green pepper, chopped
4½	tsp. canola oil
2	garlic cloves, minced
3	cups finely chopped rotisserie chicken
1½	cups shredded part-skim mozzarella cheese
½	cup Buffalo wing sauce
¼	tsp. salt
¼	tsp. pepper
5	sheets refrigerated pie crust
2	large eggs
2	Tbsp. water
1	cup heavy whipping cream
1	cup crumbled blue cheese

1. In a small skillet, saute onion and green pepper in oil until crisp-tender. Add garlic; cook 1 minute longer.

2. In a large bowl, combine the chicken, mozzarella cheese, wing sauce, salt and pepper. Stir in the onion mixture.

3. On a lightly floured surface, unroll 1 pie crust. Roll out into a 12-in. circle. Cut with a floured 3-in. biscuit cutter. Remove the excess dough and reroll scraps. Repeat with the remaining pie crusts.

4. Beat eggs and water; brush over the edges of the 3-in. pie crust circles. Place 1 heaping tsp. filling in the center of each circle. Fold crust in half over filling. Press edges with a fork to seal.

STREUSEL PUMPKIN SWEET ROLLS

My sons love anything that's pumpkin, especially these yummy sweet rolls. It wouldn't be fall without these fragrant treats, so irresistible.
—Julie Fehr, Martensville, SK

- -

Prep: 45 min. + rising • **Bake:** 20 min.
Makes: 2 dozen

 1 **pkg. (¼ oz.) active dry yeast**
1¼ **cups warm 2% milk (110° to 115°)**
 1 **cup solid-pack pumpkin**
 ½ **cup sugar**
 ½ **cup butter, melted**
 1 **tsp. salt**
4¾ **to 5¾ cups all-purpose flour**
STREUSEL
1½ **cups all-purpose flour**
 1 **cup packed brown sugar**
 1 **tsp. ground cinnamon**
 ½ **tsp. ground allspice**
 ¾ **cup cold butter, cubed**
GLAZE
 1 **cup confectioners' sugar**
 ½ **tsp. vanilla extract**
 1 **to 2 Tbsp. 2% milk**

1. In a large bowl, dissolve yeast in warm milk. Add the pumpkin, sugar, butter, salt and 4¾ cups flour. Beat until smooth. Stir in enough remaining flour to form a soft dough (dough will be sticky).
2. Turn onto a floured surface; knead until smooth and elastic, 6-8 minutes. Place in a greased bowl, turning once to grease top. Cover and let rise in a warm place until doubled, about 1 hour.
3. Punch dough down; divide in half. Roll each portion into a 12x10-in. rectangle. Combine the flour, brown sugar, cinnamon and allspice; cut in butter until crumbly. Set aside 1 cup.
4. Sprinkle remaining streusel over dough to within ½ in. of edges; press down

lightly. Roll up jelly-roll style, starting with a long side; pinch seams to seal.
5. Cut each into 12 slices. Place cut side down in two greased 13x9-in. baking pans. Sprinkle with reserved streusel. Cover and let rise until doubled, about 30 minutes.
6. Bake at 375° until golden brown, for 20-25 minutes. Meanwhile, combine the confectioners' sugar, vanilla and enough milk to achieve the desired consistency; drizzle over rolls. Serve warm.
1 roll: 285 cal., 10g fat (6g sat. fat), 26mg chol., 176mg sod., 45g carb. (19g sugars, 1g fiber), 4g pro.

TACO CRACKERS

Just one handful of these crispy oyster crackers is never enough: Partygoers always come back for more. Taco seasoning and chili powder give the munchies a fun southwestern flavor.
—Diane Earnest, Newton, IL

- -

Takes: 30 min. • **Makes:** 16 cups

 3 **pkg. (10 oz. each) oyster crackers**
 ¾ **cup canola oil**
 1 **envelope taco seasoning**
 ½ **tsp. garlic powder**
 ½ **tsp. dried oregano**
 ½ **tsp. chili powder**

1. Place the crackers in a large roasting pan; drizzle with canola oil. Combine the seasonings; sprinkle over crackers and toss to coat.
2. Bake at 350° until golden brown, for 15-20 minutes, stirring once.
½ cup: 161 cal., 8g fat (1g sat. fat), 0 chol., 352mg sod., 21g carb. (0 sugars, 1g fiber), 3g pro.

NO-KNEAD KNOT ROLLS

My mom loved to serve these light, golden rolls when I was growing up on our Iowa farm. They're extra nice to make because the dough requires no kneading. It rises in the refrigerator overnight, so there's little last-minute fuss when you want to serve fresh hot rolls with any meal.
—Toni Hilscher, Omaha, NE

- -

Prep: 25 min. + rising • **Bake:** 10 min.
Makes: 4 dozen

2   pkg. (¼ oz. each) active dry yeast
2   cups warm water (110° to 115°)
½   cup sugar
2   tsp. salt
6   to 6½ cups all-purpose flour
1   large egg, room temperature
½   cup shortening
½   cup butter, softened

1. In a large bowl, dissolve yeast in warm water. Add the sugar, salt and 2 cups flour. Beat on medium speed for 2 minutes. Beat in egg and shortening. Stir in enough of the remaining flour to form a soft dough (do not knead). Cover and refrigerate the dough overnight.

2. Punch dough down and divide into 4 portions; roll each one into a 14x12-in. rectangle. Spread 2 Tbsp. butter over dough. Fold in half lengthwise; cut into 12 strips. Tie each strip into a knot; tuck and pinch ends under. Place 2 in. apart on greased baking sheets. Repeat with remaining dough.

3. Cover and let rise until doubled, about 1 hour. Bake at 400° until golden brown, 10-12 minutes. Remove rolls to wire rack to cool.

1 roll: 102 cal., 4g fat (2g sat. fat), 10mg chol., 119mg sod., 14g carb. (2g sugars, 0 fiber), 2g pro.

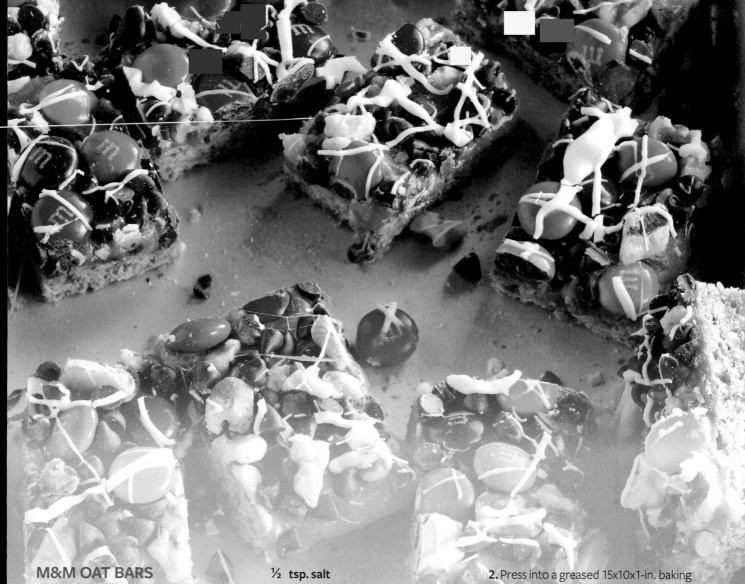

M&M OAT BARS

These irresistible, festive bars make for an easy way to sweeten any occasion.
—Renee Schwebach, Dumont, MN

Prep: 20 min. • **Bake:** 10 min. + cooling
Makes: 6 dozen

½ cup butter, softened
1 cup packed brown sugar
1 large egg, room temperature
1 tsp. vanilla extract
1¼ cups all-purpose flour
½ tsp. baking soda
½ tsp. salt
2 cups quick-cooking oats
1 pkg. (14 oz.) caramels
3 Tbsp. water
1 cup (6 oz.) miniature semisweet chocolate chips
1 cup chopped walnuts
1 cup plain M&M's
3 oz. white candy coating

1. In a large bowl, cream butter and brown sugar. Beat in the egg and vanilla. Combine flour, baking soda and salt; add to creamed mixture and mix well. Beat in oats.

2. Press into a greased 15x10x1-in. baking pan. Bake at 350° until golden brown, for about 10-15 minutes. Cool on a wire rack.

3. In a microwave, melt the caramels with water; stir until smooth. Spread over the crust. Sprinkle with the chips, nuts and M&M's. Gently press into the caramel mixture. Melt candy coating; drizzle over the top. Let stand until set, 5 minutes. Cut into bars.

1 bar: 104 cal., 5g fat (2g sat. fat), 7mg chol., 56mg sod., 15g carb. (11g sugars, 1g fiber), 2g pro.

Slow-Cooked
Big Breakfast
page 198

Slow Cooker

Everybody loves the convenience of slow-cooked dishes, especially when it's time for a potluck. These keep-warm cozy delights are always the stars of the buffet line!

ITALIAN SAUSAGE & KALE SOUP

The first time I made this colorful soup, we knew it was a keeper that would see us through the cold winter days. And it makes the house smell so wonderful.
—*Sarah Stombaugh, Chicago, IL*

- -

Prep: 20 min. • **Cook:** 8 hours
Makes: 8 servings (3½ qt.)

- 1 lb. bulk hot Italian sausage
- 6 cups chopped fresh kale
- 2 cans (15½ oz. each) great northern beans, rinsed and drained
- 1 can (28 oz.) crushed tomatoes
- 4 large carrots, finely chopped (about 3 cups)
- 1 medium onion, chopped
- 3 garlic cloves, minced
- 1 tsp. dried oregano
- ¼ tsp. salt
- ⅛ tsp. pepper
- 5 cups chicken stock
   Grated Parmesan cheese

1. In a large skillet, cook sausage over medium heat until no longer pink, about 6-8 minutes, breaking into crumbles; drain. Transfer to a 5-qt. slow cooker.
2. Add kale, beans, tomatoes, carrots, onion, garlic, seasonings and stock to the slow cooker. Cook, covered, on low until the vegetables are tender, for 8-10 hours. Top each serving with cheese.
1¾ cups: 297 cal., 13g fat (4g sat. fat), 31mg chol., 1105mg sod., 31g carb. (7g sugars, 9g fiber), 16g pro.

TEST KITCHEN TIP
Cannellini beans are a fine substitute for great northern beans, so use what you have on hand.

HOT HAM SANDWICHES

I came up with this crowd-pleasing recipe when trying to recreate a favorite sandwich from a restaurant near my hometown. The sandwiches are easy to serve in a buffet line because they don't really need condiments. They're so flavorful just as they are.
—*Susan Rehm, Grahamsville, NY*

- -

Prep: 10 min. • **Cook:** 4 hours
Makes: 12 servings

- 3 lbs. thinly sliced deli ham (about 40 slices)
- 2 cups apple juice
- ⅔ cup packed brown sugar
- ½ cup sweet pickle relish
- 2 tsp. prepared mustard
- 1 tsp. paprika
- 12 kaiser rolls, split
   Additional sweet pickle relish, optional

1. Separate ham slices and place in a 3-qt. slow cooker. In a small bowl, combine the apple juice, brown sugar, relish, mustard and paprika. Pour over ham.
2. Cover and cook on low until mixture is heated through, 4-5 hours. Place 3-4 slices of ham on each roll. Serve with additional relish if desired.
1 sandwich: 432 cal., 13g fat (4g sat. fat), 62mg chol., 1974mg sod., 52g carb. (23g sugars, 2g fiber), 27g pro.

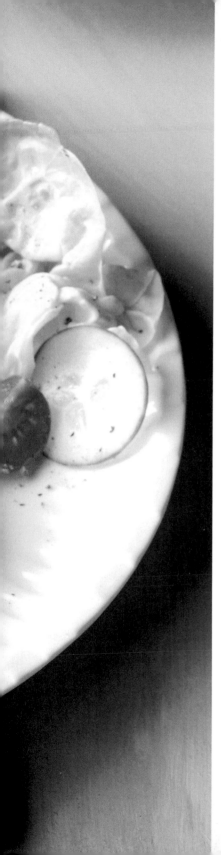

SLOW-COOKER TATER TOT CASSEROLE

What's not to love about classic Tater Tot casserole—especially when it's made in the slow cooker? You'll want to add this family-pleasing potluck favorite to your regular rotation.

—*Nick Iverson, Denver, CO*

Prep: 25 min. • **Cook:** 6 hours + standing
Makes: 12 servings

- 2 lbs. ground beef
- 1 large onion, chopped
- 1 lb. sliced fresh mushrooms
- 3 garlic cloves, minced
- 2 cans (10¾ oz. each condensed cream of mushroom soup, undiluted
- ½ tsp. salt
- ½ tsp. pepper
- 1 lb. frozen cut green beans
- 1 bag (32 oz.) frozen Tater Tots
- 1 cup shredded cheddar cheese

1. In a large skillet cook beef over medium-high heat until no longer pink, 5-6 minutes, breaking into crumbles; drain and transfer to a 5-qt. slow cooker. Add onions and mushrooms to skillet; cook over medium-high heat until the vegetables are tender, 8-10 minutes. Add garlic; cook 1 minute longer. Stir in condensed soup, salt and pepper. Place vegetable mixture in slow cooker; add the green beans and stir to combine. Top with Tater Tots and cheese.

2. Cook, covered, on low for 6 hours. Let casserole stand, uncovered, 15 minutes before serving.

1 serving: 383 cal., 22g fat (7g sat. fat), 58mg chol., 941mg sod., 27g carb. (3g sugars, 4g fiber), 20g pro.

CRANBERRY TURKEY BREAST WITH GRAVY

This recipe makes a wonderful holiday main dish because it's so convenient, plus the turkey turns out tender and moist. You can use additional slow cookers to prepare side dishes such as homemade stuffing.

—*Shirley Welch, Tulsa, OK*

Prep: 15 min. • **Cook:** 5 hours
Makes: 12 servings (3 cups gravy)

- 1 bone-in turkey breast (5 to 6 lbs.)
- 1 can (14 oz.) whole-berry cranberry sauce
- ¼ cup orange juice
- 1 envelope onion soup mix
- ¼ tsp. salt
- ¼ tsp. pepper
- 3 to 4 tsp. cornstarch
- 1 Tbsp. water

1. Place turkey in a 5-qt. slow cooker. In a small bowl, combine the cranberry sauce, orange juice, onion soup mix, salt and pepper; pour over turkey. Cover and cook on low until tender, 5-6 hours.

2. Remove the turkey to a serving platter; keep warm. Skim fat from cooking juices; transfer to a small saucepan. Bring to a boil. Combine cornstarch and water until smooth. Gradually stir into the pan. Bring to a boil; cook and stir until thickened, for 2 minutes. Serve with turkey.

5 oz. cooked turkey with ¼ cup gravy: 318 cal., 10g fat (3g sat. fat), 102mg chol., 346mg sod., 15g carb. (9g sugars, 1g fiber), 40g pro. **Diabetic exchanges:** 5 lean meat, 1 starch.

CONTEST-WINNING BAVARIAN MEATBALL HOAGIES

I use my slow cooker so much—unless my husband grills for me—and these mouthwatering meatballs are just one reason why. They're a guaranteed crowd-pleaser when I serve them as party appetizers or this way: spooned over tasty rolls and topped with melted cheese as sandwiches.
—*Peggy Rios, Mechanicsville, VA*

Prep: 15 min. • **Cook:** 3 hours
Makes: 12 servings

- 1 pkg. (32 oz.) frozen fully cooked Italian meatballs
- ½ cup chopped onion
- ¼ cup packed brown sugar
- 1 envelope onion soup mix
- 1 can (12 oz.) beer or nonalcoholic beer
- 12 hoagie buns, split
- 3 cups shredded Swiss cheese

1. In a 3-qt. slow cooker, combine the meatballs, onion, brown sugar, soup mix and beer. Cook, covered, on low until meatballs are heated through, 3-4 hours.
2. Place 5 or 6 meatballs on each bun bottom. Sprinkle each sandwich with ¼ cup cheese. Place on baking sheets. Broil 4-6 in. from the heat until cheese is melted, 2-3 minutes. Replace bun tops.
1 sandwich: 643 cal., 36g fat (18g sat. fat), 95mg chol., 1302mg sod., 49g carb. (13g sugars, 4g fiber), 29g pro.

CINNAMON ROLL CASSEROLE

Because we love cinnamon rolls, I created a slow-cooker recipe that's perfect for a weekend breakfast or brunch. This delicious, simple, no-fuss casserole is always the perfect choice for company and family.

—Joan Hallford, North Richland Hills, TX

Prep: 20 min. • **Cook:** 2½ hours
Makes: 10 servings

- 2 **tubes (12.40 oz. each) refrigerated cinnamon rolls with icing, cut into quarters**
- ½ **cup chopped toasted pecans, divided**
- ½ **cup miniature semisweet chocolate chips, divided**
- ½ **cup evaporated milk**
- 3 **Tbsp. maple syrup**
- 2 **tsp. vanilla extract**
- 1 **tsp. ground cinnamon**
- ½ **cup all-purpose flour**
- ½ **cup packed brown sugar**
- ¼ **tsp. pumpkin pie spice**
- ½ **cup cold butter, cubed**

1. Place half of the cinnamon roll pieces in a greased 4- or 5-qt. slow cooker. Sprinkle with ¼ cup of pecans and ¼ cup chocolate chips. In a small bowl, whisk the milk, syrup, vanilla and cinnamon until blended; pour over rolls. Top the first layer with the remaining cinnamon roll pieces and remaining chocolate chips. Top with one packet of icing.

2. For the topping, mix flour, brown sugar and pie spice; cut in butter until crumbly. Stir in remaining pecans. Sprinkle over the icing. Cook, covered, on low until the rolls are set, 2½ to 3 hours. Remove the insert to a cooling rack and top casserole with remaining icing. Serve warm.

1 serving: 492 cal., 25g fat (11g sat. fat), 28mg chol., 638mg sod., 65g carb. (36g sugars, 2g fiber), 5g pro.

TEST KITCHEN TIP
You'll love this ooey-gooey breakfast treat that's almost like bread pudding. The topping melts into the casserole, adding a sweet, spiced pecan layer.

SLOW-COOKED TURKEY SANDWICHES

These sandwiches have been such a hit at office potlucks that I keep copies of the recipe in my desk to hand out.

—*Diane Twait Nelsen, Ringsted, IA*

Prep: 15 min. • **Cook:** 3 hours
Makes: 18 servings

- 6 cups cubed cooked turkey
- 2 cups cubed process cheese (Velveeta)
- 1 can (10¾ oz.) condensed cream of chicken soup, undiluted
- 1 can (10¾ oz.) condensed cream of mushroom soup, undiluted
- ½ cup finely chopped onion
- ½ cup chopped celery
- 18 wheat sandwich buns, split

In a 4-qt. slow cooker, combine the first 6 ingredients. Cover and cook on low until the vegetables are tender and the cheese is melted, 3-4 hours. Stir mixture; spoon ½ cup onto each bun.

1 sandwich: 263 cal., 9g fat (3g sat. fat), 62mg chol., 680mg sod., 26g carb. (5g sugars, 4g fiber), 20g pro.

EASY CHICKEN TAMALE PIE

All you need are some simple ingredients from the pantry to put this easy dish together. I love to go fishing while my favorite meal-in-one dinner cooks.

—*Peter Halferty, Corpus Christi, TX*

Prep: 20 min. • **Cook:** 7 hours
Makes: 8 servings

- 1 lb. ground chicken
- 1 tsp. ground cumin
- 1 tsp. chili powder
- ½ tsp. salt
- ¼ tsp. pepper
- 1 can (15 oz.) black beans, rinsed and drained
- 1 can (14½ oz.) diced tomatoes, undrained
- 1 can (11 oz.) whole kernel corn, drained
- 1 can (10 oz.) enchilada sauce
- 2 green onions, chopped
- ¼ cup minced fresh cilantro
- 1 pkg. (8½ oz.) cornbread/muffin mix
- 2 large eggs, lightly beaten
- 1 cup shredded Mexican cheese blend
  Optional toppings: sour cream, salsa and minced fresh cilantro

1. In a large skillet, cook the chicken over medium heat until no longer pink, for 6-8 minutes, breaking into crumbles. Stir in seasonings.
2. Transfer to a 4-qt. slow cooker. Stir in beans, tomatoes, corn, enchilada sauce, green onions and cilantro. Cook, covered, on low until heated through, 6-8 hours.
3. In a small bowl, combine muffin mix and eggs; spoon over chicken mixture. Cook, covered, on low until a toothpick inserted in cornbread layer comes out clean, 1-1½ hours longer.
4. Sprinkle with cheese; let stand, covered, 5 minutes. If desired, serve with toppings.

1 serving: 359 cal., 14g fat (5g sat. fat), 110mg chol., 1021mg sod., 40g carb. (11g sugars, 5g fiber), 20g pro.

COFFEE-BRAISED SHORT RIBS

When the leaves start falling, I crave comfort foods like hearty stews and braised meats. I love this recipe because as the short ribs cook until tender, they smell tantalizing. And while their taste is impressive, they're so easy to make.
—*Melissa Turkington, Camano Island, WA*

Prep: 25 min. • **Cook:** 6 hours
Makes: 8 servings

- 4 lbs. bone-in beef short ribs
- 1½ tsp. salt, divided
- 1 tsp. ground coriander
- ½ tsp. pepper
- 2 Tbsp. olive oil
- 1½ lbs. small red potatoes, cut in half
- 1 medium onion, chopped
- 1 cup reduced-sodium beef broth
- 1 whole garlic bulb, cloves separated, peeled and slightly crushed
- 4 cups strong brewed coffee
- 2 tsp. red wine vinegar
- 3 Tbsp. butter

1. Sprinkle ribs with 1 tsp. salt, coriander and pepper. In a large skillet, brown the ribs in oil in batches. Using tongs, transfer the ribs to a 6-qt. slow cooker. Add the potatoes and onion.
2. Add broth to skillet, stirring to loosen browned bits. Bring to a boil; cook until liquid is reduced by half. Stir in garlic and remaining salt; add to slow cooker. Pour coffee over top. Cover and cook on low until meat is tender, 6-8 hours.
3. Remove ribs and potatoes to a serving platter; keep warm. Strain cooking juices into a small saucepan; skim fat. Bring to a boil; cook until the liquid is reduced by half. Stir in vinegar. Remove from heat; whisk in butter. Serve sauce with the ribs and potatoes.

1 serving: 320 cal., 18g fat (8g sat. fat), 66mg chol., 569mg sod., 17g carb. (2g sugars, 2g fiber), 21g pro.

GARLIC SWISS FONDUE

I've been making this irresistible fondue for years—everyone flips over the wonderful flavors. When cooled, the cheesy appetizer also can be used as a fantastic cracker spread.
—*Cleo Gonske, Redding, CA*

Prep: 10 min. • **Cook:** 2 hours
Makes: 3 cups

- 4 cups shredded Swiss cheese
- 1 can (10¾ oz.) condensed cheddar cheese soup, undiluted
- 2 Tbsp. sherry or chicken broth
- 1 Tbsp. Dijon mustard
- 2 garlic cloves, minced
- 2 tsp. hot pepper sauce
  Cubed French bread baguette, sliced apples and seedless red grapes

In a 1½-qt. slow cooker, mix the first 6 ingredients. Cook, covered, on low until the cheese is melted, 2-2½ hours, stirring every 30 minutes. Serve warm with bread cubes and fruit.

¼ cup: 159 cal., 11g fat (7g sat. fat), 35mg chol., 326mg sod., 4g carb. (2g sugars, 0 fiber), 11g pro.

PUMPKIN CRANBERRY BREAD PUDDING

Savor your favorite fall flavors with this scrumptious bread pudding, served warm with a sweet vanilla sauce. Yum!
—*Judith Bucciarelli, Newburgh, NY*

Prep: 15 min. • **Cook:** 3 hours
Makes: 8 servings (1⅓ cups sauce)

- 8 slices cinnamon bread, cut into 1-in. cubes
- 4 large eggs, beaten
- 2 cups 2% milk
- 1 cup canned pumpkin
- ¼ cup packed brown sugar
- ¼ cup butter, melted
- 1 tsp. vanilla extract
- ½ tsp. ground cinnamon
- ¼ tsp. ground nutmeg
- ½ cup dried cranberries

SAUCE
- 1 cup sugar
- ⅔ cup water
- 1 cup heavy whipping cream
- 2 tsp. vanilla extract
  Vanilla ice cream, optional

1. Place the cinnamon bread cubes in a greased 3- or 4-qt. slow cooker. Combine the next 8 ingredients; stir in cranberries. Pour over bread. Cook, covered, on low until a knife inserted in the center comes out clean, 3-4 hours.

2. For sauce, bring the sugar and water to a boil in a large saucepan over medium heat. Cook until sugar is dissolved and mixture turns golden amber, for about 20 minutes. Gradually stir in cream until smooth. Remove from heat; stir in vanilla. Serve warm with the bread pudding. If desired, add a scoop of vanilla ice cream to each serving.

1 serving: 479 cal., 23g fat (13g sat. fat), 147mg chol., 237mg sod., 61g carb. (48g sugars, 4g fiber), 9g pro.

PARTY SAUSAGES

Don't want to have any leftovers from your party? Serve these tempting sausage bites in a sweet and savory sauce. I've never had even one piece go uneaten.

—*Jo Ann Renner, Xenia, OH*

Prep: 15 min. • **Cook:** 1 hour
Makes: 16 servings

- 2 lbs. smoked sausage links
- 1 bottle (8 oz.) Catalina salad dressing
- 1 bottle (8 oz.) Russian salad dressing
- ½ cup packed brown sugar
- ½ cup pineapple juice
  Sliced green onions, optional

1. Cut sausages diagonally into ½-in. slices; cook in a skillet over medium heat until lightly browned. Transfer sausages to a 3-qt. slow cooker; discard drippings.
2. Add dressings, brown sugar and juice to skillet; cook and stir over medium-low heat until sugar is dissolved. Pour over sausages. Cover and cook on low until sausages are heated through, about 1-2 hours. If desired, sprinkle with green onions.

Note: You may substitute French salad dressing for one or both dressings.

2 pieces: 306 cal., 22g fat (7g sat. fat), 38mg chol., 1008mg sod., 18g carb. (16g sugars, 0 fiber), 8g pro.

Zesty Smoked Links: Omit dressings and pineapple juice. Increase brown sugar to 1 cup; add ½ cup ketchup and ¼ cup prepared horseradish. Cook as directed.

SLOW-COOKER BURGUNDY BEEF

When my adult children are coming over for dinner, this is their most-requested dish. All three of them, along with their significant others, love this dish.
—*Urilla Cheverie, Andover, MA*

- -

Prep: 10 min. • **Cook:** 8¼ hours
Makes: 10 servings

4	lbs. beef top sirloin steak, cut into 1-in. cubes
3	large onions, sliced
1	cup water
1	cup burgundy wine or beef broth
1	cup ketchup
¼	cup quick-cooking tapioca
¼	cup packed brown sugar
¼	cup Worcestershire sauce
4	tsp. paprika
1½	tsp. salt
1	tsp. minced garlic
1	tsp. ground mustard
2	Tbsp. cornstarch
3	Tbsp. cold water
	Hot cooked noodles

1. In a 5-qt. slow cooker, combine the first 12 ingredients. Cook, covered, on low until meat is tender, 8-9 hours.
2. Combine cornstarch and water until smooth; stir into the pan juices. Cook, covered, on high until gravy is thickened, about 15 minutes. Serve with noodles.
1 cup: 347 cal., 8g fat (3g sat. fat), 74mg chol., 811mg sod., 24g carb. (15g sugars, 1g fiber), 40g pro.

BUTTERNUT COCONUT CURRY

I love my slow cooker because it's so easy to make dinner with one! This flavorful curry was first created for a potluck, where it was a hit. I love not having to make the rice separately.
—*Jessie Apfe, Berkeley, CA*

- -

Prep: 35 min. • **Cook:** 4 hours
Makes: 9 servings

1	cup chopped carrots
1	small onion, chopped
1	Tbsp. olive oil
1½	tsp. brown sugar
1½	tsp. curry powder
1	garlic clove, minced
½	tsp. ground cinnamon
¼	tsp. ground ginger
⅛	tsp. salt
1	medium butternut squash (about 2½ lbs.), cut into 1-in. cubes
2½	cups vegetable broth
¾	cup coconut milk
½	cup uncooked basmati or jasmine rice

1. In a large skillet, saute carrots and onion in oil until onion is tender. Add the brown sugar, curry, garlic, cinnamon, ginger and salt. Cook and stir 2 minutes longer.
2. In a 3- or 4-qt. slow cooker, combine butternut squash, broth, coconut milk, rice and carrot mixture. Cover and cook on low until rice is tender, for 4-5 hours.
¾ cup: 200 cal., 6g fat (4g sat. fat), 0 chol., 312mg sod., 34g carb. (5g sugars, 5g fiber), 3g pro.

CARIBBEAN CHIPOTLE PORK SLIDERS

One of our favorite pulled pork recipes combines the heat of chipotle peppers with tropical coleslaw for coolness. The robust flavors make these little sliders a big hit with our family and guests.

—*Kadija Bridgewater, Boca Raton, FL*

- -

Prep: 35 min. • **Cook:** 8 hours
Makes: 20 servings

1 large onion, quartered
1 boneless pork shoulder
    butt roast (3 to 4 lbs.)
2 finely chopped chipotle peppers
    in adobo sauce plus 3 Tbsp. sauce
¾ cup honey barbecue sauce
¼ cup water
4 garlic cloves, minced
1 Tbsp. ground cumin
1 tsp. salt
¼ tsp. pepper
COLESLAW
2 cups finely chopped red cabbage
1 medium mango, peeled
    and chopped
1 cup pineapple tidbits, drained
¾ cup chopped fresh cilantro
1 Tbsp. lime juice
¼ tsp. salt
⅛ tsp. pepper
20 Hawaiian sweet rolls,
    split and toasted

1. Place onion in a 5-qt. slow cooker. Cut roast in half; place over onion. In a small bowl, combine chipotle peppers, adobo sauce, barbecue sauce, water, garlic, cumin, salt and pepper; pour over meat. Cook, covered, on low until meat is tender, for 8-10 hours.

2. Remove roast; cool slightly. Skim fat from cooking juices. Shred the pork with 2 forks. Return pork to the slow cooker; heat through.

3. For coleslaw, in a large bowl, combine cabbage, mango, pineapple, cilantro, lime juice, salt and pepper. Place ¼ cup of the pork mixture on each roll bottom; top with 2 Tbsp. coleslaw. Replace tops.

1 sandwich: 265 cal., 10g fat (4g sat. fat), 55mg chol., 430mg sod., 27g carb. (15g sugars, 2g fiber), 16g pro.

★ ★ ★ ★ ★ **READER REVIEW**

"Delicious! The pork was tender and full of flavor. The slaw is a must-have for that tangy crunch. I'm not a fan of cilantro, but that's an easy fix. I will be making this again!"

SUEFALK TASTEOFHOME.COM

SLOW-COOKED BIG BREAKFAST

We make this during holidays when some folks are sleeping in or on mornings when we know we're going to have a long, busy day. It's a superb dish for brunch.
—*Delisha Paris, Elizabeth City, NC*

Prep: 30 min. • **Cook:** 3 hours + standing
Makes: 12 servings

- 1 lb. bulk pork sausage
- 2 lbs. potatoes (about 4 medium), peeled and cut into ½-in. cubes
- ¼ cup water
- 1 large onion, finely chopped
- 1 medium sweet red pepper, chopped
- 2 cups fresh spinach
- 1 cup chopped fresh mushrooms
- 1 lb. cubed deli ham
- 1 cup shredded cheddar cheese
- 12 large eggs
- ½ cup 2% milk
- 1 tsp. garlic powder
- 1 tsp. pepper
- ½ tsp. salt

1. In a large skillet, cook and crumble the sausage over medium heat until no longer pink, 5-7 minutes; drain.
2. Meanwhile, place potatoes and water in a large microwave-safe dish. Microwave, covered, on high until potatoes are tender, 6 minutes, stirring halfway through cooking. Drain and add to sausage.
3. Stir in onion, sweet red pepper, spinach, mushrooms, ham and cheese. Transfer to a greased 6-qt. slow cooker.
4. Whisk together remaining ingredients until blended; pour over sausage mixture. Cook, covered, on low until eggs are set, 3-4 hours. Let stand, uncovered, 10 minutes before serving.

1 cup: 303 cal., 18g fat (6g sat. fat), 236mg chol., 873mg sod., 14g carb. (3g sugars, 1g fiber), 21g pro.

COCONUT-PECAN SWEET POTATOES

These holiday-worthy sweet potatoes cook effortlessly in the slow cooker so you can tend to other things. Coconut gives the classic dish unexpected flair.
—*Raquel Haggard, Edmond, OK*

Prep: 15 min. • **Cook:** 4 hours
Makes: 12 servings (⅔ cup each)

- ½ cup chopped pecans
- ½ cup sweetened shredded coconut
- ⅓ cup sugar
- ⅓ cup packed brown sugar
- ½ tsp. ground cinnamon
- ¼ tsp. salt
- ¼ cup reduced-fat butter, melted
- 4 lbs. sweet potatoes (about 6 medium), peeled and cut into 1-in. pieces
- ½ tsp. coconut extract
- ½ tsp. vanilla extract

1. In a bowl, combine first 6 ingredients; stir in melted butter. Place sweet potatoes in a 5-qt. slow cooker coated with cooking spray. Sprinkle with pecan mixture.
2. Cook, covered, on low until potatoes are tender, 4-4½ hours. Stir in extracts.
Note: This recipe was tested with Land O'Lakes light stick butter.
⅔ cup: 211 cal., 7g fat (3g sat. fat), 5mg chol., 103mg sod., 37g carb. (22g sugars, 3g fiber), 2g pro.

HEARTY SLOW-COOKER LASAGNA

Lasagna is a popular holiday meal, but it's hard to find time to fix it the conventional way. This slow-cooker version will allow you to enjoy time with your family and still put a much-loved and elegant dinner on the table.

—*Kathryn Conrad, Milwaukee, WI*

- -

Prep: 25 min. • **Cook:** 4 hours + standing
Makes: 8 servings

- 1 lb. ground beef
- 1 Tbsp. olive oil
- ½ cup chopped onion
- ½ cup chopped zucchini
- ½ cup chopped carrot
- 1 jar (24 oz.) marinara sauce
- 2 tsp. Italian seasoning
- ½ tsp. crushed red pepper flakes, optional
- 2 cartons (15 oz. each) part-skim ricotta cheese
- 1 cup grated Parmesan cheese
- 4 large eggs
- ½ cup loosely packed basil leaves, chopped
- 12 no-cook lasagna noodles
- 3 cups shredded part-skim mozzarella cheese
  Quartered grape tomatoes and additional chopped fresh basil, optional

1. Cut three 25x3-in. strips of heavy-duty foil; crisscross so they resemble spokes of a wheel. Place strips on bottom and up sides of a 5-qt. slow cooker. Coat strips with cooking spray.

2. In a 6-qt. stockpot, cook beef over medium heat until beef is no longer pink, 6-8 minutes; drain. Set beef aside.

3. In same pot, heat oil over medium-high heat. Add onion, zucchini and carrot; cook and stir just until tender, 2-3 minutes. Stir in beef mixture, marinara sauce, Italian seasoning and, if desired, the crushed red pepper. In a large bowl, combine ricotta, Parmesan, eggs and basil.

4. Spread ½ cup meat sauce into bottom of the slow cooker. Layer with 4 noodles, breaking to fit. Top with 1½ cups meat mixture, 1⅔ cups cheese mixture and 1 cup mozzarella cheese. Repeat layers twice. Cook, covered, on low until noodles are tender, 4 hours. Let stand 30 minutes. If desired, sprinkle with grape tomatoes and additional basil.

1 serving: 631 cal., 32g fat (15g sat. fat), 199mg chol., 1074mg sod., 40g carb. (8g sugars, 3g fiber), 43g pro.

SO-EASY SPAGHETTI SAUCE

Let the slow cooker do all the work for this hearty spaghetti sauce. All you need to do is cook the pasta and bake up some crusty garlic bread.
—*Cathy Johnson, Somerset, PA*

Prep: 30 min. • **Cook:** 5 hours
Makes: about 2¼ qt.

- 1   lb. lean ground beef (90% lean)
- 1   medium onion, finely chopped
- ¼   cup finely chopped celery
- 1   can (29 oz.) tomato sauce
- 2½ cups tomato juice
- 1   can (14½ oz.) diced tomatoes, undrained
- 1   can (12 oz.) tomato paste
- 2   tsp. sugar
- 2   tsp. chili powder
- 1   tsp. salt
- 1   tsp. garlic powder
- 1   tsp. dried basil
- 1   tsp. dried oregano
- ½   tsp. pepper
- 4   bay leaves
    Hot cooked spaghetti
    Grated Parmesan cheese, optional

1. In a large skillet, cook the beef, onion and celery over medium heat until meat is no longer pink; drain. In a 4- or 5-qt. slow cooker, combine the tomato sauce, tomato juice, tomatoes, tomato paste, sugar, seasonings and beef mixture.
2. Cover and cook on low until heated through, 5-6 hours. Discard bay leaves. Serve with spaghetti; sprinkle with the cheese if desired.
¾ cup: 125 cal., 3g fat (1g sat. fat), 19mg chol., 744mg sod., 16g carb. (10g sugars, 4g fiber), 10g pro. **Diabetic exchanges:** 1 lean meat, 1 vegetable, ½ starch, ½ fat.

JAZZED-UP GREEN BEAN CASSEROLE

After trying many variations of this old standby, I decided to give it a little extra kick. Its crunchy texture and cheesy goodness—plus bacon—make it a hit at any holiday get-together.
—*Stephan-Scott Rugh, Portland, OR*

Prep: 20 min. • **Cook:** 5½ hours
Makes: 10 servings

- 2   pkg. (16 oz. each) frozen cut green beans, thawed
- 2   cans (10¾ oz. each) condensed cream of mushroom soup, undiluted
- 1   can (8 oz.) sliced water chestnuts, drained
- 1   cup 2% milk
- 6   bacon strips, cooked and crumbled
- 1   tsp. pepper
- ⅛   tsp. paprika
- 4   oz. process cheese (Velveeta), cubed
- 1   can (2.8 oz.) French-fried onions

In a 4-qt. slow cooker, combine the green beans, soup, water chestnuts, milk, bacon, pepper and paprika. Cover and cook on low until beans are tender, 5-6 hours; stir in cheese. Cover and cook until cheese is melted, 30 minutes. Sprinkle with onions.
¾ cup: 200 cal., 11g fat (4g sat. fat), 18mg chol., 862mg sod., 19g carb. (5g sugars, 3g fiber), 7g pro.

MAKEOVER
BEEF & POTATO SOUP

Slow-cooker easy, this satisfying soup is a Christmas Eve tradition at our house after church services.
—*Sheila Holderman, Berthold, ND*

Prep: 30 min. • **Cook:** 6½ hours
Makes: 10 servings (3 qt.)

- 1½ lbs. lean ground beef (90% lean)
- ¾ cup chopped onion
- ½ cup all-purpose flour
- 2 cans (14½ oz. each) reduced-sodium chicken broth, divided
- 5 medium potatoes, peeled and cubed
- 5 medium carrots, chopped
- 3 celery ribs, chopped
- 3 tsp. dried basil
- 2 tsp. dried parsley flakes
- 1 tsp. garlic powder
- ½ tsp. pepper
- 12 oz. reduced-fat process cheese (Velveeta), cubed
- 1½ cups 2% milk
- ½ cup reduced-fat sour cream

1. In a large skillet, cook beef and onion over medium heat until meat is no longer pink; drain. Combine flour and 1 can broth until smooth. Add to beef mixture. Bring to a boil; cook and stir until thickened, about 2 minutes.
2. Transfer to a 5-qt. slow cooker. Stir in the potatoes, carrots, celery, seasonings and remaining broth. Cover and cook on low until vegetables are tender, 6-8 hours.
3. Stir in cheese and milk. Cover and cook until cheese is melted, about 30 minutes. Just before serving, stir in sour cream.
1¼ cups: 327 cal., 11g fat (5g sat. fat), 61mg chol., 832mg sod., 32g carb. (9g sugars, 3g fiber), 25g pro.

RANCH BEANS

This sweet and tangy side dish uses lots of convenient canned goods, so it's a snap to throw together. The recipe was sent to me by a friend. It's nice to serve at a group picnic.
—*Barbara Gordon, Roswell, GA*

Prep: 10 min. • **Cook:** 3 hours
Makes: 10 servings

- 1 can (16 oz.) kidney beans, rinsed and drained
- 1 can (15¾ oz.) pork and beans, undrained
- 1 can (15 oz.) lima beans, rinsed and drained
- 1 can (14½ oz.) cut green beans, drained
- 1 bottle (12 oz.) chili sauce
- ¾ cup packed brown sugar
- 1 small onion, chopped

In a 3-qt. slow cooker, combine all the ingredients. Cover and cook on high until heated through, 3-4 hours.
1 cup: 264 cal., 0 fat (0 sat. fat), 0 chol., 1300mg sod., 60g carb. (34g sugars, 8g fiber), 8g pro.

TEST KITCHEN TIP
This dish can be cooked in the oven. Cover and bake at 350° for 40 minutes. Remove cover and cook the beans 10 minutes longer.

MEATY SLOW-COOKED JAMBALAYA

This recipe makes a big batch of chicken, sausage and shrimp deliciousness.
—*Diane Smith, Pine Mountain, GA*

Prep: 25 min. • **Cook:** 7¼ hours
Makes: 12 servings (3 qt.)

- 1 **can (28 oz.) diced tomatoes, undrained**
- 1 **cup reduced-sodium chicken broth**
- 1 **large green pepper, chopped**
- 1 **medium onion, chopped**
- 2 **celery ribs, sliced**
- ½ **cup white wine or additional reduced-sodium chicken broth**
- 4 **garlic cloves, minced**
- 2 **tsp. Cajun seasoning**
- 2 **tsp. dried parsley flakes**
- 1 **tsp. dried basil**
- 1 **tsp. dried oregano**
- ¾ **tsp. salt**
- ½ **to 1 tsp. cayenne pepper**
- 2 **lbs. boneless skinless chicken thighs, cut into 1-in. pieces**
- 1 **pkg. (12 oz.) fully cooked andouille or other spicy chicken sausage links**
- 2 **lbs. uncooked medium shrimp, peeled and deveined**
- 8 **cups hot cooked brown rice**

1. In a large bowl, combine the first 13 ingredients. Place chicken and sausage in a 6-qt. slow cooker. Pour tomato mixture over top. Cook, covered, on low until the chicken is tender, 7-9 hours.

2. Stir in the shrimp. Cook, covered, until shrimp turn pink, 15-20 minutes longer. Serve with rice.

1 cup jambalaya with ⅔ cup cooked rice: 387 cal., 10g fat (3g sat. fat), 164mg chol., 674mg sod., 37g carb. (4g sugars, 4g fiber), 36g pro. **Diabetic exchanges:** 3 lean meat, 2½ starch.

BUTTERSCOTCH-PECAN BREAD PUDDING

Bread pudding fans will absolutely adore this treat. Toppings like whipped cream and a butterscotch drizzle make it utterly irresistible.
—*Lisa Varner, El Paso, TX*

Prep: 15 min. • **Cook:** 3 hours
Makes: 8 servings

- 9 **cups cubed day-old white bread (about 8 slices)**
- ½ **cup chopped pecans**
- ½ **cup butterscotch chips**
- 4 **large eggs**
- 2 **cups half-and-half cream**
- ½ **cup packed brown sugar**
- ½ **cup butter, melted**
- 1 **tsp. vanilla extract**
   Whipped cream and butterscotch ice cream topping

1. Place bread, pecans and butterscotch chips in a greased 4-qt. slow cooker. In a large bowl, whisk eggs, cream, brown sugar, melted butter and vanilla until blended. Pour over bread mixture; stir gently to combine.
2. Cook, covered, on low until a knife inserted in center comes out clean, for 3-4 hours. Serve warm with whipped cream and butterscotch topping.
1 serving: 502 cal., 30g fat (16g sat. fat), 154mg chol., 384mg sod., 47g carb. (26g sugars, 2g fiber), 10g pro.

2 Tbsp. Sriracha chili sauce
1 Tbsp. chili powder
1 tsp. smoked paprika
1 tsp. garlic powder
1 tsp. onion powder
½ tsp. salt
2 lbs. boneless skinless chicken thighs (about 8 thighs)
¾ cup brown ale
3 Tbsp. cornstarch
3 Tbsp. water
12 slider buns
Sweet pickles and additional Sriracha sauce, optional

1. In a 3- or 4-qt. slow cooker, combine the first 8 ingredients. Add chicken and ale; toss to coat. Cook, covered, on low until chicken is tender, 6-8 hours. Remove meat; when cool enough to handle, shred with 2 forks.

2. Strain cooking juices; skim fat. Transfer juices to a small saucepan; bring to a boil. In a small bowl, mix cornstarch and water until smooth; stir into saucepan. Return to a boil, stirring constantly; cook and stir until thickened, about 5 minutes. Add the chicken to the sauce; toss to coat. Serve on buns, with sweet pickles and additional Sriracha sauce if desired.

1 slider: 224 cal., 7g fat (2g sat. fat), 51mg chol., 357mg sod., 22g carb. (8g sugars, 1g fiber), 17g pro.

✳

TEST KITCHEN TIP
It's OK to be a little heavy-handed with the Sriracha if you love it spicy. Or you can always squeeze on more after you assemble your sandwich.

OVERNIGHT VEGETABLE & EGG BREAKFAST

My overnight eggs and veggies make a hearty breakfast for those who have to rush out the door. I use sliced potatoes, but frozen potatoes work, too.
—*Kimberly Clark-Thiry, Anchor Point, AK*

- -

Prep: 15 min. • **Cook:** 7 hours
Makes: 8 servings

4 lbs. potatoes, peeled and thinly sliced (about 8 cups)
1 medium green pepper, finely chopped
1 pkg. (10 oz.) frozen chopped spinach, thawed and squeezed dry
1 cup sliced fresh mushrooms
1 medium onion, finely chopped
8 large eggs
1 cup water
1 cup 2% milk
1¼ tsp. salt
¼ tsp. pepper
2 cups shredded cheddar cheese

In a greased 6-qt. slow cooker, layer the first 5 ingredients. In a large bowl, whisk the next 5 ingredients; pour over top. Sprinkle with cheese. Cook, covered, on low until potatoes are tender and eggs are set, 7-9 hours.

1½ cups: 354 cal., 15g fat (7g sat. fat), 217mg chol., 668mg sod., 37g carb. (5g sugars, 4g fiber), 19g pro.

HONEY & ALE PULLED CHICKEN SLIDERS

Score big with your guests with a little bit of sweet heat! This recipe works well for a football party—the extra liquid in the slow cooker keeps it nice and juicy all day long.
—*Julie Peterson, Crofton, MD*

- -

Prep: 20 min. • **Cook:** 6 hours
Makes: 12 servings

¼ cup honey
2 Tbsp. cider vinegar

MAKE AHEAD
LOUISIANA RED BEANS & RICE

Smoked turkey sausage and red pepper flakes add zip to this slow-cooked version of the New Orleans classic. For extra heat, add red pepper sauce.

—*Julia Bushree, Menifee, CA*

- -

Prep: 20 min. • **Cook:** 3 hours
Makes: 8 servings

- 4 cans (16 oz. each) kidney beans, rinsed and drained
- 1 can (14½ oz.) diced tomatoes, undrained
- 1 pkg. (14 oz.) smoked turkey sausage, sliced
- 3 celery ribs, chopped
- 1 large onion, chopped
- 1 cup chicken broth
- 1 medium green pepper, chopped
- 1 small sweet red pepper, chopped
- 6 garlic cloves, minced
- 1 bay leaf
- ½ tsp. crushed red pepper flakes
- 2 green onions, chopped
  Hot cooked rice

1. In a 4- or 5-qt. slow cooker, combine the first 11 ingredients. Cook, covered, on low until vegetables are tender, 3-4 hours.
2. Stir before serving. Remove bay leaf. Serve with green onions and rice.
Freeze option: Discard bay leaf and freeze cooled bean mixture in freezer containers. To use, partially thaw in refrigerator overnight. Heat mixture through in a saucepan, stirring occasionally and adding a little broth or water if necessary. Serve as directed.
1 cup: 291 cal., 3g fat (1g sat. fat), 32mg chol., 1070mg sod., 44g carb. (8g sugars, 13g fiber), 24g pro.

SHREDDED BARBECUE BEEF

I work for the Delaware Department of Transportation, and I often prepare this simple dish for storm emergencies or lunchtime get-togethers.

—*Jan Walls, Dover, DE*

- -

Prep: 20 min. • **Cook:** 6 hours
Makes: 12 servings

- 1 tsp. celery salt
- 1 tsp. garlic powder
- 1 tsp. onion powder
- 1 fresh beef brisket (3 to 4 lbs.)
- 3 Tbsp. liquid smoke, optional
- 1 Tbsp. hot pepper sauce
- 1 bottle (18 oz.) barbecue sauce
- 12 sandwich rolls, split

1. Combine the celery salt, garlic powder and onion powder; rub over brisket. Place in a 5-qt. slow cooker. Combine liquid smoke if desired and hot pepper sauce; pour over brisket. Cover and cook on low until meat is tender, 6-8 hours.
2. Remove beef and cool slightly. Discard all but ½ cup cooking juices; whisk the barbecue sauce into cooking juices. Shred meat with 2 forks; return to slow cooker and mix well. Heat through. Serve about ⅓ cup meat mixture on each roll.
Note: This is a fresh beef brisket, not corned beef brisket.
1 serving: 387 cal., 10g fat (3g sat. fat), 48mg chol., 905mg sod., 41g carb. (10g sugars, 2g fiber), 32g pro.

ROOT BEER BRATS

Here's an easy recipe that's versatile, too. Serve the saucy brats over rice for one meal and have them on buns the next. For extra punch, add a splash of root beer concentrate to the sauce.
—*Pamela Thompson, Girard, IL*

- -

Prep: 15 min. • **Cook:** 6 hours
Makes: 10 servings

- 1 can (12 oz.) root beer
- 3 Tbsp. cornstarch
- 3 tsp. ground mustard
- 3 tsp. caraway seeds
- 10 uncooked bratwurst links
- 1 large onion, coarsely chopped
- 1 bottle (12 oz.) chili sauce
- 10 hoagie buns, toasted

Thinly sliced red onion, optional
Prepared mustard, optional

1. Whisk first 4 ingredients until blended. In a nonstick skillet, brown bratwursts over medium-high heat. Transfer to a 4- or 5-qt. slow cooker. Add onion, chili sauce and root beer mixture.
2. Cook mixture, covered, on low until a thermometer inserted in sausage reads at least 160°, 6-8 hours. Serve in buns. If desired, top with onion and mustard.
1 serving: 563 cal., 30g fat (10g sat. fat), 63mg chol., 1575mg sod., 54g carb. (16g sugars, 2g fiber), 20g pro.

ROASTED RED PEPPER SAUCE

I often use Greek olives for added zest in this pasta sauce. Roast the peppers yourself if you have the time.
—*Genie Tosh, Lumberton, NJ*

- -

Prep: 15 min. • **Cook:** 4 hours
Makes: about 15 cups

- 4 lbs. plum tomatoes (about 17), coarsely chopped
- 1 large sweet onion, chopped
- 1 can (29 oz.) tomato puree
- 3 jars (7 oz. each) roasted sweet red peppers, drained and chopped
- 2 jars (6½ oz. each) marinated artichoke hearts, drained and chopped
- ½ lb. fresh mushrooms, quartered
- 2 cans (2¼ oz. each) sliced ripe olives, drained
- ¼ cup sugar
- ¼ cup balsamic vinegar
- ¼ cup olive oil
- 3 garlic cloves, minced
- 1 Tbsp. dried basil
- 1 Tbsp. dried oregano
- 1 tsp. salt
  Hot cooked pasta

In a 5-qt. slow cooker, combine the first 14 ingredients. Cover and cook on high until flavors are blended, 4 hours. Serve with pasta.
1 cup: 116 cal., 6g fat (1g sat. fat), 0 chol., 298mg sod., 14g carb. (8g sugars, 2g fiber), 2g pro.

GARLIC LOVER'S BEEF STEW

The wine gives a mellow flavor to this beef and carrot stew. We like to serve it over mashed potatoes, but you could also use noodles.

—*Alissa Brown, Fort Washington, PA*

Prep: 30 min. • **Cook:** 8 hours
Makes: 10 servings

- 1 **boneless beef chuck roast (3 lbs.), cut into 2-in. pieces**
- 1¼ **tsp. salt**
- ¾ **tsp. coarsely ground pepper**
- ½ **cup all-purpose flour**
- 2 **Tbsp. olive oil**
- 12 **garlic cloves, minced**
- 1 **cup dry red wine or reduced-sodium beef broth**
- 2 **cans (14½ oz. each) diced tomatoes, undrained**
- 1 **can (14½ oz.) reduced-sodium beef broth**
- 6 **medium carrots, thinly sliced**
- 2 **medium onions, chopped**
- 2 **Tbsp. tomato paste**
- 2 **tsp. minced fresh rosemary or ½ tsp. dried rosemary, crushed**
- 2 **tsp. minced fresh thyme or ½ tsp. dried thyme**
- 2 **bay leaves**
   Dash ground cloves
   Hot mashed potatoes

1. Sprinkle the beef with salt, pepper and flour; toss to coat.

2. In a large skillet, heat oil over medium-high heat. Brown beef in batches. Remove with a slotted spoon. Reduce the heat to medium. Add the garlic; cook and stir for 1 minute.

3. Add wine to skillet, stirring to loosen browned bits from pan. Transfer to a 5- or 6-qt. slow cooker. Stir in tomatoes, broth, carrots, onions, tomato paste, rosemary, thyme, bay leaves, cloves and beef.

4. Cook, covered, on low until the beef is tender, 8-10 hours. Remove bay leaves. Serve with mashed potatoes.

1 cup: 330 cal., 16g fat (5g sat. fat), 89mg chol., 586mg sod., 17g carb. (6g sugars, 3g fiber), 29g pro. **Diabetic exchanges:** 4 lean meat, 1 starch, 1 fat.

2. Cover and cook on low until chicken is tender, 6-8 hours; skim fat. Serve chicken with the mole sauce; if desired sprinkle with cilantro.

Freeze option: Cool chicken in mole sauce. Freeze in freezer containers. To use, partially thaw in refrigerator overnight. Heat through slowly in a covered skillet or Dutch oven until a thermometer inserted in chicken reads 165°, stirring occasionally and adding a little broth or water if necessary.

1 chicken thigh with ⅓ cup sauce: 311 cal., 18g fat (5g sat. fat), 86mg chol., 378mg sod., 12g carb. (7g sugars, 3g fiber), 26g pro.

HAWAIIAN KIELBASA SANDWICHES

If you are looking for a different way to use kielbasa, the sweet and mildly spicy flavor of these sandwiches might be a nice change of pace.

—*Judy Dames, Bridgeville, PA*

- -

Prep: 15 min. • **Cook:** 3 hours
Makes: 12 sandwiches

- 3 **lbs. smoked kielbasa or Polish sausage, cut into 3-in. pieces**
- 2 **bottles (12 oz. each) chili sauce**
- 1 **can (20 oz.) pineapple tidbits, undrained**
- ¼ **cup packed brown sugar**
- 12 **hoagie buns, split**
  Thinly sliced green onions, optional

Place kielbasa in a 3-qt. slow cooker. Combine the chili sauce, pineapple and brown sugar; pour over kielbasa. Cover and cook on low until heated through, 3-4 hours. Serve on buns. If desired, top with green onions.

1 sandwich: 663 cal., 35g fat (12g sat. fat), 76mg chol., 2532mg sod., 64g carb. (27g sugars, 1g fiber), 23g pro.

CHICKEN MOLE

If you're not familiar with mole, don't be shy to try this versatile Mexican sauce that includes nuts, chocolate and other surprises. I love sharing the recipe; it's a tasty introduction to the classic dish.

—*Darlene Morris, Franklinton, LA*

- -

Prep: 25 min. • **Cook:** 6 hours
Makes: 12 servings

- 12 **bone-in chicken thighs (about 4½ lbs.), skin removed**
- 1 **tsp. salt**
  MOLE SAUCE
- 1 **can (28 oz.) whole tomatoes, drained**
- 1 **medium onion, chopped**
- 2 **dried ancho chiles, stems and seeds removed**
- ½ **cup sliced almonds, toasted**
- ¼ **cup raisins**
- 3 **oz. bittersweet chocolate, chopped**
- 3 **Tbsp. olive oil**
- 1 **chipotle pepper in adobo sauce**
- 3 **garlic cloves, peeled and halved**
- ¾ **tsp. ground cumin**
- ½ **tsp. ground cinnamon**
  Fresh cilantro leaves, optional

1. Sprinkle chicken with salt; place in a 5- or 6-qt. slow cooker. Place tomatoes, onion, chiles, almonds, raisins, chocolate, oil, chipotle pepper, garlic, cumin and cinnamon in a food processor; cover and process until blended. Pour over chicken.

SLOW-COOKED HUNGARIAN GOULASH

You will love how easily this slow-cooked version of a beloved ethnic dish comes together. My son shared the recipe with me many years ago.
—*Jackie Kohn, Duluth, MN*

- -

Prep: 15 min. • **Cook:** 8 hours
Makes: 8 servings

- 2 lbs. beef top round steak, cut into 1-in. cubes
- 1 cup chopped onion
- 2 Tbsp. all-purpose flour
- 1½ tsp. paprika
- 1 tsp. garlic salt
- ½ tsp. pepper
- 1 can (14½ oz.) diced tomatoes, undrained
- 1 bay leaf
- 1 cup sour cream
  Hot cooked egg noodles

Place the beef and onion in a 3-qt. slow cooker. Combine the flour, paprika, garlic salt and pepper; sprinkle over beef and stir to coat. Stir in tomatoes; add bay leaf. Cover and cook on low until the meat is tender, 8-10 hours. Discard bay leaf. Just before serving, stir in the sour cream; heat through. Serve with noodles.

Freeze option: Before adding sour cream, cool goulash. Freeze in freezer containers. To use, partially thaw in refrigerator overnight. Heat through in a saucepan, stirring occasionally and adding a little broth if necessary. Remove from heat; stir in sour cream.

1 cup: 224 cal., 8g fat (5g sat. fat), 83mg chol., 339mg sod., 7g carb. (4g sugars, 1g fiber), 27g pro.

RICH & CREAMY MASHED POTATOES

It's a cinch to jazz up instant mashed potatoes with sour cream and cream cheese, then cook and serve them from a slow cooker. To add another special touch to the perfect-for-party-time potatoes, sprinkle with chopped fresh chives, canned French-fried onions or fresh grated Parmesan cheese.
—*Donna Bardocz, Howell, MI*

- -

Prep: 15 min. • **Cook:** 2 hours
Makes: 10 servings

- 3¾ cups boiling water
- 1½ cups 2% milk
- 1 pkg. (8 oz.) cream cheese, softened
- ½ cup butter, cubed
- ½ cup sour cream
- 4 cups mashed potato flakes
- 1 tsp. garlic salt
- ¼ tsp. pepper
  Minced fresh parsley, optional

In a greased 4-qt. slow cooker, whisk the boiling water, milk, cream cheese, butter and sour cream until smooth. Stir in the potato flakes, garlic salt and pepper. Cover and cook on low until heated through, 2-3 hours. Sprinkle with parsley if desired.

¾ cup: 299 cal., 20g fat (13g sat. fat), 60mg chol., 390mg sod., 25g carb. (2g sugars, 1g fiber), 6g pro.

BEEF BARLEY LENTIL SOUP

I serve this soup often to family and friends on cold nights, along with homemade rolls and a green salad. For variety, try substituting jicama for the potatoes.

—*Judy Metzentine, The Dalles, OR*

Prep: 5 min. • **Cook:** 8 hours
Makes: 10 servings

- 1   lb. lean ground beef (90% lean)
- 1   medium onion, chopped
- 2   cups cubed red potatoes (¼-in. pieces)
- 1   cup chopped celery
- 1   cup chopped carrot
- 1   cup dried lentils, rinsed
- ½   cup medium pearl barley
- 8   cups water
- 2   tsp. beef bouillon granules
- 1   tsp. salt
- ½   tsp. lemon-pepper seasoning
- 2   cans (14½ oz. each) stewed tomatoes, coarsely chopped

1. In a nonstick skillet, cook the beef and onion over medium heat until meat is no longer pink; drain.

2. Transfer to a 5-qt. slow cooker. Layer with the potatoes, celery, carrot, lentils and barley. Combine the water, bouillon, salt and lemon pepper; pour over the vegetables. Cover and cook on low until vegetables and barley are tender, about 6 hours.

3. Add the tomatoes; cook 2 hours longer.

1½ cups: 232 cal., 4g fat (2g sat. fat), 28mg chol., 603mg sod., 33g carb. (6g sugars, 6g fiber), 16g pro. **Diabetic exchanges:** 2 lean meat, 1½ starch, 1 vegetable.

CHOCOLATE ESPRESSO LAVA CAKE

My aunt inspired this cake, which can satisfy even the strongest chocolate craving. It's gooey and saucy, but not too sweet—and that really makes it the potluck-perfect dessert.
—*Lisa Renshaw, Kansas City, MO*

Prep: 15 min. • **Cook:** 3 hours + standing
Makes: 16 servings

1 pkg. chocolate fudge cake mix (regular size)
1 Tbsp. instant espresso powder
3 cups 2% milk
1 pkg. (3.9 oz.) instant chocolate pudding mix
1 cup (6 oz.) semisweet chocolate chips
1 cup white baking chips

1. Prepare cake mix batter according to the package directions, adding espresso powder before mixing. Transfer mixture to a greased 4-qt. slow cooker.
2. In a small bowl, whisk milk and pudding mix 2 minutes. Let stand until soft-set, about 2 minutes. Pour over batter. Cook, covered, on low until a toothpick inserted in cake portion comes out with moist crumbs, 3-3½ hours.
3. Sprinkle top with chocolate chips and baking chips. Turn off the slow cooker; remove insert. Let stand, uncovered, until chips are softened, 15-30 minutes. Serve cake warm.

⅔ cup: 327 cal., 15g fat (6g sat. fat), 41mg chol., 317mg sod., 45g carb. (29g sugars, 2g fiber), 5g pro.

Brown Sugar
Pound Cake
page 232

The Sweetest Treats

Time to celebrate the stars of any get-together: the pretty confections we always remind ourselves to save room for! It won't be hard when these lovely sweets are on the menu.

MAMAW EMILY'S STRAWBERRY CAKE

My husband loved his mamaw's strawberry cake. He thought no one could duplicate it. I made it, and it's just as scrumptious as he remembers.
—*Jennifer Bruce, Manitou, KY*

- -

Prep: 15 min. • **Bake:** 25 min. + cooling
Makes: 12 servings

- 1 pkg. white cake mix (regular size)
- 1 pkg. (3 oz.) strawberry gelatin
- 3 Tbsp. sugar
- 3 Tbsp. all-purpose flour
- 1 cup water
- ½ cup canola oil
- 2 large eggs, room temperature
- 1 cup finely chopped strawberries

FROSTING
- ½ cup butter, softened
- ½ cup crushed strawberries
- 4½ to 5 cups confectioners' sugar

1. Preheat oven to 350°. Line the bottoms of two greased 8-in. round baking pans with parchment; grease parchment.
2. In a large bowl, combine cake mix, gelatin, sugar and flour. Add water, oil and eggs; beat on low speed 30 seconds. Beat on medium 2 minutes. Fold in chopped strawberries. Transfer to prepared pans.
3. Bake until a toothpick inserted in center comes out clean, 25-30 minutes. Cool in pans 10 minutes before removing to wire racks; remove paper. Cool completely.
4. For frosting, in a small bowl, beat butter until creamy. Beat in crushed strawberries. Gradually beat in enough confectioners' sugar to reach desired consistency. Spread frosting between layers and over the top and sides of cake.

1 slice: 532 cal., 21g fat (7g sat. fat), 51mg chol., 340mg sod., 85g carb. (69g sugars, 1g fiber), 4g pro.

PUMPKIN SPICE CUPCAKES WITH CREAM CHEESE FROSTING

I love the flavor of pumpkin, especially during fall. Generously spiced with cinnamon, the cream cheese frosting in this recipe adds an extra-special touch.
—*Debbie Wiggins, Longmont, CO*

- -

Prep: 25 min. • **Bake:** 20 min. + cooling
Makes: 2 dozen

- ¾ cup butter, softened
- 2½ cups sugar
- 3 large eggs, room temperature
- 1 can (15 oz.) solid-pack pumpkin
- 2⅓ cups all-purpose flour
- 1 Tbsp. pumpkin pie spice
- 1 tsp. baking powder
- 1 tsp. ground cinnamon
- ¾ tsp. salt
- ½ tsp. baking soda
- ½ tsp. ground ginger
- 1 cup buttermilk

FROSTING
- 1 pkg. (8 oz.) cream cheese, softened
- ½ cup butter, softened
- 4 cups confectioners' sugar
- 1 tsp. vanilla extract
- 2 tsp. ground cinnamon

1. Preheat oven to 350°. In a large bowl, cream butter and sugar until light and fluffy. Add eggs, one at a time, beating well after each addition. Add pumpkin. Combine the flour, pie spice, baking powder, cinnamon, salt, baking soda and ginger; add to creamed mixture alternately with the buttermilk, beating well after each addition.
2. Fill 24 paper-lined muffin cups three-fourths full. Bake until a toothpick inserted in center comes out clean, 20-25 minutes. Cool 10 minutes before removing from pans to wire racks to cool completely.
3. For frosting, in a large bowl, beat the cream cheese and butter until fluffy. Add the confectioners' sugar, vanilla and cinnamon; beat until smooth. Frost the cupcakes. Refrigerate leftovers.

1 cupcake: 340 cal., 14g fat (8g sat. fat), 62mg chol., 233mg sod., 53g carb. (41g sugars, 1g fiber), 4g pro.

BROADWAY BROWNIE BARS

I named these dessert bars for Broadway because they're a hit every time I serve them. I especially like to make them for the holidays, or for hostess gifts. They're sure to please any sweet tooth!
—*Anne Frederick, New Hartford, NY*

Prep: 20 min. + chilling • **Bake:** 30 min.
Makes: 2½ dozen

FILLING
- 6 oz. cream cheese, softened
- ½ cup sugar
- ¼ cup butter, softened
- 2 Tbsp. all-purpose flour
- 1 large egg, lightly beaten, room temperature
- ½ tsp. vanilla extract

BROWNIE
- ½ cup butter, cubed
- 1 oz. unsweetened chocolate
- 2 large eggs, lightly beaten, room temperature
- 1 tsp. vanilla extract
- 1 cup sugar
- 1 cup all-purpose flour
- 1 tsp. baking powder
- 1 cup chopped walnuts

TOPPING
- 1 cup (6 oz.) semisweet chocolate chips
- ¼ cup chopped walnuts
- 2 cups miniature marshmallows

FROSTING
- ¼ cup butter
- ¼ cup milk
- 2 oz. cream cheese
- 1 oz. unsweetened chocolate
- 3 cups confectioners' sugar
- 1 tsp. vanilla extract

1. Preheat oven to 350°. In a small bowl, combine the first 6 ingredients until smooth; set aside.

2. In a large saucepan over medium heat, melt butter and chocolate. Remove from the heat and let cool. Stir in the eggs and vanilla. Add sugar, flour, baking powder and nuts, stirring until blended.

3. Spread batter in a 13x9-in. baking pan coated with cooking spray. Spread filling over batter. For topping, in small bowl, combine the chocolate chips and nuts; sprinkle over filling.

4. Bake until almost set, 28 minutes. Sprinkle with the marshmallows; bake 2 minutes longer.

5. For frosting, in a large saucepan, heat butter, milk, cream cheese and chocolate until melted, stirring until smooth. Remove from heat; stir in confectioners' sugar and vanilla. Immediately drizzle frosting over marshmallows. Chill well; cut into bars.

1 brownie: 271 cal., 15g fat (7g sat. fat), 46mg chol., 108mg sod., 33g carb. (26g sugars, 1g fiber), 4g pro.

TEST KITCHEN TIP
For easy removal of bars, line your pan with foil, letting the ends extend up the sides of the pan. Then use the foil to lift the cooled bars.

FROZEN CHOCOLATE CHEESECAKE TART

I first made this irresistible dessert for dinner guests. They were amazed by its rich flavor and appearance. My husband said it was the best dessert he had ever eaten in his whole life!
—*Heather Bennett, Dunbar, WV*

Prep: 15 min. + freezing • **Makes:** 12 servings

- 2¼ cups crushed Oreo cookies (about 22 cookies)
- ⅓ cup butter, melted

FILLING
- 2 pkg. (8 oz. each) cream cheese, softened
- ⅓ cup confectioners' sugar
- 3 cups vanilla or white chips, melted and cooled
- ⅓ cup heavy whipping cream
- 1 tsp. vanilla extract
- ½ cup miniature semisweet chocolate chips
  Additional miniature semisweet chocolate chips, optional

1. In a small bowl, combine cookie crumbs and butter. Press onto the bottom and up the sides of a greased 9-in. fluted tart pan with a removable bottom. Cover and freeze for at least 1 hour.

2. In a large bowl, beat cream cheese and sugar until smooth. Beat in the vanilla chips, cream and vanilla until well combined. Stir in chocolate chips; pour over crust. Cover and freeze for 8 hours or overnight.

3. Uncover and refrigerate 3-4 hours before serving. If desired, sprinkle with miniature chocolate chips. Refrigerate leftovers.

1 slice: 546 cal., 36g fat (20g sat. fat), 52mg chol., 291mg sod., 53g carb. (18g sugars, 2g fiber), 6g pro.

RAISIN DATE BREAD PUDDING

I put all of my leftover bread and buns in the freezer, and when I've stashed away enough, I whip up a batch of this super delicious pudding. It's the perfect dish for any occasion.
—*Dawn Green, Hopkins, MI*

Prep: 15 min. • **Bake:** 55 min.
Makes: 12 servings

- 4 cups whole milk
- 5 cups cubed day-old bread
- 1 cup sugar
- 8 large eggs, beaten
- ½ cup butter, melted
- ¼ cup chopped dates
- ¼ cup raisins
- 1 tsp. vanilla extract
- ½ tsp. ground cinnamon
  Dash salt
  Dash ground nutmeg
  Additional sugar, cinnamon and nutmeg, optional
  Whipped cream, optional

In a large bowl, pour milk over bread. Add sugar, eggs, butter, dates, raisins, vanilla, cinnamon, salt and nutmeg; stir to mix well. Pour into a greased 13x9-in. baking dish. If desired, sprinkle top with additional sugar, cinnamon and nutmeg. Bake at 350° until golden brown and a knife inserted in the center comes out clean, about 55 minutes. If desired, serve warm with whipped cream.
1 serving: 290 cal., 14g fat (8g sat. fat), 173mg chol., 250mg sod., 33g carb. (25g sugars, 1g fiber), 8g pro.

DOUBLE WHAMMY EGGNOG COOKIES

I use up leftover eggnog when I make these cookies. They've become a new family classic.

—*Teresa Morris, Laurel, DE*

- -

Prep: 30 min. + chilling
Bake: 15 min./batch
Makes: 4 dozen

1⅓ cups butter, softened
1 cup packed brown sugar
4 large egg yolks, room temperature
2 Tbsp. eggnog
½ tsp. rum extract
3 cups all-purpose flour

EGGNOG FROSTING
4½ cups confectioners' sugar
¾ cup butter, softened
1½ tsp. rum extract
½ tsp. ground nutmeg
¼ tsp. ground cinnamon
2 to 3 Tbsp. eggnog
Additional ground nutmeg

1. In a large bowl, cream butter and brown sugar until light and fluffy. Beat in the egg yolks, eggnog and extract. Gradually beat in flour. Refrigerate dough, covered, for at least 2 hours.

2. Shape into 1-in. balls; place 2 in. apart on ungreased baking sheets. Bake at 325° until bottoms are brown, 13-16 minutes. Remove to wire racks to cool completely.

3. In a bowl, beat the first 5 frosting ingredients until blended; beat in enough eggnog to reach the desired consistency. Spread frosting over cookies; sprinkle with additional nutmeg. Let stand until set. Store in airtight containers.

Note: This recipe was tested with commercially prepared eggnog.

1 cookie: 167 cal., 9g fat (5g sat. fat), 37mg chol., 66mg sod., 22g carb. (16g sugars, 0 fiber), 1g pro.

OLD-FASHIONED BANANA CREAM PIE

This fluffy no-bake pie is full of old-fashioned flavor, with only a fraction of the work. Because it uses instant pudding, it's ready in just minutes.
—*Perlene Hoekema, Lynden, WA*

- -

Takes: 10 min. • **Makes:** 8 servings

1 cup cold 2% milk
½ tsp. vanilla extract
1 pkg. (3.4 oz.) instant vanilla pudding mix
1 carton (12 oz.) frozen whipped topping, thawed, divided
1 graham cracker crust (9 in.)
2 medium firm bananas, sliced
   Additional banana slices, optional

1. In a large bowl, whisk milk, vanilla and pudding mix for 2 minutes (mixture will be thick). Fold in 3 cups whipped topping.
2. Pour 1⅓ cups of pudding mixture into pie crust. Layer with banana slices and remaining pudding mixture. Top with the remaining whipped topping. Garnish pie with additional banana slices if desired. Refrigerate until serving.
1 piece: 311 cal., 13g fat (9g sat. fat), 2mg chol., 213mg sod., 43g carb. (29g sugars, 1g fiber), 2g pro.
Chocolate & Peanut Butter Banana Cream Pie: Substitute 1 (9-in.) chocolate crumb crust for the graham cracker crust. Arrange banana slices on crust. In a microwave-safe bowl, mix ¾ cup peanut butter and 2 oz. chopped chocolate; microwave on high until blended and smooth, for 1-1½ minutes, stirring every 30 seconds. Spoon over the bananas. Pour pudding mixture over top. Garnish with remaining whipped topping. Just before serving, garnish with 2 Tbsp. chopped salted peanuts or chopped peanut butter cups.

KEY LIME BITES

Key limes don't provide much peel, so sometimes I use regular limes—for the zest only—in these bites. If you can wait, these are even better the next day.
—*Joni Larsen, Wellington, UT*

- -

Prep: 20 min.
Bake: 10 min./batch + standing
Makes: 2½ dozen

1 cup butter, softened
¼ cup confectioners' sugar
2 tsp. Key lime juice
2 tsp. grated Key lime zest
2 cups all-purpose flour
¼ tsp. salt
½ cup chopped macadamia nuts
ICING
2 cups confectioners' sugar
¼ cup Key lime juice
1 tsp. grated Key lime zest

1. Preheat oven to 400°. In a large bowl, cream butter and confectioners' sugar until light and fluffy. Beat in lime juice and zest. Combine flour and salt; gradually add to creamed mixture and mix well. Stir in chopped nuts.
2. Shape dough into 1-in. balls. Place 2 in. apart on ungreased baking sheets; flatten cookies slightly.
3. Bake until bottoms are lightly browned, 8-10 minutes. Remove to wire racks to cool completely.
4. In a bowl, combine icing ingredients. Dip cookies in icing; allow excess to drip off. Place on a wire rack; let stand until set. Store in an airtight container.
1 cookie: 136 cal., 8g fat (4g sat. fat), 16mg chol., 69mg sod., 16g carb. (9g sugars, 0 fiber), 1g pro.

LUSCIOUS LEMON CHEESECAKE

I'm always greeted with "oohs" and "aahs" when I bring out this exquisite dessert. It has a wonderful lemony flavor and silky texture with a smooth, rich sour cream topping.

—Kaaren Jurack, Manassas, VA

Prep: 20 min. • **Bake:** 1 hour + chilling
Makes: 14 servings

CRUST
- 1¼ cups graham cracker crumbs (about 20 squares)
- ¾ cup finely chopped nuts
- ¼ cup sugar
- ⅓ cup butter, melted

FILLING
- 4 pkg. (8 oz. each) cream cheese, softened
- 1¼ cups sugar
- 4 large eggs
- 1 Tbsp. lemon juice
- 2 tsp. grated lemon zest
- 1 tsp. vanilla extract

TOPPING
- 2 cups sour cream
- ¼ cup sugar
- 1 tsp. grated lemon zest
- 1 tsp. vanilla extract

1. In a bowl, combine the crumbs, nuts and sugar; stir in butter. Press onto the bottom of a greased 10-in. springform pan; set aside. in a large bowl, beat cream cheese and sugar until smooth. Add eggs, beating on low speed just until combined. Stir in the lemon juice, zest and vanilla; beat just until blended. Pour into crust.
2. Bake at 350° until center is almost set, 55 minutes. Remove from the oven; let stand for 5 minutes. Combine topping ingredients; spread over filling. Return to the oven for 5 minutes. Cool on a wire rack for 10 minutes.

3. Carefully run a knife around edge of pan to loosen; cool 1 hour longer. Refrigerate overnight. Remove sides of pan. Let cake stand at room temperature for 30 minutes before slicing.
1 slice: 352 cal., 21g fat (11g sat. fat), 112mg chol., 172mg sod., 33g carb. (27g sugars, 1g fiber), 6g pro.

CHERRY DREAM CAKE

I use cherry gelatin to give a boxed cake mix an eye-appealing marbled effect. It's so festive-looking and at the same time, it's incredibly easy, too!

—Margaret McNeil, Germantown, TN

Prep: 15 min. + chilling
Bake: 30 min. • **Makes:** 20 servings

- 1 pkg. white cake mix (regular size)
- 1 pkg. (3 oz.) cherry gelatin
- 1½ cups boiling water
- 1 pkg. (8 oz.) cream cheese, softened
- 2 cups whipped topping
- 1 can (21 oz.) cherry pie filling

1. Prepare cake mix according to package directions, using a greased 13x9-in. baking pan. Bake at 350° until a toothpick in center comes out clean, 30-35 minutes.
2. Dissolve gelatin in boiling water. Cool cake on a wire rack for 3-5 minutes. Poke holes in cake with a meat fork or wooden skewer; gradually pour gelatin over cake. Cool for 15 minutes. Cover and refrigerate for 30 minutes.
3. In a large bowl, beat cream cheese until fluffy. Fold in whipped topping. Carefully spread over cake. Top with the pie filling. Cover and refrigerate for at least 2 hours before serving.
1 piece: 164 cal., 4g fat (1g sat. fat), 1mg chol., 251mg sod., 28g carb. (0 sugars, 0 fiber), 3g pro. **Diabetic exchanges:** 1½ starch, 1 fat, ½ fruit.

GOLDEN PEACH PIE

Years ago, I entered this pie in the Park County Fair in Livingston. It won a first-place blue ribbon plus a purple ribbon for Best All Around! Family and friends agree with the judges—it's a perfectly peachy pie.
—*Shirley Olson, Polson, MT*

Prep: 20 min. • **Bake:** 50 min. + cooling
Makes: 8 servings

- 2 **sheets refrigerated pie crust**
- 5 **cups sliced peeled fresh peaches (about 5 medium)**
- 2 **tsp. lemon juice**
- ½ **tsp. grated orange zest**
- ⅛ **tsp. almond extract**
- 1 **cup sugar**
- ¼ **cup cornstarch**
- ¼ **tsp. ground nutmeg**
- ⅛ **tsp. salt**
- 2 **Tbsp. butter**

1. Line a 9-in. pie plate with 1 crust; trim, leaving a 1-in. overhang around edge. Set aside. In a large bowl, combine the peaches, lemon juice, orange zest and extract. Combine the sugar, cornstarch, nutmeg and salt. Add to peach mixture; toss gently to coat. Pour into crust; dot with butter.

2. Roll out remaining crust to a ⅛-in.-thick circle; cut into strips of various widths. Arrange over filling in a lattice pattern. Trim and seal strips to bottom crust; fold overhang over. Lightly press or flute edge. Cover the edges loosely with foil.

3. Bake at 400° for 40 minutes. Remove foil; bake until crust is golden brown and filling is bubbly, for 10-15 minutes longer. Cool on a wire rack. Store leftover pie in the refrigerator.

1 piece: 425 cal., 17g fat (8g sat. fat), 18mg chol., 267mg sod., 67g carb. (36g sugars, 2g fiber), 3g pro.

CHOCOLATE ALMOND CRESCENTS

If you like chocolate-covered almonds, you're in for a treat. These buttery, crumbly cookies are not only pretty, they also make a thoughtful gift.
—*Vicki Raatz, Waterloo, WI*

Prep: 20 min. + chilling
Bake: 10 min./batch
Makes: 6 dozen

- 1¼ cups butter, softened
- ⅔ cup sugar
- 2 cups finely chopped almonds
- 1½ tsp. vanilla extract
- 2 cups all-purpose flour
- ½ cup baking cocoa
- ⅛ tsp. salt
- 1¼ cups semisweet chocolate chips, melted
- 1 to 2 Tbsp. confectioners' sugar
  Sweetened shredded coconut, optional

1. In a large bowl, cream butter and sugar until light and fluffy. Beat in almonds and vanilla. In another bowl, whisk the flour, cocoa and salt; gradually beat into the creamed mixture. Refrigerate, covered, until firm enough to shape, 2 hours.

2. Preheat oven to 350°. Shape 2 tsp. of dough into 2-in.-long logs. Form each into a crescent. Place 2 in. apart on ungreased baking sheets. Bake cookies until set, for 10-12 minutes. Remove from pans to wire racks to cool completely.

3. Dip cookies halfway into melted chocolate, allowing excess to drip off. Place on waxed paper. If desired, sprinkle with coconut. Let stand until set. Cover the dipped sides of cookies with waxed paper; dust the undipped sides with confectioners' sugar. Store chocolate almond crescents between pieces of waxed paper in airtight containers.

1 cookie: 85 cal., 6g fat (3g sat. fat), 8mg chol., 27mg sod., 7g carb. (4g sugars, 1g fiber), 1g pro.

CARAMEL CHOCOLATE TRIFLE

A highlight of our annual family reunion is the dessert competition. The judges take their jobs very seriously! Last year's first-place winner was this tempting and eye-catching trifle.

—*Barb Hausey, Independence, MO*

Prep: 20 min. • **Bake:** 20 min. + cooling
Makes: 16 servings

- 1 pkg. (9 oz.) devil's food cake mix
- 2 pkg. (3.9 oz. each) instant chocolate pudding mix
- 1 carton (12 oz.) frozen whipped topping, thawed
- 1 jar (12¼ oz.) caramel ice cream topping
- 1 pkg. (7½ or 8 oz.) English toffee bits or almond brickle chips

1. Prepare and bake cake according to package directions for an 8-in. square baking pan. Cool on a wire rack. Prepare pudding according to package directions.
2. Cut cake into 1½-in. cubes. Place half of the cubes in a 3-qt. trifle bowl or large glass serving bowl; lightly press down to fill in gaps. Top with half of the whipped topping, pudding, caramel topping and toffee bits; repeat layers. Cover trifle and refrigerate until serving.

1 serving: 349 cal., 11g fat (7g sat. fat), 21mg chol., 533mg sod., 61g carb. (29g sugars, 1g fiber), 3g pro.

MAKE AHEAD

LEMON POUND CAKE LOAVES

Next time you are spending the weekend at a friend's house, take these luscious lemon loaves with you. You can have them for breakfast the next morning!
—*Lola Baxter, Winnebago, MN*

Prep: 20 min. • **Bake:** 35 min. + cooling
Makes: 2 mini loaves (6 slices each)

- ½ cup butter, softened
- 1 cup sugar
- 2 large eggs, room temperature
- 1 tsp. grated lemon zest
- 1 tsp. vanilla extract
- ½ tsp. lemon extract
- 1¾ cups all-purpose flour
- ½ tsp. salt
- ¼ tsp. baking soda
- ½ cup sour cream

ICING
- ¾ cup confectioners' sugar
- ½ tsp. grated lemon zest
- 1 Tbsp. lemon juice

1. Preheat oven to 350°. Grease and flour two 5¾x3x2-in. loaf pans.
2. In a large bowl, cream butter and sugar until light and fluffy. Add eggs, one at a time, beating well after each addition. Beat in lemon zest and extracts. In another bowl, whisk flour, salt and baking soda; add to the creamed mixture alternately with the sour cream, beating well after each addition.
3. Transfer to prepared pans. Bake until a toothpick inserted in center comes out clean, 35-40 minutes. Cool bread in pans 10 minutes before removing to wire racks to cool completely.
4. In a small bowl, mix icing ingredients. Spoon over loaves.

Freeze option: Do not make icing. Securely wrap cooled loaves in plastic and foil, then freeze. To use, thaw at room temperature. Prepare icing as directed.

1 slice: 262 cal., 10g fat (6g sat. fat), 58mg chol., 201mg sod., 39g carb. (25g sugars, 1g fiber), 3g pro.

For one large loaf: Make batter as directed; transfer to a greased and floured 8x4-in. loaf pan. Bake in a preheated 350° oven until a toothpick comes out clean, 40-45 minutes. Ice as directed.

JUICY PEACH & STRAWBERRY CRUMB PIE

You've had peach pie and strawberry pie, and maybe you've even had peach-strawberry pie. But throw in some garden-fresh basil and you're in for a real treat. Try it!
—*Lindsay Sprunk, Brooklyn, NY*

Prep: 25 min. • **Bake:** 45 min. + cooling
Makes: 8 servings

- 1 sheet refrigerated pie crust
- 3½ cups sliced peeled peaches (about 4 medium)
- 2½ cups sliced fresh strawberries
- 2 Tbsp. lemon juice
- ¾ cup sugar
- ¼ cup cornstarch
- 2 Tbsp. minced fresh basil
- ¾ cup all-purpose flour
- ½ cup packed brown sugar
- 6 Tbsp. cold butter

1. Preheat oven to 375°. Unroll pie crust into a 9-in. pie plate; flute edge. In a large bowl, combine peaches, strawberries and lemon juice. In a small bowl, mix sugar, cornstarch and basil. Add to fruit and toss gently to coat. Transfer to crust.
2. In a small bowl, mix the flour and brown sugar; cut in butter until crumbly. Sprinkle over filling. Place the pie on a foil-lined baking pan.
3. Bake on a lower oven rack until topping is golden brown and filling is bubbly, for 45-55 minutes. Cool on a wire rack.
1 piece: 424 cal., 16g fat (9g sat. fat), 28mg chol., 174mg sod., 69g carb. (41g sugars, 2g fiber), 3g pro.

APPLE CRISP PIZZA

While visiting a Wisconsin apple orchard bakery, I tried this tempting treat. When I got home, I put together my own recipe version. As it bakes, the enticing aroma fills my kitchen, and friends and family linger, waiting for a sample.
—*Nancy Preussner, Delhi, IA*

Prep: 15 min. • **Bake:** 35 min.
Makes: 12 servings

- Pastry for a single-crust pie
- ⅔ cup sugar
- 3 Tbsp. all-purpose flour
- 1 tsp. ground cinnamon
- 4 medium baking apples, peeled and cut into ½-in. slices

TOPPING
- ½ cup all-purpose flour
- ⅓ cup packed brown sugar
- ⅓ cup rolled oats
- 1 tsp. ground cinnamon
- ¼ cup butter, softened
- ¼ to ½ cup caramel ice cream topping or caramel apple dip
- Vanilla ice cream, optional

1. Roll pastry to fit a 12-in. pizza pan; fold under or flute the edges. Combine sugar, flour and cinnamon in a bowl. Add apples and toss. Arrange the apples in a single layer in a circular pattern to completely cover pastry. Combine the first 5 topping ingredients; sprinkle over apples.
2. Bake at 350° until apples are tender, for 35-40 minutes. Remove from the oven and immediately drizzle with caramel topping or dip. Serve warm with vanilla ice cream if desired.
1 piece: 286 cal., 12g fat (7g sat. fat), 30mg chol., 159mg sod., 44g carb. (26g sugars, 2g fiber), 3g pro.

PEANUT BUTTER TRUFFLE CUPCAKES

Cupcakes are so popular now, and these have a wonderful hidden treasure inside. They're rich and delicious!
—*Marlene Schollenberger, Bloomington, IN*

Prep: 40 min. • **Bake:** 15 min. + cooling
Makes: 1 dozen

- 6 oz. white baking chocolate, coarsely chopped
- ¼ cup creamy peanut butter
- 2 Tbsp. baking cocoa

BATTER
- ½ cup butter, softened
- ¾ cup sugar
- 2 large eggs, room temperature
- 1 tsp. vanilla extract
- ¾ cup all-purpose flour
- ½ cup baking cocoa
- ½ tsp. baking soda
- ¼ tsp. salt
- ½ cup buttermilk
- ½ cup strong brewed coffee

FROSTING
- 3 oz. semisweet chocolate, chopped
- ⅓ cup heavy whipping cream
- 3 Tbsp. creamy peanut butter

1. For truffles, in a microwave-safe bowl, melt chocolate at 70% power for 1 minute; stir. Microwave chocolate for additional 10- to 20-second intervals, stirring until smooth. Stir in peanut butter. Cover and refrigerate for 15-20 minutes or until firm enough to form into balls. Shape into twelve 1-in. balls; roll in cocoa. Set aside.

2. In a large bowl, cream butter and sugar until light and fluffy. Add eggs, one at a time, beating well after each. Beat in vanilla. Combine the flour, cocoa, baking soda and salt; gradually add to creamed mixture alternately with buttermilk and coffee and mix well.

3. Fill paper-lined muffin cups two-thirds full. Top each with a truffle (do not press truffle down).

4. Bake at 350° until a toothpick inserted in cake portion comes out clean, about 15-20 minutes. Cool for 10 minutes before removing cupcakes from pan to a wire rack to cool completely.

5. In a heavy saucepan over low heat, melt chocolate with cream, stirring constantly. Remove from heat; stir in peanut butter until smooth. Transfer to a small bowl; chill until mixture reaches desired spreading consistency. Frost the cupcakes. Store in the refrigerator.

1 cupcake: 277 cal., 18g fat (8g sat. fat), 66mg chol., 249mg sod., 26g carb. (16g sugars, 2g fiber), 6g pro.

CITRUS CORNMEAL CAKE

Cornmeal adds a rustic quality to this delicate dessert flavored with citrus and almond. It's sure to be a staple in your recipe collection. It makes a great hostess gift, too.

—*Roxanne Chan, Albany, CA*

- -

Prep: 25 min. • **Bake:** 25 min.
Makes: 8 servings

½ **cup lemon yogurt**
⅓ **cup honey**

¼ cup olive oil
1 large egg, room temperature
2 large egg whites, room temperature
¼ tsp. almond extract
¾ cup all-purpose flour
½ cup cornmeal
1 tsp. baking powder
½ tsp. grated orange zest
1 can (15 oz.) mandarin oranges, drained
3 Tbsp. sliced almonds

1. Coat a 9-in. fluted tart pan with removable bottom with cooking spray.

In a bowl, beat the yogurt, honey, oil, egg, egg whites and extract until well blended. Combine the flour, cornmeal and baking powder; gradually beat into yogurt mixture until blended. Stir in orange zest.
2. Pour into prepared pan. Arrange oranges over batter; sprinkle with the almonds. Bake at 350° until a toothpick inserted in the center comes out clean, .25-30 minutes. Cool on a wire rack for 10 minutes before cutting. Serve warm or at room temperature.

1 slice: 240 cal., 9g fat (1g sat. fat), 27mg chol., 85mg sod., 36g carb. (20g sugars, 2g fiber), 5g pro.

3. Transfer to prepared pan. Bake until a toothpick inserted in center comes out clean, 55-65 minutes. Cool in pan for 10 minutes before removing to a wire rack to cool completely.

4. For glaze, combine butter and pecans in a saucepan over medium heat, stirring constantly, until the butter is light golden brown, 4-5 minutes. Stir mixture into the confectioners' sugar. Add vanilla, salt and cream to reach a drizzling consistency. Drizzle glaze over cake, allowing some to drip down sides. Let stand until set.

Note: To remove cakes easily, always use solid shortening to grease plain and fluted tube pans.

1 slice: 473 cal., 25g fat (15g sat. fat), 121mg chol., 193mg sod., 57g carb. (38g sugars, 1g fiber), 5g pro.

CHERRY COKE GELATIN

This sparkling sweet is as popular at potlucks as cherry-flavored cola. It'll become your new go-to dish.
—*Judy Nix, Toccoa, GA*

Prep: 10 min. + chilling
Makes: 12 servings

  1 can (20 oz.) crushed pineapple
  ½ cup water
  2 pkg. (3 oz. each) cherry gelatin
  1 can (21 oz.) cherry pie filling
  ¾ cup cola

1. Drain pineapple, reserving juice; set fruit aside. In a saucepan or microwave, bring pineapple juice and water to a boil. Add gelatin; stir until dissolved. Stir in pie filling and cola.

2. Pour into a serving bowl. Refrigerate until slightly thickened. Fold in reserved pineapple. Refrigerate until firm.

1 serving: 118 cal., 0 fat (0 sat. fat), 0 chol., 26mg sod., 29g carb. (26g sugars, 1g fiber), 1g pro.

BROWN SUGAR POUND CAKE

This tender pound cake is the first one I mastered. You'll want to eat the browned butter icing by the spoonful. It tastes just like pralines but with a cake bonus.
—*Shawn Barto, Winter Garden, FL*

Prep: 20 min. • **Bake:** 55 min. + cooling
Makes: 16 servings

  1½ cups unsalted butter, softened
  2¼ cups packed brown sugar
  5 large eggs, room temperature
  2 tsp. vanilla extract
  3 cups all-purpose flour
  1 tsp. baking powder
  ¼ tsp. salt
  1 cup sour cream
GLAZE
  3 Tbsp. unsalted butter
  ¼ cup chopped pecans
  1 cup confectioners' sugar
  ¼ tsp. vanilla extract
    Dash salt
  2 to 3 Tbsp. half-and-half cream

1. Preheat oven to 350°. Grease and flour a 10-in. fluted tube pan.

2. Cream butter and brown sugar until light and fluffy. Add eggs, one at a time, beating well after each addition. Beat in vanilla. In another bowl, whisk flour, baking powder and salt; add to creamed mixture alternately with sour cream, beating after each addition just until combined.

CHEWY PEANUT BUTTER BARS

These yummy bars are great for lunches and bake sales. I appreciate that they're made with kitchen staples.
—Beverly Swihart, Marion, OH

Prep: 20 min. • **Bake:** 15 min. + chilling
Makes: 2 to 2½ dozen

- ½ cup butter, softened
- ⅔ cup packed brown sugar
- 2 large egg yolks, room temperature
- 1 tsp. vanilla extract
- 1½ cups all-purpose flour
- ½ tsp. baking powder
- ½ tsp. salt
- ¼ tsp. baking soda
- 3 cups miniature marshmallows

TOPPING
- ⅔ cup light corn syrup
- ¼ cup butter
- 1 pkg. (10 oz.) peanut butter chips
- 2 tsp. vanilla extract
- 2 cups Rice Krispies
- 2 cups salted peanuts

1. In a bowl, cream butter and sugar. Add egg yolks and vanilla; mix well. Combine flour, baking powder, salt and baking soda; add to creamed mixture and mix well. Press into a greased 13x9-in. baking pan.

2. Bake at 350° until golden, about 12-15 minutes. Sprinkle with marshmallows; bake just until the marshmallows begin to puff, 2 minutes. Cool. Meanwhile, combine corn syrup, butter, chips and vanilla in a large saucepan; cook and stir over low heat until chips are melted and mixture is smooth. Remove from the heat; stir in cereal and peanuts. Spread warm topping over the marshmallow layer. Chill until set.

1 bar: 232 cal., 13g fat (5g sat. fat), 26mg chol., 199mg sod., 27g carb. (15g sugars, 2g fiber), 5g pro.

AUNT MARION'S FRUIT SALAD DESSERT

Aunt Marion, my namesake, is like a grandma to me. She gave me this luscious salad recipe, which I like to use as a dessert. It's on the table at all our family reunions, hunt club suppers and snowmobile club picnics...and I never come home with leftovers!
—Marion LaTourette, Honesdale, PA

Prep: 20 min. + chilling
Makes: 10 servings (2½ qt.)

- 1 can (20 oz.) pineapple chunks, drained
- 1 can (15¼ oz.) sliced peaches, drained and cut into bite-size pieces
- 1 can (11 oz.) mandarin oranges, drained
- 3 bananas, sliced
- 2 unpeeled red apples, cut into bite-sized pieces

FRUIT SAUCE
- 1 cup cold whole milk
- ¾ cup sour cream
- ⅓ cup thawed orange juice concentrate
- 1 pkg. (3.4 oz.) instant vanilla pudding mix

In a large bowl, combine the fruits; set aside. Whisk sauce ingredients until smooth. Gently fold into fruits. Chill 3-4 hours before serving.

1 cup: 218 cal., 5g fat (3g sat. fat), 7mg chol., 86mg sod., 44g carb. (37g sugars, 3g fiber), 2g pro.

RHUBARB MANDARIN CRISP

An attractive and unique dessert, this crisp is also a popular breakfast dish at our house, served with a glass of milk rather than topped with ice cream. Since it calls for lots of rhubarb, it's a great use for the bounty you harvest.

—*Rachael Vandendool, Barry's Bay, ON*

- -

Prep: 20 min. + standing • **Bake:** 40 min.
Makes: 12 servings

- 6 **cups chopped fresh or frozen rhubarb**
- 1½ **cups sugar**
- 5 **Tbsp. quick-cooking tapioca**
- 1 **can (11 oz.) mandarin oranges, drained**
- 1 **cup packed brown sugar**
- 1 **cup quick-cooking oats**
- ½ **cup all-purpose flour**
- ½ **tsp. salt**
- ½ **cup cold butter, cubed**
  Ice cream, optional

1. In a large bowl, toss the rhubarb, sugar and tapioca; let stand for 15 minutes, stirring occasionally. Pour into a greased 13x9-in. baking pan. Top with the oranges.
2. In a large bowl, combine the brown sugar, oats, flour and salt. Cut in butter until mixture resembles coarse crumbs; sprinkle evenly over oranges.
3. Bake at 350° until top is golden brown, 40 minutes. Serve the crisp with ice cream if desired.

Note: If using frozen rhubarb, measure rhubarb while still frozen, then thaw completely. Drain in a colander, but do not press liquid out.

1 serving: 323 cal., 8g fat (5g sat. fat), 20mg chol., 187mg sod., 62g carb. (48g sugars, 2g fiber), 2g pro.

GINGERBREAD SNOWFLAKES

Our tradition is to make snowflake cookies to eat in the car on our way to fetch a Christmas tree.
—*Shelly Rynearson, Oconomowoc, WI*

Prep: 30 min. + chilling
Bake: 10 min./batch
Makes: 5 dozen

- 1 **cup butter, softened**
- 1 **cup sugar**
- 1 **cup molasses**
- ¼ **cup water**
- 5 **cups all-purpose flour**
- 2½ **tsp. ground ginger**
- 1½ **tsp. baking soda**
- 1½ **tsp. ground cinnamon**
- ½ **tsp. ground allspice**
- ¼ **tsp. salt**

FROSTING

- 3¾ **cups confectioners' sugar**
- ¼ **cup water**
- 1½ **tsp. light corn syrup**
- ½ **tsp. vanilla extract**

1. In a large bowl, cream butter and sugar until light and fluffy. Beat in molasses and water. Combine the flour, ginger, baking soda, cinnamon, allspice and salt; gradually add to creamed mixture and mix well. Cover and refrigerate until easy to handle, about 1 hour.

2. On a lightly floured surface, roll out to ¼-in. thickness. Cut with 2½-in. cookie cutters dipped in flour. Place 2 in. apart on ungreased baking sheets.

3. Bake at 350° until the edges are firm, 10-12 minutes. Remove cookies to wire racks to cool.

4. In a small bowl, combine frosting ingredients; beat until smooth. Transfer to a pastry bag fitted with a tip; pipe the frosting onto cookies in desired designs.

1 cookie: 124 cal., 3g fat (2g sat. fat), 8mg chol., 68mg sod., 23g carb. (15g sugars, 0 fiber), 1g pro.

NUTTY CHEESECAKE SQUARES

These bars are easy enough to make for everyday occasions but special enough to serve company. They also travel well to potlucks and picnics.

—*Ruth Simon, Buffalo, NY*

Prep: 20 min. • **Bake:** 20 min. + cooling
Makes: 20 servings

- 2 cups all-purpose flour
- 1 cup finely chopped walnuts
- ⅔ cup packed brown sugar
- ½ tsp. salt
- ⅔ cup cold butter

FILLING

- 2 pkg. (8 oz. each) cream cheese, softened
- ½ cup sugar
- 2 large eggs, lightly beaten
- ¼ cup milk
- 1 tsp. vanilla extract

1. In a large bowl, combine the flour, walnuts, brown sugar and salt; cut in butter until mixture resembles coarse crumbs. Set half aside; press remaining crumb mixture onto the bottom of a greased 13x9-in. baking pan. Bake at 350° until lightly browned, 10-15 minutes.
2. In a large bowl, beat filling ingredients until smooth; pour over crust. Sprinkle with reserved crumb mixture.
3. Bake at 350° until a knife inserted in the center comes out clean, 20-25 minutes. Cool on a wire rack for 1 hour. Store bars in the refrigerator.

1 square: 233 cal., 14g fat (7g sat. fat), 50mg chol., 165mg sod., 23g carb. (13g sugars, 1g fiber), 4g pro.

REESE'S CHOCOLATE SNACK CAKE

My family constantly requests this cake all year, though its yellow and orange toppings make it the perfect dessert for a Halloween party.

—*Eileen Travis, Ukiah, CA*

Prep: 15 min. • **Bake:** 30 min. + cooling
Makes: 20 servings

- 3⅓ cups all-purpose flour
- ⅔ cup sugar
- ⅔ cup packed brown sugar
- ½ cup baking cocoa
- 2 tsp. baking soda
- 1 tsp. salt
- 2 cups water
- ⅓ cup canola oil
- ⅓ cup unsweetened applesauce
- 2 tsp. white vinegar
- 1 tsp. vanilla extract
- 1 cup Reese's pieces
- ½ cup coarsely chopped salted peanuts

1. Preheat oven to 350°. Coat a 13x9-in. pan with cooking spray.
2. Whisk together first 6 ingredients. In another bowl, whisk together water, oil, applesauce, vinegar and vanilla. Add to flour mixture, stirring just until blended. Transfer to prepared pan. Sprinkle with Reese's pieces and peanuts.
3. Bake until a toothpick inserted in center comes out clean, 30-35 minutes. Cool on a wire rack.

1 piece: 240 cal., 8g fat (2g sat. fat), 0 chol., 280mg sod., 38g carb. (19g sugars, 2g fiber), 5g pro.

ORANGE DREAM ANGEL FOOD CAKE

A basic angel food cake becomes a heavenly indulgence thanks to a hint of orange flavor swirled into the orange colored half. Slices of the two-tone cake look so pretty when arranged on individual dessert plates.
—*Lauren Osborne, Holtwood, PA*

- -

Prep: 25 min. • **Bake:** 30 min. + cooling
Makes: 16 servings

- 12 large egg whites
- 1 cup all-purpose flour
- 1¾ cups sugar, divided
- 1½ tsp. cream of tartar
- ½ tsp. salt
- 1 tsp. almond extract
- 1 tsp. vanilla extract
- 1 tsp. grated orange zest
- 1 tsp. orange extract
- 6 drops red food coloring, optional
- 6 drops yellow food coloring, optional

1. Place the egg whites in a large bowl; let stand at room temperature 30 minutes. Sift flour and ¾ cup sugar together twice; set aside.

2. Add cream of tartar, salt and almond and vanilla extracts to egg whites; beat on medium speed until soft peaks form. Gradually add the remaining sugar, about 2 Tbsp. at a time, beating on high until stiff glossy peaks form and the sugar is dissolved. Gradually fold in flour mixture, about ½ cup at a time.

3. Gently spoon half of the batter into an ungreased 10-in. tube pan. To the remaining batter, stir in the orange zest, orange extract and, if desired, food colorings. Gently spoon orange batter over white batter. Cut through both layers with a knife to swirl the orange and white and remove air pockets.

4. Bake on the lowest oven rack at 375° until lightly browned and the entire top appears dry, 30-35 minutes. Immediately invert pan; cool completely, about 1 hour.

5. Run a knife around side and center tube of pan. Remove cake to a serving plate.

1 slice: 130 cal., 0 fat (0 sat. fat), 0 chol., 116mg sod., 28g carb. (22g sugars, 0 fiber), 4g pro. **Diabetic exchanges:** 2 starch.

★ ★ ★ ★ ★ **READER REVIEW**

"My entire family of 12 loved this cake! I made it for Easter & then it was requested for three summer birthday celebrations. Even I liked it, and I rarely like angel food cake—got too much of it when I was growing up. This one has a wonderful orange flavor and is light and airy. It's so easy to make, too!"

SUE ZAPPA TASTEOFHOME.COM

CONTEST-WINNING CHOCOLATE MINT COOKIES

My dad sandwiches thin mint patties between two tender chocolate cookies to create these chewy treats. The blend of chocolate and mint is a big hit at our house. Best of all, these cookies are easy and fun to make.

—*Christina Burbage, Spartanburg, SC*

Prep: 15 min.
Bake: 10 min./batch + cooling
Makes: 32 cookies

1¼ cups butter, softened
2 cups sugar
2 large eggs, room temperature
2 tsp. vanilla extract
2 cups all-purpose flour
¾ cup baking cocoa
1 tsp. baking soda
½ tsp. salt
32 chocolate-covered thin mints

1. In a bowl, cream butter and sugar. Add eggs, one at a time, beating well after each addition. Beat in vanilla. Combine the flour, cocoa, baking soda and salt; gradually add to the creamed mixture, beating until well-combined.

2. Drop by tablespoonfuls 2 in. apart onto ungreased baking sheets. Bake at 350° until puffy and the tops are cracked, for 8-9 minutes. Invert half of the cookies onto wire racks. Immediately place a mint patty on each one, then top with the remaining cookies. Press lightly to seal. Cool completely.

1 cookie: 179 cal., 8g fat (5g sat. fat), 32mg chol., 154mg sod., 25g carb. (18g sugars, 1g fiber), 2g pro.

PINEAPPLE UPSIDE-DOWN CUPCAKES

I have baked cupcakes for years. These easy-to-make treats are an attractive dessert for special occasions. You can tote them easily in a covered 13x9 pan.
—*Barbara Hahn, Park Hills, MO*

Prep: 30 min. • **Bake:** 30 min. + cooling
Makes: 1 dozen jumbo cupcakes

- 6 Tbsp. butter, cubed
- 1 cup packed light brown sugar
- 2 Tbsp. light corn syrup
- 1 small pineapple, peeled, cored and cut into ½-in. slices
- 12 maraschino cherries, well drained
- 3 large eggs, room temperature

- 2 cups sugar
- 1 cup canola oil
- 1 cup sour cream
- 2 tsp. vanilla extract
- 2½ cups all-purpose flour
- ½ tsp. baking powder
- ½ tsp. baking soda
- ½ tsp. salt
  Whipped topping, optional

1. Line the bottom of 12 greased jumbo muffin cups with waxed paper; grease the paper and set aside.

2. In a small saucepan, melt butter over low heat; stir in brown sugar and corn syrup. Cook and stir over medium heat until sugar is dissolved. Remove from the heat. Spoon 1 tablespoonful into each muffin cup; top each with a pineapple slice and a cherry.

3. In a large bowl, beat eggs and sugar until thickened and lemon-colored. Beat in the oil, sour cream and vanilla until smooth. Combine the flour, baking powder, baking soda and salt. Add to the egg mixture and mix well.

4. Fill muffin cups two-thirds full. Bake at 350° until a toothpick inserted in the center comes out clean, 28-32 minutes. Cool for 5 minutes before inverting onto wire racks to cool completely. Garnish with whipped topping if desired.

1 serving: 602 cal., 29g fat (9g sat. fat), 82mg chol., 264mg sod., 82g carb. (61g sugars, 1g fiber), 5g pro.

cocoa until butter is melted; remove from heat. Add confectioners' sugar; stir until smooth. Pour immediately over hot cake.

1 piece: 491 cal., 20g fat (12g sat. fat), 74mg chol., 346mg sod., 78g carb. (63g sugars, 1g fiber), 4g pro.

ICEBOX APPLE PIE

A lot of people drive here from many miles to pick their own apples. This recipe is handy because I can make it so fast.
—*Johanna King, Sparta, WI*

Prep: 15 min. • **Cook:** 10 min. + chilling
Makes: 8 servings

4½ cups sliced peeled tart apples
1½ cups water
1 Tbsp. butter
¼ tsp. ground cinnamon
¼ tsp. ground nutmeg
1 pkg. (3 oz.) peach or orange gelatin
1 pkg. (3 oz.) cook-and-serve vanilla pudding mix
1 pastry shell (9 in.), baked
TOPPING
¼ cup graham cracker crumbs
1 Tbsp. butter, melted
1½ tsp. sugar

1. In a large saucepan, combine the apples, water, butter, cinnamon and nutmeg; bring to a boil. Reduce heat; simmer, uncovered, until the apples are tender, 5 minutes. Gradually stir in gelatin and pudding; bring to a boil. Remove from the heat; let stand 5 minutes.
2. Pour into pie shell. Combine topping ingredients; sprinkle over filling. Chill for 3-4 hours or until firm.

1 slice: 272 cal., 10g fat (5g sat. fat), 13mg chol., 234mg sod., 44g carb. (27g sugars, 1g fiber), 2g pro.

COKECOLA CAKE

We live in Coca-Cola country, where everyone loves a chocolaty, moist sheet cake made with the iconic soft drink. Our rich version does the tradition proud.
—*Heidi Jobe, Carrollton, GA*

Prep: 25 min. • **Bake:** 25 min.
Makes: 15 servings

2 cups all-purpose flour
2 cups sugar
1 tsp. baking soda
½ tsp. salt
½ tsp. ground cinnamon
1 can (12 oz.) cola
1 cup butter, cubed
¼ cup baking cocoa
2 large eggs, room temperature
½ cup buttermilk
1 tsp. vanilla extract

GLAZE
1 can (12 oz.) cola
½ cup butter, cubed
¼ cup baking cocoa
4 cups confectioners' sugar, sifted

1. Preheat oven to 350°. Grease a 13x9-in. baking pan.
2. In a bowl, whisk the first 5 ingredients. In a small saucepan, combine cola, butter and cocoa; bring just to a boil, stirring occasionally. Add to flour mixture, stirring just until moistened.
3. In a small bowl, whisk eggs, buttermilk and vanilla until blended; add to the flour mixture, whisking constantly.
4. Transfer to prepared pan. Bake until a toothpick inserted in center comes out clean, 25-30 minutes.
5. About 15 minutes before cake is done, prepare glaze. In a small saucepan, bring cola to a boil; cook until liquid is reduced to ½ cup, 12-15 minutes. Stir in butter and

JELLY BEAN BARK

Homemade Easter candy really doesn't get any simpler than this. It's so easy when all you need are three ingredients, a microwave and a pan! Little kids love to help make this candy, as well as help make it disappear.
—Mavis Dement, Marcus, IA

- -

Prep: 15 min. + standing • **Makes:** 2 lbs.

- 1 Tbsp. butter
- 1¼ lbs. white candy coating, coarsely chopped
- 2 cups small jelly beans

1. Line a 15x10x1-in. pan with foil; grease foil with butter. In a microwave, melt candy coating; stir until smooth. Spread into prepared pan. Top with jelly beans, pressing to adhere. Let stand until set.
2. Cut or break bark into pieces. Store in an airtight container.

1 oz.: 154 cal., 5g fat (5g sat. fat), 1mg chol., 10mg sod., 27g carb. (23g sugars, 0 fiber), 0 pro.

CHERRY CHEESE BLINTZES

These elegant blintzes are attractive for brunch or dessert. The bright cherry sauce gives them a pop of fresh flavor. Sometimes I substitute other fruits, such as raspberries, blueberries or peaches.
—Jessica Vantrease, Anderson, AK

- -

Prep: 30 min. + chilling • **Bake:** 10 min.
Makes: 9 servings

- 1½ cups 2% milk
- 3 large eggs, room temperature
- 2 Tbsp. butter, melted
- ⅔ cup all-purpose flour
- ½ tsp. salt

FILLING
- 1 cup 4% cottage cheese
- 3 oz. cream cheese, softened
- ¼ cup sugar
- ½ tsp. vanilla extract

CHERRY SAUCE
- 1 lb. fresh or frozen pitted sweet cherries
- ⅔ cup plus 1 Tbsp. water, divided
- ¼ cup sugar
- 1 Tbsp. cornstarch

1. In a small bowl, combine the milk, eggs and butter. Combine flour and salt; add to the milk mixture and mix well. Cover and refrigerate for 2 hours.
2. Heat a lightly greased 8-in. nonstick skillet; pour 2 Tbsp. batter into the center of skillet. Lift and tilt pan to evenly coat bottom. Cook until top appears dry; turn and cook 15-20 seconds longer. Remove to a wire rack. Repeat with remaining batter. When cool, stack crepes with waxed paper or paper towels in between. Wrap in foil; refrigerate crepes.
3. In a blender, process cottage cheese until smooth. Transfer to a small bowl; add cream cheese and beat until smooth. Beat in the sugar and vanilla. Spread about 1 rounded tablespoonful onto each crepe. Fold opposite sides of crepe over filling, forming a little bundle.
4. Place seam side down in a greased 15x10x1-in. baking pan. Bake, uncovered, at 350° until heated through, for about 10 minutes.
5. Meanwhile, in a large saucepan, bring cherries, ⅔ cup water and sugar to a boil over medium heat. Reduce heat; cover and simmer for 5 minutes. Combine cornstarch and remaining water until smooth; stir into cherry mixture. Bring to a boil; cook and stir until thickened, 2 minutes. Serve with crepes.

2 blintzes: 245 cal., 10g fat (6g sat. fat), 97mg chol., 306mg sod., 31g carb. (21g sugars, 1g fiber), 8g pro.

PEANUT BUTTER BROWNIE CRISPY BARS

To make a dairy-free dessert, I created chocolate peanutty bars. My kids and their friends eat them up.

—*Dawn Pasco, Overland Park, KS*

Prep: 15 min. • **Bake:** 25 min. + chilling
Makes: 2 dozen

- 1 **pkg. fudge brownie mix (13x9-in. pan size)**
- 1½ **cups chunky peanut butter**
- 2 **cups (12 oz.) semisweet chocolate chips**
- 1 **cup creamy peanut butter**
- 3 **cups Rice Krispies**

1. Line a 13x9-in. baking pan with parchment, letting ends extend up sides. Prepare and bake brownie mix according to package directions, using prepared pan. Cool brownies in pan on a wire rack for 30 minutes. Refrigerate until cold.
2. Spread chunky peanut butter over the brownies. Place the chocolate chips and creamy peanut butter in a microwave-safe bowl. Microwave in 30-second intervals until melted; stir until smooth. Stir in Rice Krispies; spread over chunky peanut butter layer. Refrigerate, covered, until set, at least 30 minutes.
3. Lifting with parchment, remove the brownies from pan. Cut into bars. Store in an airtight container in the refrigerator.

1 bar: 390 cal., 27g fat (6g sat. fat), 16mg chol., 234mg sod., 35g carb. (21g sugars, 3g fiber), 9g pro.

SALTED CARAMEL & NUT CUPS

These indulgent cookie cups, with four kinds of nuts, have helped make many of my get-togethers even more special.
—*Roxanne Chan, Albany, CA*

Prep: 30 min. + chilling
Bake: 20 min.
Makes: 1½ dozen

½ cup butter, softened
3 oz. cream cheese, softened
2 Tbsp. sugar
1 cup all-purpose flour
1 large egg
¼ cup hot caramel ice cream topping
¼ to ½ tsp. ground allspice
¼ cup chopped pecans
¼ cup chopped slivered almonds
¼ cup chopped macadamia nuts
¼ cup chopped pistachios
    Coarse sea salt
    Sweetened whipped cream, optional

1. In a small bowl, beat butter, cream cheese and sugar until blended. Gradually beat in flour. Refrigerate, covered, until firm, about 30 minutes.

2. Preheat oven to 350°. Shape 1 level Tbsp. of dough into balls; press evenly onto bottoms and up sides of greased mini muffin cups.

3. In a small bowl, whisk the egg, caramel topping and allspice until blended. Stir in nuts. Place about 2 tsp. mixture in each dough cup.

4. Bake until edges are golden and filling is set, 20-22 minutes. Immediately sprinkle tops with salt. Cool in pans 10 minutes. Remove to wire racks to cool. If desired, serve with whipped cream.

1 cookie cup: 149 cal., 11g fat (5g sat. fat), 29mg chol., 89mg sod., 11g carb. (5g sugars, 1g fiber), 2g pro.

ANGEL SUGAR CRISPS

Whenever I've taken these to church coffees, I've had women come into the kitchen and want me to share the recipe. You'll enjoy this sugar cookie's secret ingredient—brown sugar!
—*Annabel Cox, Olivet, SD*

- -

Prep: 25 min. • **Bake:** 10 min.
Makes: 4 dozen

 - ½   cup butter, softened
 - ½   cup shortening
 - ½   cup sugar
 - ½   cup packed brown sugar
 - 1   large egg, room temperature
 - 1   tsp. vanilla extract
 - 2   cups all-purpose flour
 - 1   tsp. baking soda
 - 1   tsp. cream of tartar
 - ½   tsp. salt
       Water
       Additional white or colored sugar

In a bowl, cream butter, shortening, sugars, egg and vanilla until light and fluffy. Sift together flour, soda, cream of tartar and salt.

Add to creamed mixture; mix until blended. Shape into large marble-size balls. Dip half of ball into water, then in sugar. Place, sugared side up, on ungreased baking sheets. Bake at 400° for 6 minutes or until done. Cool.

2 cookies: 161 cal., 8g fat (3g sat. fat), 19mg chol., 145mg sod., 21g carb. (13g sugars, 0 fiber), 1g pro.

DOUBLE-LAYER PUMPKIN CHEESECAKE

I thought cheesecake and pumpkin pie would be amazing together. This creamy combo was awarded a prize in our local pie contest, so I guess the judges agreed!
—*Noel Ferry, Perkasie, PA*

- -

Prep: 25 min. • **Bake:** 55 min. + cooling
Makes: 10 servings

 - 1½ cups crushed gingersnap cookies (about 30 cookies)
 - ¾   cup chopped pecans, toasted
 - 1   Tbsp. sugar
 - ⅛   tsp. salt
 - ¼   cup butter, melted

CHEESECAKE LAYER
 - 1   pkg. (8 oz.) cream cheese, softened
 - ⅓   cup sugar
 - 1   large egg, lightly beaten
 - 1   tsp. vanilla extract

PUMPKIN LAYER
 - 2   large eggs, lightly beaten
 - 1⅓ cups canned pumpkin
 - ½   cup sugar
 - 1   tsp. pumpkin pie spice
 - ⅛   tsp. salt
 - ⅔   cup heavy whipping cream
       Sweetened whipped cream, optional
       Toasted chopped pecans, optional

1. Preheat oven to 325°. Pulse the first 4 ingredients in a food processor until ground. Add the butter; pulse to blend. Press mixture onto bottom and up sides of an ungreased 9-in. deep-dish pie plate. Refrigerate while preparing filling.
2. For the cheesecake layer, beat all the ingredients until smooth. For pumpkin layer, whisk together the eggs, pumpkin, sugar, pie spice and salt; gradually whisk in cream. Spread the cheesecake mixture onto crust; cover with pumpkin mixture.
3. Bake on a lower oven rack until filling is set, 55-65 minutes. Cool at least 1 hour on a wire rack; serve or refrigerate within 2 hours. If desired, top with whipped cream and pecans.

Note: To toast nuts, bake in a shallow pan in a 350° oven for 5-10 minutes or cook in a skillet over low heat until lightly browned, stirring occasionally.

1 piece: 422 cal., 28g fat (13g sat. fat), 115mg chol., 313mg sod., 40g carb. (25g sugars, 2g fiber), 6g pro.

Double-Layer Pumpkin Cheesecake Squares: Press crumb mixture onto bottom of an ungreased 8-in. square baking pan. Prepare and add layers as directed; bake in a preheated 325° oven until filling is set, 55-65 minutes. Cool as directed. Cut into squares.

PUMPKIN BARS

What could be a more appropriate fall treat than a big pan of pumpkin-flavored bars? Actually, my family loves these any time of year.

—*Brenda Keller, Andalusia, AL*

Prep: 20 min. • **Bake:** 25 min. + cooling
Makes: 2 dozen

- 4 large eggs, room temperature
- 1⅔ cups sugar
- 1 cup canola oil
- 1 can (15 oz.) solid-pack pumpkin
- 2 cups all-purpose flour
- 2 tsp. ground cinnamon
- 2 tsp. baking powder
- 1 tsp. baking soda
- 1 tsp. salt

ICING
- 6 oz. cream cheese, softened
- 2 cups confectioners' sugar
- ¼ cup butter, softened
- 1 tsp. vanilla extract
- 1 to 2 Tbsp. whole milk

1. In a bowl, beat the eggs, sugar, oil and pumpkin until well blended. Combine the flour, cinnamon, baking powder, baking soda and salt; gradually add to pumpkin mixture and mix well. Pour into an ungreased 15x10x1-in. baking pan. Bake at 350° for 25-30 minutes or until set. Cool bars completely.
2. For the icing, beat the cream cheese, confectioners' sugar, butter and vanilla in a small bowl. Add enough milk to achieve spreading consistency. Spread over bars. Store in the refrigerator.

1 bar: 260 cal., 13g fat (3g sat. fat), 45mg chol., 226mg sod., 34g carb. (24g sugars, 1g fiber), 3g pro.

COOKIE ICE CREAM PIE

Because you use your freezer to prepare this crunchy, creamy treat—not your oven—it won't heat up the kitchen on sweltering days. Whip it up and serve to company or the neighborhood kids.

—*Debbie Walsh, Madison, WI*

Prep: 25 min. + freezing
Makes: 8 servings

- 10 Oreo cookies, crushed
- 3 Tbsp. butter, melted
- 14 whole Oreo cookies

FILLING
- ½ gallon white chocolate raspberry truffle ice cream, softened, divided
- ½ cup prepared fudge topping, divided
- Fresh raspberries, optional

1. In a small bowl, combine the crushed cookies and butter; press onto bottom of a 9-in. pie plate. Stand whole cookies up around edges, pressing lightly into crust. Freeze until set, about 1 hour.
2. For filling, spread half of ice cream over crushed cookies. Drizzle with ¼ cup of fudge topping. Freeze until set, about 1 hour. Spread remaining ice cream on top. Drizzle with remaining fudge topping. Freeze several hours or overnight.
3. Garnish with fresh raspberries if desired. Let the pie stand at room temperature for 15 minutes before cutting.

1 piece: 763 cal., 45g fat (24g sat. fat), 201mg chol., 448mg sod., 81g carb. (62g sugars, 3g fiber), 11g pro.

PISTACHIO CAKE WITH WALNUTS

It didn't take long for this dessert to become my husband's favorite cake, including for birthdays.
—Patty LaNoue Stearns, Traverse City, MI

Prep: 20 min. • **Bake:** 40 min. + cooling
Makes: 12 servings

- 1 pkg. white cake mix (regular size)
- 1 pkg. (3.4 oz.) instant pistachio pudding mix
- 3 large eggs
- 1 cup club soda
- ¾ cup canola oil
- 1 cup chopped walnuts

FROSTING
- 1 pkg. (3.4 oz.) instant pistachio pudding mix
- 1 cup 2% milk
- 1 carton (8 oz.) frozen whipped topping, thawed

1. Preheat oven to 350°. Grease and flour a 10-in. fluted tube pan.
2. In a bowl, combine first 5 ingredients; beat on low speed 30 seconds. Beat on medium 2 minutes. Fold in walnuts. Transfer to prepared pan. Bake until a toothpick inserted in center comes out clean, 40-45 minutes. Cool cake in pan for 10 minutes before removing to a wire rack to cool completely.
3. For frosting, in a large bowl, combine pudding mix and milk; beat on low speed 1 minute. Fold in whipped topping. Spread over cake. Refrigerate leftovers.
Note: For easier removal of cakes, use solid shortening to grease plain and fluted tube pans.
1 slice: 476 cal., 27g fat (6g sat. fat), 54mg chol., 534mg sod., 51g carb. (31g sugars, 1g fiber), 5g pro.

MICROWAVE OATMEAL BARS

My mother shared this speedy recipe with me. There aren't many ingredients, making these microwave treats easy enough for kids to whip up.
—Annette Self, Junction City, OH

Prep: 20 min. + chilling
Makes: 10 servings

- 2 cups quick-cooking oats
- ½ cup packed brown sugar
- ½ cup butter, melted
- ¼ cup corn syrup
- 1 cup (6 oz.) semisweet chocolate chips

1. In a large bowl, combine oats and brown sugar. Stir in butter and corn syrup. Press the mixture into a greased 9-in. square microwave-safe dish.
2. Microwave, uncovered, on high for 1½ minutes. Rotate a half turn; microwave 1½ minutes longer. Sprinkle oat mixture with the chocolate chips. Microwave at 30% power for 4½ minutes or until chips are glossy; spread melted chocolate evenly over top.
3. Refrigerate dessert for 15-20 minutes before cutting.
1 piece: 287 cal., 15g fat (9g sat. fat), 25mg chol., 109mg sod., 38g carb. (24g sugars, 3g fiber), 3g pro.

PEACH CAKE

I first tasted this cake over 15 years ago when a dear aunt brought it to a family reunion. I knew I had to have the recipe, and I was thrilled to discover how easy it is to make.

—*Donna Britsch, Tega Cay, SC*

Prep: 15 min. • **Bake:** 30 min. + cooling
Makes: 12 serving

- ¾ **cup cold butter, cubed**
- 1 **pkg. yellow cake mix (regular size)**
- 2 **large egg yolks**
- 2 **cups sour cream**
- 1 **can (29 oz.) sliced peaches, drained**
- ½ **tsp. ground cinnamon**
- 1 **carton (8 oz.) frozen whipped topping, thawed**

1. In a large bowl, cut butter into cake mix until mixture resembles coarse crumbs. Pat into a greased 13x9-in. baking pan.

2. In another bowl, beat egg yolks; add sour cream and stir until smooth. Set aside 6-8 peach slices for garnish. Cut remaining peaches into 1-in. pieces; stir into the sour cream mixture. Spread over crust; sprinkle with cinnamon.

3. Bake at 350° until the edges begin to brown and a toothpick inserted in the center comes out clean, 25-30 minutes. Cool on a wire rack. Spread with whipped topping; top with reserved peaches. Store in the refrigerator.

1 slice: 440 cal., 25g fat (16g sat. fat), 71mg chol., 420mg sod., 51g carb. (33g sugars, 1g fiber), 3g pro.

RED VELVET PEPPERMINT THUMBPRINTS

I love red velvet cookies and cakes. In this pretty thumbprint cookie, I added my favorite holiday ingredient: peppermint. It's a fun seasonal twist!

—*Priscilla Yee, Concord, CA*

Prep: 30 min.
Bake: 10 min./batch + cooling
Makes: about 4 dozen

- 1 cup butter, softened
- 1 cup sugar
- 1 large egg, room temperature
- 4 tsp. red food coloring
- 1 tsp. peppermint extract
- 2½ cups all-purpose flour
- 3 Tbsp. baking cocoa
- 1 tsp. baking powder
- ¼ tsp. salt
- 2 cups white baking chips
- 2 tsp. canola oil
- ¼ cup crushed peppermint candies

1. Preheat oven to 350°. In a large bowl, cream the butter and sugar until light and fluffy. Beat in egg, food coloring and extract. In another bowl, whisk the flour, cocoa, baking powder and salt; gradually beat into creamed mixture.
2. Shape dough into 1-in. balls. Place 1 in. apart on ungreased baking sheets. Press a deep indentation in center of each ball with the end of a wooden spoon handle.
3. Bake 9-11 minutes or until set. Remove the cookies from pans to wire racks to cool completely.
4. In a microwave, melt baking chips with oil; stir until smooth. Spoon a scant tsp. filling into each cookie. Drizzle tops with the remaining mixture. Sprinkle with peppermint candies. Let stand until set.
1 cookie: 118 cal., 7g fat (4g sat. fat), 16mg chol., 63mg sod., 14g carb. (9g sugars, 0 fiber), 1g pro.

DATE NUT BARS

I've had this recipe since I was a young woman, when my co-workers gave me a bridal shower. One of their presents was a box filled with their favorite recipes. Inside, I found this one, and I've used it for just about every occasion since. These old-fashioned bars are always well-received.

—*Margaret Asselin, Port Huron, MI*

Prep: 10 min. • **Bake:** 20 min. + cooling
Makes: 5 dozen

- 2 cups sugar
- 2 cups all-purpose flour
- 2 tsp. baking powder
- ¼ tsp. salt
- 2 cups chopped dates
- 2 cups chopped walnuts or pecans
- 4 large eggs, lightly beaten
- 2 Tbsp. butter, melted
- 1 tsp. vanilla extract
  Confectioners' sugar

1. In a large bowl, combine the sugar, flour, baking powder, salt, dates and nuts. Add the eggs, butter and vanilla; stir just until dry ingredients are moistened (batter will be very stiff).
2. Spread in a greased 15x10x1-in. baking pan. Bake at 350° until golden brown, for 20-25 minutes. Cool bars on a wire rack. Dust with confectioners' sugar.
2 bars: 182 cal., 6g fat (1g sat. fat), 30mg chol., 63mg sod., 30g carb. (21g sugars, 2g fiber), 4g pro.

CHOCOLATE-CRANBERRY CRISPY BARS

I created this recipe by accident when I wanted to make Rice Krispie bars with dried fruit. All I had in my cupboard were dried cranberries and chocolate chips, so I tossed them in.
—*Grace Laird, Barker, TX*

Takes: 15 min. • **Makes:** 1½ dozen

5½ cups Rice Krispies
½ cup semisweet chocolate chips
½ cup dried cranberries
¼ cup toasted wheat germ
1 pkg. (10½ oz.) miniature marshmallows
2 tsp. canola oil
2 tsp. milk

1. In a large bowl, combine the cereal, chocolate chips, cranberries and wheat germ; set aside.
2. In a large microwave-safe bowl, combine the marshmallows, oil and milk. Microwave, uncovered, on high for 45 seconds; stir. Microwave 30-45 seconds longer or until marshmallows are puffed and melted; stir until smooth.
3. Pour over cereal mixture; stir until chips are melted. Spread into a lightly greased 13x9-in. pan. Cut into bars.
1 bar: 126 cal., 2g fat (1g sat. fat), 0 chol., 87mg sod., 27g carb. (15g sugars, 1g fiber), 1g pro.

CHUNKY APPLE-CINNAMON CAKE

Here's a nice change of pace from the usual apple pie that's tasty and worthy of a special get-together— and it's very easy to make! Add a scoop of ice cream if you like.
—*Ellen Ruzinsky, Yorktown Heights, NY*

Prep: 25 min. • **Bake:** 45 min. + cooling
Makes: 15 servings

2¾ lbs. McIntosh, Jonathan or Granny Smith apples, peeled and thinly sliced (11 cups)
½ cup packed brown sugar
3 tsp. ground cinnamon, divided
1 cup plus 1 Tbsp. sugar, divided
1 cup canola oil
4 large eggs, room temperature
3 Tbsp. orange juice
2 tsp. vanilla extract
2½ cups all-purpose flour
2 tsp. baking powder
½ tsp. kosher salt

1. Preheat oven to 425°. In a large bowl, toss the apples with brown sugar and 2 tsp. cinnamon.
2. In a large bowl, beat 1 cup sugar, oil, eggs, orange juice and vanilla until well blended. In another bowl, whisk flour, baking powder and salt; gradually beat into sugar mixture.
3. Transfer half of the batter to an ungreased 13x9-in. baking pan. Top with apples; spread with remaining batter. Mix remaining sugar and cinnamon; sprinkle over top. Bake for 10 minutes.
4. Reduce oven temperature to 375°. Bake cake until golden brown and apples are tender, 35-45 minutes. Cool cake on a wire rack.
1 piece: 349 cal., 17g fat (2g sat. fat), 56mg chol., 138mg sod., 47g carb. (30g sugars, 2g fiber), 4g pro.

HEAVENLY BLUEBERRY TART

Mmm—this tart is bursting with the fresh flavor of blueberries! Not only do I bake berries with the crust, but I also top the tart with more just-picked fruit after I take it out of the oven.
—*Lyin Schramm, Berwick, ME*

Prep: 20 min. • **Bake:** 40 min. + cooling
Makes: 6 servings

1	cup all-purpose flour
2	Tbsp. sugar
⅛	tsp. salt
½	cup cold butter
1	Tbsp. vinegar

FILLING

4	cups fresh blueberries, divided
⅔	cup sugar
2	Tbsp. all-purpose flour
½	tsp. ground cinnamon
⅛	tsp. ground nutmeg

1. In a small bowl, combine flour, sugar and salt; cut in butter until crumbly. Add vinegar, tossing with a fork to moisten. Press onto bottom and up the sides of a lightly greased 9-in. tart pan with removable bottom.

2. For the filling, lightly smash 2 cups of blueberries in a bowl. Combine the sugar, flour, cinnamon and nutmeg; stir into the smashed blueberries. Spread mixture evenly into the crust; sprinkle with 1 cup of the remaining whole blueberries. Place tart pan on a baking sheet.

3. Bake at 400° until crust is browned and filling is bubbly, 40-45 minutes. Remove from the oven; arrange remaining berries over top. Cool on a wire rack. Store tart in the refrigerator.

1 slice: 380 cal., 16g fat (10g sat. fat), 41mg chol., 173mg sod., 59g carb. (36g sugars, 3g fiber), 3g pro.

HOMEMADE LEMON BARS

My husband remembers these sweet bars from his childhood. Today, family meals aren't complete without them.
—*Denise Baumert, Dalhart, TX*

Prep: 25 min. • **Bake:** 25 min. + cooling
Makes: 9 servings

- 1 **cup all-purpose flour**
- ⅓ **cup butter, softened**
- ¼ **cup confectioners' sugar**

TOPPING

- 2 **large eggs, room temperature**
- 1 **cup sugar**
- 2 **Tbsp. all-purpose flour**
- 2 **Tbsp. lemon juice**
- ¾ **tsp. lemon extract**
- ½ **tsp. baking powder**
- ¼ **tsp. salt**
  Confectioners' sugar

1. Preheat oven to 350°. In a large bowl, beat flour, butter and confectioners' sugar until blended. Press onto bottom of an ungreased 8-in. square baking dish. Bake 15-20 minutes or until lightly browned.

2. For topping, in a large bowl, beat eggs, sugar, flour, lemon juice, extract, baking powder and salt until frothy; pour over the hot crust.

3. Bake 10-15 minutes longer or until light golden brown. Cool completely in dish on a wire rack. Dust with confectioners' sugar.

1 piece: 235 cal., 8g fat (5g sat. fat), 65mg chol., 171mg sod., 38g carb. (25g sugars, 0 fiber), 3g pro.

DUTCH APPLE CAKE

My husband and I came to Canada from Holland over 40 years ago. This traditional Dutch recipe is a family favorite and has frequently gone along with me to potluck suppers and other get-togethers.
—*Elizabeth Peters, Martintown, ON*

Prep: 15 min. + standing
Bake: 1½ hours + cooling
Makes: 12 servings

- 3 medium tart apples, peeled and cut into ¼-in. slices (3 cups)
- 3 Tbsp. plus 1 cup sugar, divided
- 1 tsp. ground cinnamon
- ⅔ cup butter, softened
- 4 large eggs, room temperature
- 1 tsp. vanilla extract
- 2 cups all-purpose flour
- ⅛ tsp. salt

1. In a large bowl, combine the apples, 3 Tbsp. sugar and cinnamon; let stand for 1 hour.
2. In another bowl, cream butter and remaining sugar until light and fluffy. Add 1 egg at a time, beating well after each addition. Add vanilla. Combine flour and salt; gradually add to creamed mixture and beat until smooth.
3. Transfer to a greased 9x5-in. loaf pan. Push apple slices vertically into batter, placing them close together.
4. Bake at 300° for 1½-1¾ hours or until a toothpick inserted in the center comes out clean. Cool for 10 minutes before removing from pan to a wire rack. Serve warm.
1 slice: 282 cal., 12g fat (7g sat. fat), 97mg chol., 120mg sod., 40g carb. (24g sugars, 1g fiber), 4g pro.

MAKE AHEAD

BLACKBERRY NECTARINE PIE

Blackberries are a big crop in my area, so I've prepared this pretty double-fruit pie many times. I can tell when my husband wants me to make it because he brings home berries that he picked behind his office.
—*Linda Chinn, Enumclaw, WA*

Prep: 25 min. + chilling • **Makes:** 8 servings

- ¼ cup cornstarch
- 1 can (12 oz.) frozen apple juice concentrate, thawed
- 2 cups fresh blackberries, divided
- 5 medium nectarines, peeled and coarsely chopped
- 1 reduced-fat graham cracker crust (8 in.) Reduced-fat whipped topping, optional

1. In a small saucepan, mix cornstarch and apple juice concentrate until smooth. Bring to a boil. Add ½ cup blackberries; cook and stir 2 minutes or until thickened. Remove from heat.
2. In a large bowl, toss nectarines with remaining blackberries; transfer to crust. Pour apple juice mixture over fruit (crust will be full). Refrigerate, covered, 8 hours or overnight. If desired, serve slices with whipped topping.
1 piece: 240 cal., 4g fat (1g sat. fat), 0 chol., 106mg sod., 50g carb. (32g sugars, 4g fiber), 3g pro.

Fruit Charcuterie Board
page 288

No-Cook Recipe Rescue

Whether you're a beginner cook or you're just in a hurry, sometimes you need an easy recipe that doesn't require cooking at all. Here you'll find dozens of delicious dishes that require a quick stir or a little dicing or slicing.

FOCACCIA SANDWICHES

Slices of this pretty sandwich make any casual get-together special. Add or change ingredients to your taste.

—*Peggy Woodward, Shullsburg, WI*

Takes: 15 min. • **Makes:** 2 dozen

- ⅓ cup mayonnaise
- 1 can (4¼ oz.) chopped ripe olives, drained
- 1 focaccia bread (about 12 oz.), split
- 4 romaine leaves
- ¼ lb. shaved deli ham
- 1 medium sweet red pepper, thinly sliced into rings
- ¼ lb. shaved deli turkey
- 1 large tomato, thinly sliced
- ¼ lb. thinly sliced hard salami
- 1 jar (7 oz.) roasted sweet red peppers, drained
- 4 to 6 slices provolone cheese

In a small bowl, combine mayonnaise and olives; spread over the bottom half of bread. Layer with remaining ingredients; replace the bread top. Cut into 24 wedges; secure with toothpicks.

1 piece: 113 cal., 6g fat (2g sat. fat), 13mg chol., 405mg sod., 9g carb. (1g sugars, 1g fiber), 5g pro.

TEST KITCHEN TIP
A rectangular-shaped focaccia bread, measuring about 12x8 in., works best for this sandwich.

NUTTY RICE KRISPIE COOKIES

My mom and I used to make these treats for Christmas every year. The no-stovetop prep means the kids can help you mix up this easy batch of fun!

—*Savanna Chapdelaine, Orlando, FL*

Takes: 15 min. • **Makes:** about 2 dozen

- 1 pkg. (10 to 12 oz.) white baking chips
- ¼ cup creamy peanut butter
- 1 cup miniature marshmallows
- 1 cup Rice Krispies
- 1 cup salted peanuts

In a large microwave-safe bowl, melt baking chips; stir until smooth. Stir in peanut butter until blended. Add marshmallows, Rice Krispies and peanuts. Drop by heaping tablespoonfuls onto waxed paper-lined baking sheets. Cool completely. Store in an airtight container.

1 cookie: 127 cal., 8g fat (3g sat. fat), 2mg chol., 49mg sod., 11g carb. (9g sugars, 1g fiber), 3g pro.

MAKE AHEAD

HAM & CHERRY PINWHEELS

When I served these roll-ups at my annual Christmas party, people really liked the smokiness of the ham and the sweet surprise of the cherries. I enjoy making them for different occasions because most of the prep can be done ahead. On party day, all you have to do is slice and arrange on a pretty tray.
—*Kate Dampier, Quail Valley, CA*

- -

Prep: 20 min. + chilling
Makes: about 3½ dozen

1	pkg. (8 oz.) cream cheese, softened
4	tsp. minced fresh dill
1	Tbsp. lemon juice
2	tsp. Dijon mustard
	Dash salt and pepper
½	cup dried cherries, chopped
¼	cup chopped green onions
5	flour tortillas (10 in.), room temperature
½	lb. sliced deli Black Forest ham
½	lb. sliced Swiss cheese

1. In a small bowl, beat cream cheese, dill, lemon juice, mustard, salt and pepper until blended. Stir in cherries and onions. Spread over each tortilla; layer with ham and cheese.
2. Roll up tightly; wrap in plastic. Refrigerate for 2 hours or overnight. Cut into ½-in. slices.
1 pinwheel: 78 cal., 4g fat (2g sat. fat), 13mg chol., 151mg sod., 6g carb. (2g sugars, 0 fiber), 4g pro.

Appetizer Pinwheels: Beat the cream cheese with 1 cup sour cream, 1 can (4¼ oz.) drained chopped ripe olives, 1 can (4 oz.) well-drained chopped green chiles, 1 cup shredded cheddar cheese, ½ cup chopped green onions, dash garlic powder and dash salt until blended. Spread over tortillas and roll up.
Reuben Pinwheels: Beat the cream cheese with 3 Tbsp. spicy brown mustard and ¼ tsp. prepared horseradish. Spread 1 heaping Tbsp. cream cheese mixture over each tortilla; layer each with 8 thin slices deli corned beef, 3 thin slices Swiss cheese and 1 heaping Tbsp. additional cream cheese mixture. Top each with ½ cup well-drained sauerkraut. Roll up.

MAKE AHEAD

MALTED MILK PIES

Malted milk balls provide the delightful flavor you'll find in each cool bite of this light dessert. Easy to make, the pies feed a crowd and are a longtime favorite of my family.
—*Jann Marie Foster, Minneapolis, MN*

Prep: 10 min. + freezing
Makes: 2 pies (8 servings each)

- 1 pkg. (7 oz.) malted milk balls, chopped
- 1 pint vanilla ice cream, softened
- 1 carton (8 oz.) frozen whipped topping, thawed
- 2 chocolate crumb crusts (9 in.)
  Additional whipped topping, optional

1. Set aside ¼ cup malted milk balls for topping. Place ice cream in a large bowl; fold in whipped topping and remaining malted milk balls. Spoon into crusts. Cover and freeze.
2. Remove from freezer 20 minutes before serving. If desired, garnish with additional whipped topping. Top with reserved malted milk balls.
1 slice: 234 cal., 11g fat (7g sat. fat), 7mg chol., 150mg sod., 31g carb. (21g sugars, 1g fiber), 2g pro.

GREEK DELI KABOBS

For an easy Mediterranean-style appetizer, marinate broccoli and mozzarella, then skewer with sweet red peppers and salami. Everybody loves food on a stick!
—*Vikki Spengler, Ocala, FL*

Prep: 30 min. + marinating • **Makes:** 2 dozen

- 1 lb. part-skim mozzarella cheese, cut into 48 cubes
- 24 fresh broccoli florets (about 10 oz.)
- ½ cup Greek vinaigrette
- 24 slices hard salami
- 2 jars (7½ oz. each) roasted sweet red peppers, drained and cut into 24 strips

1. In a shallow dish, combine cheese, broccoli and vinaigrette. Turn to coat; cover and refrigerate 4 hours or overnight.
2. Drain cheese and broccoli, reserving vinaigrette. On 24 appetizer skewers, alternately thread cheese, salami, broccoli and peppers. Brush with reserved vinaigrette.
1 kabob: 109 cal., 7g fat (4g sat. fat), 19mg chol., 374mg sod., 2g carb. (1g sugars, 0 fiber), 8g pro.

CHOCOLATE CHIP DIP

Is there a kid alive (or a kid at heart) who wouldn't gobble up this creamy dip for graham crackers? It beats dunking them in milk, hands down! You can also use apple wedges for dipping.

—*Heather Koenig, Prairie Du Chien, WI*

- -

Takes: 15 min. • **Makes:** 2 cups

1 pkg. (8 oz.) cream cheese, softened
½ cup butter, softened
¾ cup confectioners' sugar
2 Tbsp. brown sugar
1 tsp. vanilla extract
1 cup miniature semisweet chocolate chips
Graham cracker sticks

In a small bowl, beat cream cheese and butter until light and fluffy. Add the sugars and vanilla; beat until smooth. Stir in chocolate chips. Serve with graham cracker sticks.

2 Tbsp.: 180 cal., 14g fat (9g sat. fat), 31mg chol., 84mg sod., 14g carb. (13g sugars, 1g fiber), 2g pro.

TEST KITCHEN TIP
If you have a hankering for cookies and cream, replace the chocolate chips with crushed cookies.

BUTTERY LEMON SANDWICH COOKIES

 My grandson approves of these lemony sandwich cookies made with crackers and prepared frosting. Decorate with whatever sprinkles you like.

—*Nancy Foust, Stoneboro, PA*

- -

Prep: 20 min. + standing • **Makes:** 2½ dozen

¾ cup lemon frosting
60 Ritz crackers

24 oz. white candy coating, melted
Nonpareils, jimmies or sprinkles, optional

Spread frosting on bottoms of half of the crackers; cover with remaining crackers. Dip sandwiches in melted candy coating; allow excess to drip off. Place on waxed paper; decorate as desired. Let stand until set. Store in an airtight container in the refrigerator.

1 sandwich cookie: 171 cal., 9g fat (6g sat. fat), 0 chol., 70mg sod., 23g carb. (19g sugars, 0 fiber), 0 pro.

S'MORES NO-BAKE COOKIES

There's no easier way to get that s'mores goodness in your kitchen. Mix these cookies together and chill until you're ready to share.
—Taste of Home *Test Kitchen*

Prep: 15 min. + chilling • **Makes:** 2½ dozen

- 1⅔ **cups milk chocolate chips**
- 2 **Tbsp. canola oil**
- 3 **cups Golden Grahams**
- 2 **cups miniature marshmallows**

In a large microwave-safe bowl, microwave chocolate chips and oil, uncovered, at 50% power until chocolate is melted, stirring every 30 seconds for 1-1½ minutes. Stir in cereal until blended; fold in marshmallows. Drop by rounded tablespoonfuls onto waxed paper-lined baking sheets. Refrigerate until firm, about 15 minutes.

1 cookie: 79 cal., 4g fat (2g sat. fat), 2mg chol., 39mg sod., 11g carb. (8g sugars, 1g fiber), 1g pro.

CUCUMBER PARTY SANDWICHES

This is one of my favorite appetizers. We have lots of pig roasts here in Kentucky, and these small sandwiches are perfect to serve while the pig is cooking.
—*Rebecca Rose, Mount Washington, KY*

- -

Prep: 20 min. + standing • **Makes:** 2½ dozen

- 1   **pkg. (8 oz.) cream cheese, softened**
- 2   **Tbsp. mayonnaise**
- 2   **tsp. Italian salad dressing mix**
- 30   **slices cocktail rye or pumpernickel bread**
- 60   **thin cucumber slices**
      Fresh dill sprigs and slivered red pearl onions, optional

1. Beat cream cheese, mayonnaise and dressing mix until blended; let stand for 30 minutes.

2. Spread cream cheese mixture on bread. Top each with 2 cucumber slices and, if desired, dill and red onion slivers. Refrigerate, covered, until serving.

1 open-faced sandwich: 53 cal., 4g fat (2g sat. fat), 8mg chol., 92mg sod., 4g carb. (1g sugars, 1g fiber), 1g pro.

SHRIMP TARTLETS

Fill mini tart shells with a cream cheese mixture, then top it off with seafood sauce and shrimp for a picture-perfect look and delightful taste. The recipe makes a fantastic appetizer, or you can serve several for a quick, light meal.
—*Gina Hutchison, Smithville, MO*

Takes: 20 min. • **Makes:** 2½ dozen

- 1 pkg. (8 oz.) cream cheese, softened
- 1½ tsp. Worcestershire sauce
- 1 to 2 tsp. grated onion
- 1 tsp. garlic salt
- ⅛ tsp. lemon juice
- 2 pkg. (1.9 oz. each) frozen miniature phyllo tart shells
- ½ cup seafood cocktail sauce
- 30 peeled and deveined cooked shrimp (31-40 per lb.), tails removed
  Minced fresh parsley and lemon wedges, optional

1. Beat the first 5 ingredients until blended. Place tart shells on a serving plate. Fill with cream cheese mixture; top with cocktail sauce and shrimp.
2. Refrigerate until serving. If desired, sprinkle with parsley and serve with lemon wedges.
1 tartlet: 61 cal., 4g fat (2g sat. fat), 23mg chol., 143mg sod., 4g carb. (1g sugars, 0 fiber), 3g pro.

PEAR WALDORF PITAS

Here's a guaranteed table brightener for a shower, luncheon or party. Just stand back and watch these sandwiches vanish. For an eye-catching presentation, I tuck each one into a colorful paper napkin.
—*Roxann Parker, Dover, DE*

Prep: 20 min. + chilling • **Makes:** 20 mini pitas

- 2 medium ripe pears, diced
- ½ cup thinly sliced celery
- ½ cup halved seedless red grapes
- 2 Tbsp. finely chopped walnuts
- 2 Tbsp. lemon yogurt
- 2 Tbsp. mayonnaise
- ⅛ tsp. poppy seeds
- 20 miniature pita pocket halves
  Lettuce leaves

1. In a large bowl, combine the pears, celery, grapes and walnuts. In another bowl, whisk the yogurt, mayonnaise and poppy seeds. Add to pear mixture; toss to coat. Refrigerate for 1 hour or overnight.
2. Line pita halves with lettuce; fill each with 2 Tbsp. pear mixture.
1 pita half: 67 cal., 2g fat (0 sat. fat), 0 chol., 86mg sod., 12g carb. (3g sugars, 1g fiber), 2g pro. **Diabetic exchanges:** 1 starch.

SANDWICH FOR A CROWD

My husband and I live on a 21-acre horse ranch. We love to invite friends over to enjoy it with us. When entertaining, I rely on no-fuss, make-ahead entrees like this satisfying sandwich.
—Helen Hougland, Spring Hill, KS

Prep: 10 min. + chilling
Makes: 14 servings

- 2 loaves (1 lb. each) unsliced Italian bread (about 11 in. long)
- 1 pkg. (8 oz.) cream cheese, softened
- 1 cup shredded cheddar cheese
- ¾ cup sliced green onions
- ¼ cup mayonnaise
- 1 Tbsp. Worcestershire sauce
- 1 lb. thinly sliced fully cooked ham
- 1 lb. thinly sliced roast beef
- 14 thin slices dill pickle

1. Cut the bread in half lengthwise. Hollow out both halves of each loaf, leaving a ½-in. shell (discard removed bread or save for another use).
2. Combine cheeses, onions, mayonnaise and Worcestershire sauce; spread over cut sides of bread. Layer the ham and roast beef on bottom and top halves; place pickles on bottom halves. Gently press halves together.
3. Wrap and refrigerate for at least 2 hours. Cut each loaf into 7 slices.

1 slice: 297 cal., 15g fat (7g sat. fat), 53mg chol., 1141mg sod., 21g carb. (3g sugars, 1g fiber), 21g pro.

BEER DIP

Ranch dressing mix flavors this easy dip packed with cheddar cheese. It's perfect paired with pretzels. Be aware, though—it's addictive. Once you start eating it, it's very hard to stop!
—Michelle Long, New Castle, CO

Takes: 5 min. • **Makes:** 3½ cups

- 2 pkg. (8 oz. each) cream cheese, softened
- ⅓ cup beer or nonalcoholic beer
- 1 envelope ranch salad dressing mix
- 2 cups shredded cheddar cheese
  Pretzels

In a large bowl, beat the cream cheese, beer and dressing mix until smooth. Stir in cheddar cheese. Serve with pretzels.

2 Tbsp.: 89 cal., 8g fat (5g sat. fat), 26mg chol., 177mg sod., 1g carb. (0 sugars, 0 fiber), 3g pro.

BLACKBERRY BRANDY SLUSH

We wanted a grown-up twist on a favorite slushy, so we spiked it with blackberry brandy. The deep red color makes it perfect for a merry celebration.
—*Lindsey Spinler, Sobieski, WI*

Prep: 10 min. + freezing
Makes: 28 servings (1 cup each)

8 cups water
2 cups sugar
3 cups blackberry brandy
1 can (12 oz.) frozen lemonade concentrate, thawed
1 can (12 oz.) frozen grape juice concentrate, thawed
14 cups lemon-lime soda, chilled

1. In a very large bowl, stir water and sugar until sugar is dissolved. Stir in brandy and juice concentrates. Transfer to freezer containers; freeze overnight.

2. To serve, place about ½ cup brandy mixture in each glass; top with ½ cup soda.

1 cup: 235 cal., 0 fat (0 sat. fat), 0 chol., 18mg sod., 51g carb. (48g sugars, 0 fiber), 0 pro.

MARINATED CHEESE

This special appetizer always makes it to our neighborhood parties and is the first to disappear at the buffet table. It's attractive, delicious—and so easy!
—*Laurie Casper, Coraopolis, PA*

- -

Prep: 30 min. + marinating
Makes: about 2 lbs.

- 2 blocks (8 oz. each) white cheddar cheese
- 2 pkg. (8 oz. each) cream cheese
- ¾ cup chopped roasted sweet red peppers
- ½ cup olive oil
- ¼ cup white wine vinegar
- ¼ cup balsamic vinegar
- 3 Tbsp. chopped green onions
- 3 Tbsp. minced fresh parsley
- 2 Tbsp. minced fresh basil
- 1 Tbsp. sugar
- 3 garlic cloves, minced
- ½ tsp. salt
- ½ tsp. pepper
  Assorted crackers or toasted sliced French bread

1. Slice each block of cheddar cheese into twenty ¼-in. slices. Cut each block of cream cheese into 18 slices. Create four 6-in.-long blocks of stacked cheese, sandwiching 9 cream cheese slices between 10 cheddar slices for each stack. Place in a 13x9-in. dish.

2. In a small bowl, combine the roasted peppers, oil, vinegars, onions, herbs, sugar, garlic, salt and pepper; pour over cheese stacks.

3. Cover and refrigerate overnight, turning cheese blocks once. Drain excess marinade. Serve cheese with crackers or toasted bread.

1 oz.: 121 cal., 11g fat (6g sat. fat), 30mg chol., 153mg sod., 1g carb. (0 sugars, 0 fiber), 5g pro.

★ ★ ★ ★ ★ **READER REVIEW**

"My 11-year-old daughter made this to bring to Christmas Eve dinner and got rave reviews 2 years in a row. Definitely takes some time to combine the cheeses and smooth out the 'stacks,' but it's well worth it!"

MARNIE12 TASTEOFHOME.COM

REFRIGERATOR LIME CHEESECAKE

I made this for a Father's Day party, and it was a hit! I guarantee compliments when you serve this fantastic dessert.
—*Cher Anjema, Kleinburg, ON*

Prep: 30 min. + chilling • **Makes:** 12 servings

- 32 soft ladyfingers, split
- 1 envelope unflavored gelatin
- ¼ cup lime juice, chilled
- 2 pkg. (8 oz. each) cream cheese, softened
- 1 cup sugar
- 6 oz. white baking chocolate, melted and cooled
- 2 tsp. grated lime zest
- 1 cup heavy whipping cream, whipped
  Fresh strawberry and lime slices, optional

1. Arrange 20 ladyfingers around the edges and 12 ladyfingers on the bottom of an ungreased 8-in. springform pan; set aside. In a small saucepan, sprinkle gelatin over cold lime juice; let stand for 1 minute. Heat over low heat, stirring until gelatin is completely dissolved; cool.

2. Meanwhile, beat cream cheese and sugar until smooth. Gradually beat in the melted chocolate, lime zest and gelatin mixture. Fold in whipped cream. Pour into prepared pan. Cover and refrigerate until set, about 3 hours. Remove sides of pan. If desired, garnish with strawberry and lime slices.

1 slice: 408 cal., 25g fat (16g sat. fat), 100mg chol., 267mg sod., 42g carb. (35g sugars, 0 fiber), 6g pro.

NO-BAKE COOKIE BUTTER BLOSSOMS

Chewy and sweet, these easy treats mix Rice Krispies, cookie spread and chocolate in an unforgettable spin on an old favorite.
—*Jessie Sarrazin, Livingston, MT*

Prep: 25 min. + standing
Makes: about 2½ dozen

- 1 cup Biscoff creamy cookie spread
- ½ cup corn syrup
- 3 cups Rice Krispies
- 32 milk chocolate kisses

In a large saucepan, combine cookie spread and corn syrup. Cook and stir over low heat until blended. Remove from heat; stir in Rice Krispies until coated. Shape level tablespoons of mixture into balls; place onto waxed paper. Immediately press a kiss into center of each cookie. Let stand until set.

1 cookie: 93 cal., 4g fat (1g sat. fat), 1mg chol., 22mg sod., 14g carb. (10g sugars, 0 fiber), 1g pro.

PARTY CHEESE BALLS

These tangy cheese balls are guaranteed to spread cheer at your next gathering. The ingredients create a colorful presentation and a savory combination of flavors.
—*Shirley Hoerman, Nekoosa, WI*

- -

Prep: 20 min. + chilling
Makes: 2 cheese balls (1¾ cups each)

- 1   pkg. (8 oz.) cream cheese, softened
- 2   cups shredded cheddar cheese
- 1   jar (5 oz.) sharp American cheese spread
- 1   jar (5 oz.) pimiento cheese spread
- 3   Tbsp. finely chopped onion
- 1   Tbsp. lemon juice
- 1   tsp. Worcestershire sauce
-     Dash garlic salt
- ½   cup chopped pecans, toasted
- ½   cup minced fresh parsley
-     Assorted crackers

1. In a large bowl, beat the first 8 ingredients until blended. Cover and refrigerate for 45 minutes or until easily handled.

2. Shape into 2 balls; roll in parsley and pecans. Cover and refrigerate. Remove from the refrigerator 15 minutes before serving with crackers.

2 Tbsp.: 99 cal., 9g fat (5g sat. fat), 25mg chol., 188mg sod., 2g carb. (1g sugars, 0 fiber), 4g pro.

SOUTH DAKOTA FRITO TREATS

Yep, they're made with corn chips! These salty sweets were a staple after meetings at the quilt guild I belonged to in South Dakota.
—*Carol Tramp, Wynot, NE*

Prep: 15 min. + standing • **Makes:** 2 dozen

- 2 pkg. (9¾ oz. each) corn chips, divided
- 2 cups semisweet chocolate chips, divided
- 1 cup sugar
- 1 cup light corn syrup
- 1 cup creamy peanut butter

1. Spread 1 package of corn chips on the bottom of a greased 13x9-in. baking pan; sprinkle with 1 cup chocolate chips.

2. In a large heavy saucepan, combine sugar and corn syrup. Bring to a boil; cook and stir 1 minute. Remove from heat; stir in peanut butter. Pour half the peanut butter mixture over chip mixture. Top with remaining corn chips and chocolate chips; drizzle with the remaining peanut butter mixture. Let stand until set. Cut into bars.

1 bar: 337 cal., 18g fat (5g sat. fat), 0 chol., 196mg sod., 43g carb. (29g sugars, 2g fiber), 5g pro.

FRUIT WITH POPPY SEED DRESSING

Easy to prepare, cool and colorful, this refreshing, good-for-you fruit salad is a springtime favorite.
—*Peggy Mills, Texarkana, AR*

- -

Prep: 20 min. + standing
Makes: 12 servings (1 cup each)

- 3 **Tbsp. honey**
- 1 **Tbsp. white vinegar**
- 1 **tsp. ground mustard**
- ¼ **tsp. salt**
- ¼ **tsp. onion powder**
- ⅓ **cup canola oil**
- 1 **tsp. poppy seeds**
- 1 **fresh pineapple, cut into 1½-in. cubes**
- 3 **medium kiwifruit, halved and sliced**
- 2 **cups fresh strawberries, halved**

1. In a small bowl, whisk first 5 ingredients. Gradually whisk in oil until blended. Stir in poppy seeds; let stand 1 hour.
2. In a large bowl, combine fruits. Drizzle with dressing; toss gently to coat.
1 cup: 129 cal., 7g fat (0 sat. fat), 0 chol., 51mg sod., 19g carb. (14g sugars, 2g fiber), 1g pro.
Diabetic exchanges: 1½ fat, 1 fruit.

APRICOT-RICOTTA STUFFED CELERY

This healthful, satisfying filling can double as a dip for sliced apples. I often make the ahead so the kids can help themselves to an after-school snack.
—*Dorothy Reinhold, Malibu, CA*

- -

Takes: 15 min. • **Makes:** about 2 dozen

- 3 **dried apricots**
- ½ **cup part-skim ricotta cheese**
- 2 **tsp. brown sugar**
- ¼ **tsp. grated orange zest**
- ⅛ **tsp. salt**
- 5 **celery ribs, cut into 1½-in. pieces**

Place apricots in a food processor. Cover and process until finely chopped. Add the ricotta cheese, brown sugar, orange zest and salt; cover and process until blended. Stuff or pipe into celery. Chill until serving.
1 piece: 12 cal., 0 fat (0 sat. fat), 2mg chol., 25mg sod., 1g carb. (1g sugars, 0 fiber), 1g pro.

SPRUCED-UP CHEESE SPREAD

A neighbor who's a wonderful cook gave me the recipe for this zippy cracker spread. Not only does it look enticing in a bowl, but also it's easy to shape into a Christmas tree for the holidays.

—*Judy Grimes, Brandon, MS*

Takes: 20 min. • **Makes:** 4 cups

- 1 cup mayonnaise
- 1 small onion, grated
- 1 to 2 Tbsp. prepared mustard
- 1 Tbsp. Worcestershire sauce
- 1 tsp. celery seed
- ½ tsp. paprika
- ¼ tsp. garlic salt
- 1 jar (4 oz.) diced pimientos, drained, divided
- 3 cups finely shredded sharp cheddar cheese
  Minced fresh parsley
- 2 Tbsp. finely chopped pecans
  Assorted crackers

1. Mix the first 7 ingredients and ⅓ cup pimientos. Stir in cheese.

2. Transfer to a serving dish. Sprinkle with parsley, pecans and remaining pimientos. Serve with crackers.

2 Tbsp. spread: 93 cal., 9g fat (3g sat. fat), 11mg chol., 131mg sod., 1g carb. (0 sugars, 0 fiber), 3g pro.

★ ★ ★ ★ ★ **READER REVIEW**

"Base is great. Here in the Southwest, this is how we make pimiento cheese spread for sandwiches. Oh, add one seeded, diced fresh jalapeno or the equivalent in seeded, diced pickled jalapeno."

TEXAN2000 TASTEOFHOME.COM

DREAMY FRUIT DIP

Everyone will love this thick cream cheese fruit dip. Serve it alongside apple wedges, pineapple chunks, strawberries and grapes.
—*Anna Beiler, Strasburg, PA*

- -

Takes: 10 min. • **Makes:** about 4 cups

- 1   pkg. (8 oz.) cream cheese, softened
- ½   cup butter, softened
- ½   cup marshmallow creme
- 1   carton (8 oz.) frozen whipped topping, thawed
  Assorted fresh fruit

In a small bowl, beat cream cheese and butter until smooth. Beat in marshmallow creme.

Fold in whipped topping. Serve with fruit. Store in the refrigerator.
2 Tbsp.: 75 cal., 6g fat (5g sat. fat), 15mg chol., 51mg sod., 3g carb. (2g sugars, 0 fiber), 1g pro.

TEST KITCHEN TIP
You can use the leftover dip as a tasty topping for toast or bagels the next morning.

MAKE AHEAD
BLACK BEAN DIP

This appealing Southwest-inspired dip can be made well in advance. If we don't have tortilla chips on hand, we serve it with crackers.
—*Ashley Donovan, Glasgow, KY*

- -

Prep: 10 min. + chilling • **Makes:** 3 cups

- 2   pkg. (8 oz. each) fat-free cream cheese, cubed
- 1   can (15 oz.) black beans, rinsed and drained, divided
- ¾   cup shredded reduced-fat cheddar cheese
- 6   green onions, chopped
- 1½ tsp. ground cumin
  Dash cayenne pepper

TOPPING

- ¼   cup shredded reduced-fat cheddar cheese
- 2   Tbsp. diced fresh tomato
- 2   Tbsp. chopped green onion
  Tortilla chips

1. In a food processor, cover and process cream cheese until smooth. Add half of the beans; cover and pulse until blended. Transfer to a bowl; stir in the cheddar cheese, onions, cumin, cayenne and remaining beans. Cover and refrigerate for 8 hours or overnight.
2. Just before serving, garnish with cheddar, tomato and onion. Serve with tortilla chips.
¼ cup: 95 cal., 3g fat (2g sat. fat), 10mg chol., 335mg sod., 8g carb. (1g sugars, 2g fiber), 10g pro. **Diabetic exchanges:** 1 lean meat, ½ starch.

ANTIPASTO APPETIZER SALAD

Use a slotted spoon to serve this as an appetizer with baguette toasts, or ladle it over romaine lettuce to enjoy as a salad.
—*Tamra Duncan, Lincoln, AR*

- -

Prep: 10 min. + chilling • **Makes:** 6 cups

1 jar (16 oz.) roasted sweet red pepper strips, drained
½ lb. part-skim mozzarella cheese, cubed
1 cup grape tomatoes
1 jar (7½ oz.) marinated quartered artichoke hearts, undrained
1 jar (7 oz.) pimiento-stuffed olives, drained
1 can (6 oz.) pitted ripe olives, drained
1 tsp. dried basil
1 tsp. dried parsley flakes
Pepper to taste
Toasted baguette slices or romaine lettuce, torn

1. In a large bowl, combine first 9 ingredients; toss to coat. Cover and refrigerate at least 4 hours before serving.
2. Serve with baguette slices or over lettuce.
Note: This recipe was tested with Vlasic roasted red pepper strips.
½ cup: 132 cal., 11g fat (3g sat. fat), 15mg chol., 651mg sod., 6g carb. (2g sugars, 1g fiber), 4g pro.

SALMON APPETIZERS

As a cook for a commercial salmon fishing crew, I found this recipe to be an innovative use of salmon. The roll-ups are a terrific addition to a festive Mexican meal or as a prelude to steak dinner.
—*Evelyn Gebhardt, Kasilof, AK*

Prep: 15 min. + chilling
Makes: about 4 dozen

- 1 can (15 oz.) salmon, drained, bones and skin removed or 2 cups flaked cooked salmon
- 1 pkg. (8 oz.) cream cheese, softened
- 4 Tbsp. salsa
- 2 Tbsp. chopped fresh parsley
- 1 tsp. dried cilantro
- ¼ tsp. ground cumin, optional
- 8 flour tortillas (8 in.)

1. Drain salmon; remove any bones. In a small bowl, combine salmon, cream cheese, salsa, parsley and cilantro. Add cumin if desired. Spread about 2 Tbsp. of the salmon mixture over each tortilla.
2. Roll up each tortilla tightly and wrap individually. Refrigerate 2-3 hours. Slice each tortilla into bite-sized pieces.
1 piece: 58 cal., 3g fat (1g sat. fat), 12mg chol., 95mg sod., 5g carb. (0 sugars, 0 fiber), 3g pro.

SHRIMP COCKTAIL SPREAD

There's no secret to this creamy seafood appetizer—it's simply delicious! I originally tasted it at a friend's house and liked it so much, I requested the recipe.
—*Brenda Buhler, Abbotsford, BC*

Takes: 20 min. • **Makes:** 20 servings

- 1 pkg. (8 oz.) cream cheese, softened
- ½ cup sour cream
- ¼ cup mayonnaise
- 1 cup seafood cocktail sauce
- 12 oz. frozen cooked salad shrimp, thawed
- 2 cups shredded mozzarella cheese
- 1 medium green pepper, chopped
- 1 small tomato, chopped
- 3 green onions with tops, sliced Assorted crackers

1. In a large bowl, beat the cream cheese, sour cream and mayonnaise until smooth.
2. Spread mixture on a round 12-in. serving platter. Top with seafood sauce. Sprinkle with shrimp, mozzarella, green pepper, tomato and onions. Refrigerate until serving. Serve with crackers.
2 Tbsp.: 136 cal., 10g fat (5g sat. fat), 62mg chol., 372mg sod., 4g carb. (3g sugars, 1g fiber), 8g pro.

ORANGE COCONUT BALLS

When my mother first made these slightly sweet morsels years ago, we immediately fell in love with their unique flavor.
—*Helen Youngers, Kingman, KS*

Takes: 20 min. • **Makes:** 4½ dozen

- 1 pkg. (12 oz.) vanilla wafers, crushed
- ¾ cup confectioners' sugar
- ¾ cup sweetened shredded coconut
- ½ cup finely chopped pecans
- ½ cup thawed orange juice concentrate
  Additional confectioners' sugar

In a large bowl, combine first 5 ingredients. Roll into 1-in. balls, then roll in confectioners' sugar. Store in the refrigerator. Roll in additional confectioners' sugar before serving.

2 pieces: 98 cal., 4g fat (1g sat. fat), 1mg chol., 46mg sod., 15g carb. (9g sugars, 1g fiber), 1g pro.

AVOCADO DIP

I created this creamy dip because I couldn't find a guacamole that appealed to me. My husband doesn't generally like avocado dip, but we both really enjoy this one!
—*Kay Dunham, Amity, MO*

Takes: 15 min. • **Makes:** 2½ cups

- 2 medium ripe avocados, peeled and pitted
- 1 pkg. (8 oz.) fat-free cream cheese
- ⅓ cup plain yogurt
- ⅓ cup picante sauce
- 1 Tbsp. lime juice
- ½ tsp. salt
- ¼ tsp. garlic powder
  Tortilla chips

In a small bowl, mash avocados and cream cheese until smooth. Stir in the yogurt, picante sauce, lime juice, salt and garlic powder. Serve with chips. Refrigerate leftovers.

¼ cup: 73 cal., 5g fat (1g sat. fat), 2mg chol., 258mg sod., 5g carb. (1g sugars, 2g fiber), 4g pro. **Diabetic exchanges:** 1 fat.

GRASSHOPPER CHEESECAKE

What do you get when you combine a popular mint chocolate drink with a cheesecake? Pure delight! Garnish the top with piped whipped cream and crushed cookie crumbs.

—*Marie Rizzio, Interlochen, MI*

Prep: 25 min. + chilling • **Makes:** 12 servings

35	chocolate wafers, finely crushed (about 1⅔ cups)
¼	cup butter, melted
1	Tbsp. plus ¾ cup sugar, divided
1	envelope unflavored gelatin
½	cup cold water
1	pkg. (8 oz.) cream cheese, softened
⅓	cup green creme de menthe
2	cups heavy whipping cream, whipped

1. In a small bowl, combine the cookie crumbs, butter and 1 Tbsp. sugar. Press half the mixture onto the bottom of a greased 9-in. springform pan. Refrigerate until chilled.

2. In a small saucepan, sprinkle gelatin over cold water; let stand for 1 minute. Heat over low heat, stirring until gelatin is completely dissolved. Cool.

3. In a large bowl, beat cream cheese and remaining sugar until fluffy. Gradually beat in the gelatin mixture. Stir in creme de menthe. Set aside ½ cup whipped cream for garnish. Fold remaining whipped cream into cream cheese mixture.

4. Pour half of the filling over crust. Top with remaining crumb mixture, reserving 2 Tbsp. for garnish. Pour remaining filling into pan; garnish with reserved whipped cream. Sprinkle with reserved crumbs. Chill until set. Remove sides of the pan before slicing.

To make ahead: Cheesecake can be made a few days in advance. Cover and refrigerate until ready to serve.

1 slice: 394 cal., 27g fat (16g sat. fat), 75mg chol., 204mg sod., 32g carb. (25g sugars, 1g fiber), 4g pro.

FRUIT CHARCUTERIE BOARD

Who says cheese and sausage get to have all the fun? Make this a party favorite with any fruits that are in season.
—Taste of Home *Test Kitchen*

- -

Takes: 25 minutes • **Makes:** 14 servings

10	fresh strawberries, halved
8	fresh or dried figs, halved
2	small navel oranges, thinly sliced
12	oz. seedless red grapes (about 1½ cups)
1	medium mango, halved and scored
½	cup fresh blueberries
1	cup fresh blackberries
½	cup dried banana chips
2	large kiwifruit, peeled, halved and thinly sliced
12	oz. seedless watermelon (about 6 slices)
½	cup unblanched almonds
8	oz. Brie cheese
8	oz. mascarpone cheese
½	cup honey

On a large platter or cutting board, arrange fruit, almonds and cheese. Place honey in a small jar and tuck jar among fruit.

1 serving: 304 cal., 17g fat (8g sat. fat), 36mg chol., 116mg sod., 36g carb. (30g sugars, 4g fiber), 7g pro.

MAKE AHEAD

ITALIAN MARINATED SHRIMP

Dress up your holiday buffet table with this tasty shrimp recipe. You'll have time to enjoy your party— this appetizer is that easy.

—*Phyllis Schmalz, Kansas City, KS*

- -

Prep: 15 min. + marinating • **Makes:** 6 cups

¾ cup water
½ cup red wine vinegar
¼ cup olive oil
¾ tsp. salt
¾ tsp. minced fresh oregano
  or ¼ tsp. dried oregano
¾ tsp. minced fresh thyme
  or ¼ tsp. dried thyme
1 garlic clove, minced
¼ tsp. pepper
1½ lbs. peeled and deveined cooked shrimp (16-20 per lb.)
1 can (14 oz.) water-packed artichoke hearts, rinsed, drained and halved
½ lb. small fresh mushrooms, halved

In a large bowl, combine first 8 ingredients. Add shrimp, artichokes and mushrooms; turn to coat. Cover and refrigerate 8 hours or overnight, turning occasionally.

⅓ cup: 81 cal., 4g fat (0 sat. fat), 57mg chol., 210mg sod., 3g carb. (0 sugars, 0 fiber), 9g pro. **Diabetic exchanges:** 1 lean meat, ½ fat.

BROWNIE BATTER DIP

I'm all about the sweeter side of dips, and this brownie-batter variety fits in with my life's philosophy: Chocolate makes anything better. Grab some fruit, cookies or salty snacks and start dunking.
—*Mel Gunnell, Boise, ID*

Takes: 10 min. • **Makes:** 2½ cups

- 1   pkg. (8 oz.) cream cheese, softened
- ¼   cup butter, softened
- 2   cups confectioners' sugar
- ⅓   cup baking cocoa
- ¼   cup 2% milk
- 2   Tbsp. brown sugar
- 1   tsp. vanilla extract
     M&M's minis, optional
     Pretzels, sliced apples and/or
     animal crackers

In a large bowl, beat cream cheese and butter until smooth. Beat in confectioners' sugar, cocoa, milk, brown sugar and vanilla until smooth. If desired, sprinkle with M&M's minis. Serve with dippers of your choice.

2 Tbsp.: 117 cal., 6g fat (4g sat. fat), 19mg chol., 62mg sod., 15g carb. (14g sugars, 0 fiber), 1g pro.

★ ★ ★ ★ ★ **READER REVIEW**

"This was delicious. My family really likes it topped with M&M's."

ANGEL182009 TASTEOFHOME.COM

EASY CINNAMON THINS

When a co-worker's husband came home after serving in Iraq, we had a potluck party for him. These spicy-sweet cookies with coarse red sugar matched our patriotic theme.
—*Janet Whittington, Heath, OH*

Prep: 20 min. + standing • **Makes:** 2½ dozen

- 12   oz. white candy coating, chopped
- 1   tsp. cinnamon extract
- 30   Ritz crackers
- 12   finely crushed cinnamon hard candies
     Red colored sugar

1. In a microwave, melt candy coating; stir until smooth. Stir in extract.
2. Dip crackers in candy coating mixture; allow excess to drip off. Place on waxed paper. Decorate with candies and colored sugar as desired. Let stand until set.

1 cookie: 75 cal., 4g fat (3g sat. fat), 0 chol., 36mg sod., 10g carb. (8g sugars, 0 fiber), 0 pro.

White Seafood
Lasagna
page 312

Popular Parties

Here's a roundup of awesome recipes you can make and take to these common get-togethers.

Super Bowl

To defeat hunger in a hurry, you'll need a guaranteed-to-please game plan. Turn to these fan favorites the next time you need a dish to pass.

SPICY ALMONDS

These delicious spiced nuts are so versatile—they make a nutritious snack for camping, and they're a must for Super Bowl munching.
—*Gina Myers, Spokane, WA*

Prep: 10 min. • **Bake:** 30 min. + cooling
Makes: 2½ cups

- 1 Tbsp. sugar
- 1½ tsp. kosher salt
- 1 tsp. paprika
- ½ tsp. ground cinnamon
- ½ tsp. ground cumin
- ½ tsp. ground coriander
- ¼ tsp. cayenne pepper
- 1 large egg white, room temperature
- 2½ cups unblanched almonds

Preheat the oven to 325°. In a small bowl, combine the first 7 ingredients. In another small bowl, whisk egg white until foamy. Add the almonds; toss to coat. Sprinkle with spice mixture; toss to coat. Spread in a single layer in a greased 15x10x1-in. baking pan. Bake for 30 minutes, stirring every 10 minutes. Spread on waxed paper to cool completely. Store in an airtight container.

¼ cup: 230 cal., 20g fat (2g sat. fat), 0 chol., 293mg sod., 9g carb. (3g sugars, 4g fiber), 8g pro.

HOT PEPPER-BEEF SANDWICHES

If you like your shredded beef with a little kick, then this recipe is for you. For an even zestier version, add another jar of jalapeno slices or use hot peppers instead of the pepperoncini.

—*Kristen Langmeier, Faribault, MN*

- -

Prep: 15 min. • **Cook:** 8 hours
Makes: 12 servings

- 1 boneless beef chuck roast (4 to 5 lbs.)
- 2 medium onions, coarsely chopped
- 1 jar (16 oz.) sliced pepperoncini, undrained
- 1 jar (8 oz.) pickled jalapeno slices, drained
- 1 bottle (12 oz.) beer or nonalcoholic beer
- 1 envelope onion soup mix
- 5 garlic cloves, minced
- ½ tsp. pepper
- 12 kaiser rolls, split
- 12 slices provolone cheese

1. Place roast in a 4- or 5-qt. slow cooker. Add the onions, pepperoncini, jalapenos, beer, soup mix, garlic and pepper.
2. Cover and cook on low until meat is tender, 8-10 hours.
3. Remove meat. Skim fat from cooking liquid. When cool enough to handle, shred the meat with 2 forks and return to slow cooker; heat through. Serve ½ cup meat mixture on each roll with a slice of cheese.
Note: Look for pepperoncini (pickled peppers) in the pickle and olive section of your grocery store.
1 sandwich: 534 cal., 23g fat (9g sat. fat), 113mg chol., 1187mg sod., 38g carb. (3g sugars, 3g fiber), 41g pro.

SWEET POTATO CHIPS & CILANTRO DIP

This cool, creamy dip is a great partner for spiced sweet potato chips. They're made for each other!

—*Elizabeth Godecke, Chicago, IL*

Prep: 20 min. • **Bake:** 25 min./batch
Makes: 12 servings (1½ cups dip)

- 2 to 3 large sweet potatoes (1¾ lbs.), peeled and cut into ⅛-in. slices
- 2 Tbsp. canola oil
- 1 tsp. chili powder
- ½ tsp. garlic powder
- ½ tsp. taco seasoning
- ¼ tsp. salt
- ¼ tsp. ground cumin
- ¼ tsp. pepper
- ⅛ tsp. cayenne pepper

DIP
- ¾ cup mayonnaise
- ½ cup sour cream
- 2 oz. cream cheese, softened
- 4½ tsp. minced fresh cilantro
- 1½ tsp. lemon juice
- ½ tsp. celery salt
- ⅛ tsp. pepper

1. Preheat oven to 400°. Place the sweet potatoes in a large bowl. In a small bowl, mix oil and seasonings; drizzle over potatoes and toss to coat.

2. Arrange half of the potatoes in a single layer in 2 ungreased 15x10x1-in. baking pans. Bake 25-30 minutes or until golden brown, turning once. Repeat with the remaining sweet potatoes.

3. In a small bowl, beat dip ingredients until blended. Serve with chips.

½ cup chips with about 1 Tbsp. dip: 285 cal., 16g fat (4g sat. fat), 8mg chol., 217mg sod., 33g carb. (14g sugars, 4g fiber), 3g pro.

TURKEY CAPRESE SANDWICHES

At a friend's party, I had bruschetta with Caprese salad on top. I loved the taste and started serving it at my own parties. Once I had no bread, only bagels. I added turkey and a few other items, and this sandwich was born. My young daughter thought it was great. Now I make them for parties and everyone loves them!

—*Maria Higginson, Bountiful, UT*

Takes: 30 min. • **Makes:** 12 sandwiches

- 6 garlic cloves, peeled and halved
- 12 Asiago cheese bagels, split and toasted
- ¼ cup mayonnaise
- 2 lbs. sliced deli turkey
- 2 lbs. fresh mozzarella cheese, sliced
- 4 plum tomatoes, thinly sliced
- 1 large red onion, thinly sliced
- 12 fresh basil leaves, thinly sliced
- 2 Tbsp. olive oil

1. Rub garlic cloves over cut sides of bagels.
2. For each sandwich, spread 1 tsp. mayonnaise over bagel bottom. Layer with turkey, cheese, tomatoes, onion and basil. Drizzle with olive oil. Replace tops. Cut sandwiches in half if desired.

1 sandwich: 709 cal., 29g fat (15g sat. fat), 96mg chol., 1444mg sod., 66g carb. (8g sugars, 3g fiber), 45g pro.

BEER & BRATS NACHOS

Savor some favorite flavors of the Midwest when you serve a big platter of these nachos. They have a rich beer-and-cheese sauce, peppers, onions and irresistible sausage.
—*Kelly Boe, Whiteland, IN*

- -

Takes: 30 min. • **Makes:** 12 servings

- 1 **pkg. (14 oz.) fully cooked smoked bratwurst links, sliced**
- 2¼ **cups frozen pepper and onion stir-fry blend**
- 3 **cups shredded cheddar cheese**
- 2½ **tsp. all-purpose flour**
- 1 **cup chopped onion**
- 1 **Tbsp. olive oil**
- 1 **garlic clove, minced**
- ¾ **cup beer or beef broth**
- 12 **cups tortilla chips**

1. In a large skillet, saute the bratwurst for 1 minute. Add stir-fry blend; cook 3-5 minutes longer or until the vegetables are tender. Set aside and keep warm.

2. In a large bowl, combine cheese and flour. In a large saucepan, saute onion in oil until tender. Add garlic; cook 1 minute longer. Stir in beer; heat over medium heat until bubbles form around sides of pan.

3. Reduce heat to medium-low; add a handful of cheese mixture. Stir constantly, using a figure-8 motion, until almost completely melted. Continue adding cheese, 1 handful at a time, allowing cheese to almost completely melt between additions.

4. Arrange the tortilla chips on a large serving platter. Spoon cheese mixture over chips. Top with bratwurst mixture. Serve immediately.

1 serving: 348 cal., 24g fat (10g sat. fat), 54mg chol., 544mg sod., 20g carb. (1g sugars, 1g fiber), 13g pro.

BITE-SIZED APPLE PIES

These little bites are fun for kids to make. Simply wrap strips of pastry around apple wedges and shake on some cinnamon-sugar. Then bake and watch them disappear!
—Taste of Home *Test Kitchen*

- -

Prep: 20 min. • **Bake:** 15 min.
Makes: 16 servings

- ½ **cup sugar**
- 2 **tsp. ground cinnamon**
- 2 **sheets refrigerated pie crust**
- 3 **Tbsp. butter, melted, divided**
- 2 **medium tart apples**
  Caramel sauce, optional

1. Preheat oven to 425°. In a small bowl, mix sugar and cinnamon; reserve 1 Tbsp.. On a lightly floured surface, unroll pie crusts; roll and trim each to an 8-in. square. Brush with 2 Tbsp. butter; sprinkle with the remaining sugar mixture. Cut each square into eight 1-in. strips.

2. Cut each apple into 8 wedges; wrap 1 strip of pastry around each wedge, placing sugared side of pastry against the apple.

3. Place on a parchment-lined baking sheet. Brush tops with the remaining butter; sprinkle with reserved sugar mixture. Bake until pastry is golden brown, 13-15 minutes. Serve with caramel sauce if desired.

1 serving: 163 cal., 9g fat (4g sat. fat), 10mg chol., 108mg sod., 21g carb. (9g sugars, 0 fiber), 1g pro.

Spring Brunch

Celebrate the season with fresh strawberry and lemon desserts, an impressive overnight casserole, springy vegetables and more.

EGGS BENEDICT CASSEROLE

Here's a casserole as tasty as eggs Benedict, but without the hassle. Simply assemble the ingredients ahead, and bake it the next morning for an elegant brunch.
—*Sandie Heindel, Liberty, MO*

- -

Prep: 25 min. + chilling • **Bake:** 45 min.
Makes: 12 servings (1⅔ cups sauce)

- 12 oz. Canadian bacon, chopped
- 6 English muffins, split and cut into 1-in. pieces
- 8 large eggs
- 2 cups 2% milk
- 1 tsp. onion powder
- ¼ tsp. paprika

HOLLANDAISE SAUCE
- 4 large egg yolks
- ½ cup heavy whipping cream
- 2 Tbsp. lemon juice
- 1 tsp. Dijon mustard
- ½ cup butter, melted

1. Place half of the Canadian bacon in a greased 3-qt. or 13x9-in. baking dish; top with English muffins and remaining bacon. In a large bowl, whisk eggs, milk and onion powder; pour over top. Refrigerate overnight.
2. Preheat oven to 375°. Remove casserole from refrigerator while oven heats. Sprinkle top with paprika. Bake, covered, 35 minutes. Uncover; bake 10-15 minutes longer or until a knife inserted in the center comes out clean.
3. In top of a double boiler or a metal bowl over simmering water, whisk the egg yolks, whipping cream, lemon juice and Dijon mustard until blended; cook until the mixture is just thick enough to coat a metal spoon and the temperature reaches 160°, whisking constantly. Reduce heat to very low. Very slowly drizzle in warm melted butter, whisking constantly. Serve immediately with casserole.
1 piece: 286 cal., 19g fat (10g sat. fat), 256mg chol., 535mg sod., 16g carb. (4g sugars, 1g fiber), 14g pro.

LEMON SUPREME PIE

A friend and I often visit a local restaurant for pie and coffee. When they stopped carrying our favorite, I created this version, which we think tastes even better! The combination of cream cheese and lemon filling is wonderful.
—*Jana Beckman, Wamego, KS*

- -

Prep: 25 min. + cooling
Bake: 25 min. + chilling • **Makes:** 8 servings

Pastry for deep-dish pie (9 in.)
LEMON FILLING
1¼ cups sugar, divided
6 Tbsp. cornstarch
½ tsp. salt
1¼ cups water
2 Tbsp. butter
2 tsp. grated lemon zest
4 to 5 drops yellow food coloring, optional
½ cup lemon juice
CREAM CHEESE FILLING
11 oz. cream cheese, softened
¾ cup confectioners' sugar
1½ cups whipped topping
1 Tbsp. lemon juice
Additional whipped topping, optional

1. On a lightly floured surface, roll pie dough to a ⅛-in.-thick circle; transfer to a 9-in. deep dish pie plate. Trim crust to ½ in. beyond rim of plate; flute edge. Refrigerate 30 minutes.
2. Preheat oven to 425°. Line crust with a double thickness of foil. Fill with pie weights, dried beans or uncooked rice. Bake on a lower oven rack 20-25 minutes or until edges are golden brown. Remove foil and weights; bake 3-6 minutes longer or until bottom is golden brown. Cool on a wire rack.

3. For lemon filling, combine ¾ cup sugar, cornstarch and salt in a small saucepan. Stir in water until smooth. Bring to a boil over medium-high heat. Reduce the heat; add remaining sugar. Cook and stir until thickened and bubbly, about 2 minutes. Remove from heat; stir in butter, lemon zest and, if desired, food coloring. Gently stir in lemon juice. Cool to room temperature, about 1 hour.
4. Beat the cream cheese and confectioners' sugar until smooth. Fold in whipped topping and lemon juice.
5. Spread cream cheese filling into pie shell; top with lemon filling. Chill pie overnight.
6. If desired, dollop additional whipped topping over lemon filling.
1 slice: 735 cal., 42g fat (26g sat. fat), 107mg chol., 604mg sod., 84g carb. (48g sugars, 1g fiber), 7g pro.

BACON & EGG LASAGNA

My sister-in-law served this special dish for Easter breakfast one year, and our whole family loved the mix of bacon, eggs, pasta and cheese. Now I sometimes make it for my own holiday brunches.
—*Dianne Meyer, Graniteville, VT*

Prep: 45 min. • **Bake:** 35 min. + standing
Makes: 12 servings

- 1 lb. bacon strips, diced
- 1 large onion, chopped
- ⅓ cup all-purpose flour
- ½ to 1 tsp. salt
- ¼ tsp. pepper
- 4 cups 2% milk
- 12 lasagna noodles, cooked and drained
- 12 hard-boiled large eggs, sliced
- 2 cups shredded Swiss cheese
- ⅓ cup grated Parmesan cheese
- 2 Tbsp. minced fresh parsley, optional

1. In a large skillet, cook bacon until crisp. Remove with a slotted spoon to paper towels. Drain, reserving ⅓ cup drippings. In the drippings, saute onion until tender. Stir in the flour, salt and pepper until blended. Gradually stir in milk. Bring to a boil; cook and stir for 2 minutes or until thickened. Remove from the heat.

2. Spread ½ cup sauce in a greased 13x9-in. baking dish. Layer with 4 noodles, a third of the eggs and bacon, Swiss cheese and white sauce. Repeat layers twice. Sprinkle with the Parmesan cheese.

3. Bake, uncovered, at 350° until bubbly, 35-40 minutes. If desired, sprinkle with parsley. Let lasagna stand for 15 minutes before cutting.

1 piece: 386 cal., 20g fat (9g sat. fat), 252mg chol., 489mg sod., 28g carb. (7g sugars, 1g fiber), 23g pro.

SPRINGTIME SPINACH SALAD

I came up with this recipe as a way to use early spring produce. Toasted walnuts add a rich, hearty accent.
—*Trisha Kruse, Eagle, ID*

Takes: 25 min. • **Makes:** 10 servings

- 1 lb. fresh asparagus, trimmed and cut into 1-in. pieces
- 1 Tbsp. olive oil
- 1 pkg. (10 oz.) fresh spinach, torn
- 2 cups fresh strawberries, sliced
- ½ cup chopped walnuts, toasted
- ⅓ cup canola oil
- 3 Tbsp. raspberry vinegar
- 1 tsp. sugar
- ½ tsp. salt

1. Place asparagus in a foil-lined 15x10x1-in. baking pan; drizzle with olive oil and toss to coat. Bake at 400° for 15 minutes or until crisp-tender, turning occasionally. Cool.

2. In a large bowl, combine the asparagus, chopped spinach, strawberries and walnuts. In a small bowl, whisk the canola oil, vinegar, sugar and salt. Drizzle over salad and toss to coat. Serve immediately.

1 cup: 137 cal., 12g fat (1g sat. fat), 0 chol., 143mg sod., 5g carb. (2g sugars, 2g fiber), 3g pro.

SLOW-COOKED HAM WITH PINEAPPLE SAUCE

We serve this dish during the holidays because everyone is crazy about it. But we also enjoy it all year long because it's super simple to prepare.

—*Terry Roberts, Yorktown, VA*

- -

Prep: 10 min. • **Cook:** 6 hours
Makes: 12 servings

- 1 **fully cooked boneless ham (4 to 5 lbs.)**
- 1 **Tbsp. cornstarch**
- 2 **Tbsp. lemon juice**
- 1 **cup packed brown sugar**
- 1 **Tbsp. yellow mustard**
- ¼ **tsp. salt**
- 1 **can (20 oz.) unsweetened crushed pineapple, undrained**

1. Place ham in a 5-qt. slow cooker. In a small saucepan, mix cornstarch and lemon juice until smooth. Stir in remaining ingredients; bring to a boil, stirring occasionally. Pour over ham, covering completely.

2. Cook, covered, on low for 6-8 hours (a thermometer inserted in ham should read at least 140°).

Note: This recipe is not recommended for a spiral-sliced ham.

4 oz. ham with ¼ cup sauce: 262 cal., 6g fat (2g sat. fat), 77mg chol., 1638mg sod., 27g carb. (25g sugars, 0 fiber), 28g pro.

HEAVENLY FILLED STRAWBERRIES

These luscious stuffed berries are the perfect bite-sized dessert.

—*Stephen Munro, Beaverbank, NS*

- -

Takes: 20 min. • **Makes:** 3 dozen

- 3 **dozen large fresh strawberries**
- 11 **oz. cream cheese, softened**
- ½ **cup confectioners' sugar**
- ¼ **tsp. almond extract**
    Grated chocolate, optional

1. Remove stems from strawberries; cut a deep "X" in the tip of each berry. Gently spread berries open.

2. In a small bowl, beat the cream cheese, confectioners' sugar and extract until light and fluffy. Pipe or spoon about 2 tsp. into each berry; if desired, sprinkle with chocolate. Chill until serving.

1 serving: 41 cal., 3g fat (2g sat. fat), 10mg chol., 26mg sod., 3g carb. (2g sugars, 0 fiber), 1g pro.

Girl Time

Whether it's a weekend at the lake house or a laid-back evening in the neighborhood, here are the perfect foods for a girls' getaway.

SPICED WHITE SANGRIA

I've been making this recipe for more than 20 years. My husband and I are in the wine and spirit business, and we served it at one of our first dinner parties after we were married. It's a refreshing change from traditional red sangria.

—Ellen Folkman, Crystal Beach, FL

- -

Prep: 15 min. + chilling • **Makes:** 10 servings

- 2 medium oranges, seeded and sliced
- 1 medium lemon, seeded and sliced
- 1 medium lime, seeded and sliced
- ⅔ cup brandy
- ½ cup sugar
- 2 cinnamon sticks (3 in.)
- 2 bottles (750 ml each) white wine
- 1 bottle (1 liter) club soda, chilled

Combine first 7 ingredients in a large pitcher. Refrigerate, covered, stirring occasionally, about 4 hours. Discard the cinnamon sticks. Refrigerate, covered, 2 hours longer. Just before serving, stir in chilled club soda. Serve over ice with fruit slices in each glass.
¾ cup: 207 cal., 0 fat (0 sat. fat), 0 chol., 28mg sod., 17g carb. (13g sugars, 0 fiber), 0 pro.

ASIAN PULLED PORK SANDWICHES

My pulled pork is a happy flavor mashup of Vietnamese pho noodle soup and a banh mi sandwich. This is one seriously delicious slow-cooker dish.

—*Stacie Anderson, Virginia Beach, VA*

Prep: 15 min. • **Cook:** 7 hours
Makes: 18 servings

- ½ cup hoisin sauce
- ¼ cup seasoned rice vinegar
- ¼ cup reduced-sodium soy sauce
- ¼ cup honey
- 2 Tbsp. tomato paste
- 1 Tbsp. Worcestershire sauce
- 2 garlic cloves, minced
- 4 lbs. boneless pork shoulder roast
- 18 French dinner rolls (about 1¾ oz. each), split and warmed
  Optional toppings: Shredded cabbage, julienned carrot, sliced jalapeno pepper, fresh cilantro or basil and Sriracha chili sauce

1. Whisk the first 7 ingredients until blended. Place roast in a 4- or 5-qt. slow cooker. Pour sauce mixture over top. Cook, covered, on low until pork is tender, 7-9 hours.
2. Remove roast; cool slightly. Skim fat from cooking juices. Coarsely shred pork with 2 forks. Return pork to slow cooker; heat through. Using tongs, serve pork on rolls, adding toppings as desired.
Freeze option: Freeze cooled meat mixture in freezer containers. To use, partially thaw in the refrigerator overnight. Heat through in a saucepan, stirring occasionally; add a little broth if necessary. Serve as directed.
1 sandwich: 350 cal., 12g fat (4g sat. fat), 60mg chol., 703mg sod., 35g carb. (8g sugars, 1g fiber), 23g pro.

CORNY CHOCOLATE CRUNCH

This sweet treat tastes almost like candy, and it's gone just about as fast!

—Delores Ward, Decatur, IN

Takes: 20 min. • **Makes:** about 5 qt.

3	qt. popped popcorn
3	cups Corn Chex
3	cups broken corn chips
1	pkg. (10 to 11 oz.) butterscotch chips
12	oz. dark chocolate candy coating, coarsely chopped

1. In a large bowl, combine the popcorn, cereal and corn chips; set aside. In a microwave, melt butterscotch chips and candy coating; stir until smooth.

2. Pour over popcorn mixture and toss to coat. Spread into 2 greased 15x10x1-in. baking pans. When cool enough to handle, break into pieces.

1 cup: 283 cal., 12g fat (8g sat. fat), 0 chol., 194mg sod., 40g carb. (20g sugars, 2g fiber), 3g pro.

CRISP CUCUMBER SALSA

Here's a fantastic way to use cucumbers. You'll love the creamy and crunchy texture and super fresh flavors.

—Charlene Skjerven, Hoople, ND

Takes: 20 min. • **Makes:** 2½ cups

2	cups finely chopped seeded peeled cucumber
½	cup finely chopped seeded tomato
¼	cup chopped red onion
2	Tbsp. minced fresh parsley
1	jalapeno pepper, seeded and chopped
4½	tsp. minced fresh cilantro
1	garlic clove, minced
¼	cup reduced-fat sour cream
1½	tsp. lemon juice
1½	tsp. lime juice
¼	tsp. ground cumin
¼	tsp. seasoned salt
	Baked tortilla chip scoops

In a small bowl, combine first 7 ingredients. Combine the sour cream, juices, cumin and seasoned salt; pour over cucumber mixture and stir to coat. Serve immediately with chips.

Note: Wear disposable gloves when cutting hot peppers; the oils can burn skin. Avoid touching your face.

¼ cup: 16 cal., 1g fat (0 sat. fat), 2mg chol., 44mg sod., 2g carb. (1g sugars, 0 fiber), 1g pro. **Diabetic exchanges:** Free food.

SIMPLE SALMON DIP

This is my go-to dip recipe for summer barbecues. The secret is the green chiles—they add just enough heat.

—Susan Jordan, Denver, CO

Prep: 15 min. + chilling • **Makes:** 1¼ cups

1	pkg. (8 oz.) reduced-fat cream cheese
2	Tbsp. canned chopped green chiles
1½	tsp. lemon juice
2	green onions, chopped, divided
2	oz. smoked salmon fillet
	Assorted crackers or toasted French bread baguette slices

Mix cream cheese, green chiles, lemon juice and half of the green onions. Flake salmon into small pieces; stir into the cream cheese mixture. Chill at least 2 hours before serving. Top with remaining green onion. Serve with crackers or baguette slices.

3 Tbsp.: 107 cal., 8g fat (5g sat. fat), 29mg chol., 246mg sod., 2g carb. (1g sugars, 0 fiber), 6g pro.

BRIE WITH APRICOT TOPPING

Baked Brie is one of our favorite quick and tasty appetizers. This one features a dried apricot topping, but don't be shy when it comes to experimenting with other dried fruits, such as cherries or figs.
—Taste of Home *Test Kitchen*

Takes: 25 min. • **Makes:** 8 servings

- ½ cup chopped dried apricots
- 2 Tbsp. brown sugar
- 2 Tbsp. water
- 1 tsp. balsamic vinegar
  Dash salt
- ½ to 1 tsp. minced fresh rosemary or ¼ tsp. dried rosemary, crushed
- 1 round Brie cheese (8 oz.)
  Assorted crackers

1. Preheat oven to 400°. In a small saucepan, bring first 5 ingredients to a boil. Cook and stir over medium heat until slightly thickened. Remove from heat; stir in rosemary.
2. Trim rind from top of cheese. Place cheese in an ungreased ovenproof serving dish. Spoon apricot mixture over cheese. Bake, uncovered, 10-12 minutes or until cheese is softened. Serve warm, with crackers.
1 serving: 129 cal., 8g fat (5g sat. fat), 28mg chol., 204mg sod., 9g carb. (7g sugars, 1g fiber), 6g pro.
Chutney-Topped Brie: Omit the topping ingredients. Trim Brie as directed and spread with ¼ cup chutney. Sprinkle with 2 Tbsp. bacon bits. Bake as directed.
Cherry-Brandy Baked Brie: Omit topping ingredients. Trim Brie as directed. Mix ½ cup dried cherries, ½ cup chopped walnuts, ¼ cup packed brown sugar and ¼ cup brandy or apple juice; spoon over cheese. Bake as directed, increasing time to 15 minutes.

WATERMELON PIZZA

Start with grilled melon slices and layer on the tangy, salty and sweet toppings for a summer-fresh app.
—*Ellen Riley, Murfreesboro, TN*

Prep: 25 min. • **Grill:** 10 min. + chilling
Makes: 8 servings

- 8 wedges seedless watermelon, about 1 in. thick
- 1 cup heirloom cherry tomatoes, sliced
- 1 cup fresh baby arugula
- ½ cup fresh blueberries
- ⅓ cup crumbled feta cheese
- ⅓ cup pitted Greek olives, halved
- 1 Tbsp. olive oil
- ⅛ tsp. kosher salt
- ⅛ tsp. coarsely ground pepper
  Balsamic glaze, optional

1. Grill watermelon, covered, on a greased grill rack over medium-high direct heat until seared, 5-6 minutes on each side. Remove from heat; transfer to a platter. Chill.
2. To serve, top chilled watermelon with tomatoes, arugula, blueberries, feta and olives. Drizzle with olive oil; season with salt and pepper. If desired, drizzle with a little balsamic glaze.
1 wedge: 91 cal., 4g fat (1g sat. fat), 3mg chol., 169mg sod., 13g carb. (11g sugars, 1g fiber), 2g pro. **Diabetic exchanges:** 1 fruit, 1 fat.

Backyard BBQ

Summertime calls for lazy backyard gatherings with friends, neighbors and family. Bring one of these standouts, which are sure to star on the buffet.

JERSEY-STYLE HOT DOGS

I grew up in northern New Jersey, where this way of eating hot dogs—with cooked potatoes, peppers and onions—was created. My husband never had them as a kid but has come to love them even more than I do. The combination of ingredients and flavors is simple, but just right!

—*Suzanne Banfield, Basking Ridge, NJ*

Prep: 20 min. • **Grill:** 40 min.
Makes: 12 servings (10 cups potato mixture)

- 6   medium Yukon Gold potatoes (about 3 lbs.), halved and thinly sliced
- 3   large sweet red peppers, thinly sliced
- 3   large onions, halved and thinly sliced
- ⅓   cup olive oil
- 6   garlic cloves, minced
- 3   tsp. salt
- 1½ tsp. pepper
- 12 bun-length beef hot dogs
- 12 hot dog buns, split

1. In a large bowl, combine the potatoes, red peppers and onions. In a small bowl, mix oil, garlic, salt and pepper; add to potato mixture and toss to coat.

2. Transfer to two 13x9-in. disposable foil pans; cover with foil. Place the pans on grill rack over medium heat; cook, covered, until potatoes are tender, 30-35 minutes. Remove from heat.

3. Grill hot dogs, covered, over medium heat 7-9 minutes or until heated through, turning occasionally. Place the buns on grill, cut side down; grill until lightly toasted. Place hot dogs and potato mixture in buns. Serve with the remaining potato mixture.

1 serving: 453 cal., 24g fat (8g sat. fat), 35mg chol., 1261mg sod., 48g carb. (8g sugars, 4g fiber), 13g pro.

SANGRIA GELATIN RING

This gelatin is enjoyed by everyone because you just can't go wrong with fresh berries.
—*Nicole Nemeth, Komoka, ON*

Prep: 15 min. + chilling • **Makes:** 10 servings

- 1½ cups boiling white wine or white grape juice
- 2 pkg. (3 oz. each) lemon gelatin
- 2 cups club soda, chilled
- 1 cup sliced fresh strawberries
- 1 cup fresh or frozen blueberries
- 1 cup fresh or frozen raspberries
- ½ cup green grapes, halved

In a large heatproof bowl, add boiling wine to gelatin; stir 2 minutes to completely dissolve. Stir in the chilled club soda. Refrigerate until thickened but not firm, about 45 minutes. Stir in berries and grapes. Pour into a 6-cup ring mold coated with cooking spray. Refrigerate until set, about 4 hours. Unmold onto a serving platter.

1 slice: 117 cal., 0 fat (0 sat. fat), 0 chol., 52mg sod., 22g carb. (19g sugars, 2g fiber), 2g pro.

SWEET & SPICY BAKED BEANS

This recipe is a hit with guests and family. It's sweet, simple and delicious, and someone always asks for the recipe.
—*Elliot Wesen, Arlington, TX*

Prep: 15 min. • **Bake:** 50 min.
Makes: 14 servings

- 2 cans (28 oz. each) baked beans
- 1 can (20 oz.) unsweetened crushed pineapple, drained
- 1 cup spicy barbecue sauce
- ½ cup molasses
- 2 Tbsp. prepared mustard
- ½ tsp. pepper
- ¼ tsp. salt
- 1 can (6 oz.) french-fried onions, crushed, divided
- 5 bacon strips, cooked and crumbled, divided

1. In a large bowl, combine the first 7 ingredients. Stir in half of the onions and bacon. Transfer to a greased 13x9-in. baking dish.
2. Cover and bake at 350° for 45 minutes. Sprinkle with remaining onions and bacon. Bake, uncovered, 5-10 minutes longer or until bubbly.

¾ cup: 285 cal., 9 g fat (3 g sat. fat), 10 mg chol., 860 mg sod., 46 g carb., 7 g fiber, 7 g pro.

CHIPOTLE SLIDERS

This recipe has to be the ultimate in a fast-fix mini burger. Creamy mayo, cheese and sweet Hawaiian rolls help tame the heat of the chipotle peppers.
—*Shawn Singleton, Vidor, TX*

Takes: 30 min. • **Makes:** 10 sliders

- 1 pkg. (12 oz.) Hawaiian sweet rolls, divided
- 1 tsp. salt
- ½ tsp. pepper
- 8 tsp. minced chipotle peppers in adobo sauce, divided
- 1½ lbs. ground beef
- 10 slices pepper jack cheese
- ½ cup mayonnaise

1. Place 2 rolls in a food processor; process until crumbly. Transfer to a large bowl; add the salt, pepper and 6 tsp. chipotle peppers. Crumble beef over mixture and mix well. Shape into 10 patties.
2. Grill the burgers, covered, over medium heat for 3-4 minutes on each side or until a thermometer reads 160° and juices run clear. Top with cheese. Grill 1 minute longer or until cheese is melted.
3. Split the remaining rolls and grill, cut side down, over medium heat for 30-60 seconds or until toasted. Combine mayonnaise and remaining chipotle peppers; spread over roll bottoms. Top each with a burger. Replace roll tops.
1 slider: 377 cal., 25g fat (8g sat. fat), 67mg chol., 710mg sod., 16g carb. (3g sugars, 1g fiber), 20g pro.

CAMPERS' FAVORITE DIP

Our family craves this cheesy chili dip so much we make two batches, one especially for the guys. If you're not grilling out, bake it in the oven or heat in the microwave.
—*Valorie Ebie, Bel Aire, KS*

Takes: 15 min. • **Makes:** 3½ cups

- 1 pkg. (8 oz.) reduced-fat cream cheese
- 1 can (15 oz.) chili with beans
- 2 cups shredded cheddar cheese
- 2 thinly sliced green onions, optional
  Tortilla chip scoops

1. Prepare campfire or grill for medium-low heat. Spread cream cheese in the bottom of a 9-in. disposable foil pie pan. Top with chili; sprinkle with cheese.
2. Place pan on a grill grate over a campfire or on grill until cheese is melted, 5-8 minutes. If desired, sprinkle with green onion. Serve with chips.
Note: To make in a microwave, spread cream cheese in the bottom of a 9-in. pie plate. Top with chili; sprinkle with cheese. Microwave on high for 3-4 minutes or until cheese is mostly melted. Let stand in microwave 2 minutes before serving. Serve with chips.
¼ cup: 250 cal., 17g fat (7g sat. fat), 32mg chol., 403mg sod., 15g carb. (2g sugars, 2g fiber), 9g pro.

TOMATOES WITH BUTTERMILK VINAIGRETTE

We make the most of tomatoes when they are in season and plentiful, and I love an old-fashioned homemade buttermilk dressing. Fresh herbs give this salad a summery taste.

—*Judith Foreman, Alexandria, VA*

Takes: 20 min.
Makes: 12 servings

- ¾ cup buttermilk
- ¼ cup minced fresh tarragon
- ¼ cup white wine vinegar
- 3 Tbsp. canola oil
- 1½ tsp. sugar
- ½ tsp. ground mustard
- ¼ tsp. celery salt
- ¼ tsp. pepper
- 4 lbs. cherry tomatoes, halved
- ⅓ cup minced fresh chives

1. In a small bowl, whisk first 8 ingredients until blended. Refrigerate mixture, covered, until serving.
2. Just before serving, arrange tomatoes on a platter; drizzle with vinaigrette. Sprinkle with chives.

¾ cup: 79 cal., 4g fat (0 sat. fat), 1mg chol., 63mg sod., 10g carb. (6g sugars, 2g fiber), 2g pro. **Diabetic exchanges:** 1 vegetable, ½ starch, ½ fat.

POT OF S'MORES

This easy Dutch-oven version of the popular campout treat is so good and gooey. The hardest part is waiting for it to cool a bit so you can dig in. Yum!

—*June Dress, Meridian, ID*

Takes: 25 min. • **Makes:** 12 servings

- 1 pkg. (14½ oz.) graham crackers, crushed
- ½ cup butter, melted
- 1 can (14 oz.) sweetened condensed milk
- 2 cups (12 oz.) semisweet chocolate chips
- 1 cup butterscotch chips
- 2 cups miniature marshmallows

1. Prepare grill or campfire for low heat, using 16-18 charcoal briquettes or large wood chips.
2. Line a cast-iron Dutch oven with heavy-duty aluminum foil. Combine cracker crumbs and butter; press into bottom of pan. Pour milk over the crust and sprinkle with chocolate and butterscotch chips. Top with marshmallows.
3. Cover Dutch oven. When briquettes or wood chips are covered with white ash, place Dutch oven directly on top of 6 of them. Using long-handled tongs, place the remaining briquettes on pan cover.
4. Cook until marshmallows begin to melt, about 15 minutes. To check for doneness, use the tongs to carefully lift the cover.

1 serving: 584 cal., 28g fat (17g sat. fat), 31mg chol., 326mg sod., 83g carb. (47g sugars, 3g fiber), 8g pro.

Family Feast

Many hands make light work, and these recipes make putting on a showstopping holiday spread a snap. Savor the time with your family.

KALAMATA CHEESECAKE APPETIZER

The savory cheesecake filling tames the bold flavor of kalamata olives, so even those who shy away from kalamatas will be glad they sampled this dish. For a milder flavor, use the more common black or green olives.
—*Theresa Kreyche, Tustin, CA*

- -

Prep: 30 min. • **Bake:** 25 min. + chilling
Makes: 24 servings

1¼ cups seasoned bread crumbs
½ cup finely chopped pecans
⅓ cup butter, melted
FILLING
11 oz. cream cheese, softened
1 cup sour cream
1 Tbsp. all-purpose flour
¼ tsp. salt
¼ tsp. pepper
1 large egg, room temperature
1 large egg yolk, room temperature
½ cup pitted kalamata olives, chopped
2 tsp. minced fresh rosemary
Optional: Halved pitted kalamata olives and fresh rosemary sprigs

1. In a small bowl, combine bread crumbs and pecans; stir in butter. Press onto the bottom of a greased 9-in. springform pan. Place the pan on a baking sheet. Bake at 350° for 12 minutes. Cool on a wire rack.
2. In a large bowl, beat the cream cheese, sour cream, flour, salt and pepper until smooth. Add egg and egg yolk; beat on low speed just until combined. Fold in chopped olives and minced rosemary. Pour over crust. Return pan to baking sheet.
3. Bake for 25-30 minutes or until center is almost set. Cool on a wire rack 10 minutes. Loosen edges of cheesecake from pan with a knife. Cool 1 hour longer. Chill overnight.
4. Remove rim from pan. Top cheesecake with olives and rosemary if desired.

1 slice: 142 cal., 12g fat (6g sat. fat), 45mg chol., 223mg sod., 6g carb. (1g sugars, 0 fiber), 3g pro.

SPARKLING CRANBERRY KISS

Cranberry and orange juices are a terrific pairing with ginger ale in this party punch. We use cranberry juice cocktail, but other blends like cranberry-apple also sparkle.
—*Shannon Copley, Upper Arlington, OH*

- -

Takes: 5 min.
Makes: 14 servings

6 cups cranberry juice
1½ cups orange juice
3 cups ginger ale
Ice cubes
Orange slices, optional

In a pitcher, combine juices. Just before serving, stir in ginger ale; serve over ice. If desired, serve with orange slices.

¾ cup: 81 cal., 0 fat (0 sat. fat), 0 chol., 9mg sod., 21g carb. (20g sugars, 0 fiber), 1g pro.
Mock Champagne Punch: Substitute 3 cups white grape juice for cranberry and orange juices. Garnish with fresh raspberries. Makes 8 servings.
Orange Juice Spritzer: Omit cranberry juice; increase the orange juice to 3 cups and add 3 Tbsp. maraschino cherry juice. Garnish with maraschino cherries and orange slices. Makes 8 servings.

1 cup shredded part-skim
  mozzarella cheese
½ cup grated Parmesan cheese
½ cup seasoned bread crumbs
1 large egg, lightly beaten

TOPPING
1 cup shredded part-skim
  mozzarella cheese
¼ cup grated Parmesan cheese
  Minced fresh parsley

WHITE SEAFOOD LASAGNA

We make lasagna with shrimp and scallops as part of the traditional Italian Feast of the Seven Fishes. Every bite delivers a tasty jewel from the sea.
—*Joe Colamonico, North Charleston, SC*

Prep: 1 hour • **Bake:** 40 min. + standing
Makes: 12 servings

9 uncooked lasagna noodles
1 Tbsp. butter
1 lb. uncooked shrimp (31 to 40 per lb.), peeled and deveined
1 lb. bay scallops
5 garlic cloves, minced
¼ cup white wine
1 Tbsp. lemon juice
1 lb. fresh crabmeat

CHEESE SAUCE
¼ cup butter, cubed
¼ cup all-purpose flour
3 cups 2% milk
1 cup shredded part-skim mozzarella cheese
½ cup grated Parmesan cheese
½ tsp. salt
¼ tsp. pepper
  Dash ground nutmeg

RICOTTA MIXTURE
1 carton (15 oz.) part-skim ricotta cheese
1 pkg. (10 oz.) frozen chopped spinach, thawed and squeezed dry

1. Preheat oven to 350°. Cook noodles according to package directions; drain.
2. Meanwhile, in a large skillet, heat butter over medium heat. Add shrimp and scallops in batches; cook 2-4 minutes or until shrimp turn pink and scallops are firm and opaque. Remove from pan.
3. Add garlic to same pan; cook 1 minute. Add wine and lemon juice, stirring to loosen browned bits from pan. Bring to a boil; cook 1-2 minutes or until liquid is reduced by half. Add the crab; heat through. Stir in the shrimp and scallops.
4. For cheese sauce, melt butter over medium heat in a large saucepan. Stir in flour until smooth; gradually whisk in milk. Bring to a boil, stirring constantly; cook and stir until thickened, 1-2 minutes. Remove from heat; stir in remaining cheese sauce ingredients. In a large bowl, combine ricotta mixture ingredients; stir in 1 cup cheese sauce.
5. Spread ½ cup cheese sauce into a greased 13x9-in. baking dish. Layer with 3 noodles, half of the ricotta mixture, half of the seafood mixture and ⅔ cup cheese sauce. Repeat layers. Top with the remaining noodles and cheese sauce. Sprinkle the top with 1 cup mozzarella cheese and ¼ cup Parmesan.
6. Bake, uncovered, 40-50 minutes or until bubbly and top is golden brown. Let lasagna stand 10 minutes before serving. Sprinkle with parsley.

1 piece: 448 cal., 19g fat (11g sat. fat), 158mg chol., 957mg sod., 29g carb. (5g sugars, 2g fiber), 39g pro.

CHOCOLATE CROISSANT PUDDING

This new twist on traditional bread pudding is a decadent and delicious family favorite!
—*Sonya Labbe, West Hollywood, CA*

- -

Prep: 15 min. + standing
Bake: 1 hour + standing • **Makes:** 15 servings

- 6 day-old croissants, split
- 1 cup (6 oz.) semisweet chocolate chips
- 5 large eggs
- 12 large egg yolks
- 5 cups half-and-half cream
- 1½ cups sugar
- 1½ tsp. vanilla extract
- 1 Tbsp. coffee liqueur, optional

1. Preheat oven to 350°. Arrange croissant bottoms in a greased 13x9-in. baking dish. Sprinkle with chocolate chips; replace the croissant tops.

2. In a large bowl, whisk the eggs, egg yolks, cream, sugar, vanilla and, if desired, coffee liqueur; pour over croissants. Let stand until croissants are softened, 15 minutes.

3. Bake, covered, 30 minutes. Uncover; bake until puffed, golden and a knife inserted near the center comes out clean, 30-40 minutes longer. Cool in pan on a wire rack 10 minutes before cutting. Serve warm.

1 piece: 400 cal., 21g fat (12g sat. fat), 265mg chol., 178mg sod., 41g carb. (32g sugars, 1g fiber), 9g pro.

RUSTIC CRANBERRY TARTS

For gatherings with family and friends, we love a dessert with a splash of red. These beautiful tarts are filled with cranberry and citrus. They are surprisingly easy to make and serve.
—*Holly Bauer, West Bend, WI*

- -

Prep: 15 min. • **Bake:** 20 min./batch
Makes: 2 tarts (6 servings each)

- 1 cup orange marmalade
- ¼ cup sugar
- ¼ cup all-purpose flour
- 4 cups fresh or frozen cranberries, thawed
- 2 sheets refrigerated pie crust
- 1 large egg white, lightly beaten
- 1 Tbsp. coarse sugar

1. Preheat oven to 425°. In a large bowl, mix marmalade, sugar and flour; stir in the cranberries.

2. Unroll 1 pie crust onto a parchment-lined baking sheet. Spoon half of the cranberry mixture over crust to within 2 in. of edge. Fold the edge over filling, pleating as you go and leaving a 5-in. opening in the center. Brush folded crust with egg white; sprinkle with half of the coarse sugar.

3. Bake 18-22 minutes or until crust is golden and filling is bubbly. Repeat with remaining ingredients. Transfer the tarts to wire racks to cool.

1 piece: 260 cal., 9g fat (4g sat. fat), 6mg chol., 144mg sod., 45g carb. (24g sugars, 2g fiber), 2g pro.

Recipe Index

Dreamy Fruit Dip
page 282

Jersey-Style
Hot Dogs
page 306

Rustic
Cranberry Tarts
page 313

White Seafood Lasagna
page 312

EQUIVALENT MEASURES

3 TEASPOONS	= 1 tablespoon	**16 TABLESPOONS**	= 1 cup
4 TABLESPOONS	= ¼ cup	**2 CUPS**	= 1 pint
5⅓ TABLESPOONS	= ⅓ cup	**4 CUPS**	= 1 quart
8 TABLESPOONS	= ½ cup	**4 QUARTS**	= 1 gallon

FOOD EQUIVALENTS

MACARONI		1 cup (3½ ounces) uncooked	= 2½ cups cooked
NOODLES, MEDIUM		3 cups (4 ounces) uncooked	= 4 cups cooked
POPCORN		3 cups (4 ounces) uncooked	= 8 cups popped
RICE, LONG GRAIN		1 cup uncooked	= 3 cups cooked
RICE, QUICK-COOKING		1 cup uncooked	= 2 cups cooked
SPAGHETTI		1 cup uncooked	= 4 cups cooked
BREAD		1 slice	= ¾ cup soft crumbs, ¼ cup fine dry crumbs
GRAHAM CRACKERS		7 squares	= ½ cup finely crushed
BUTTERY ROUND CRACKERS		12 crackers	= ½ cup finely crushed
SALTINE CRACKERS		14 crackers	= ½ cup finely crushed
BANANAS		1 medium	= ⅓ cup mashed
LEMONS		1 medium	= 3 tablespoons juice, 2 teaspoons grated zest
LIMES		1 medium	= 2 tablespoons juice, 1½ teaspoons grated zest
ORANGES		1 medium	= ¼-⅓ cup juice, 4 teaspoons grated zest
CABBAGE	1 head = 5 cups shredded	**GREEN PEPPER**	1 large = 1 cup chopped
CARROTS	1 pound = 3 cups shredded	**MUSHROOMS**	½ pound = 3 cups sliced
CELERY	1 rib = ½ cup chopped	**ONIONS**	1 medium = ½ cup chopped
CORN	1 ear fresh = ⅔ cup kernels	**POTATOES**	3 medium = 2 cups cubed
ALMONDS	1 pound = 3 cups chopped	**PECAN HALVES**	1 pound = 4½ cups chopped
GROUND NUTS	3¾ ounces = 1 cup	**WALNUTS**	1 pound = 3¾ cups chopped

EASY SUBSTITUTIONS

WHEN YOU NEED...		USE...
BAKING POWDER	1 teaspoon	½ teaspoon cream of tartar + ¼ teaspoon baking soda
BUTTERMILK	1 cup	1 tablespoon lemon juice or vinegar + enough milk to measure 1 cup (let stand 5 minutes before using)
CORNSTARCH	1 tablespoon	2 tablespoons all-purpose flour
HONEY	1 cup	1¼ cups sugar + ¼ cup water
HALF-AND-HALF CREAM	1 cup	1 tablespoon melted butter + enough whole milk to measure 1 cup
ONION	1 small, chopped (⅓ cup)	1 teaspoon onion powder or 1 tablespoon dried minced onion
TOMATO JUICE	1 cup	½ cup tomato sauce + ½ cup water
TOMATO SAUCE	2 cups	¾ cup tomato paste + 1 cup water
UNSWEETENED CHOCOLATE	1 square (1 ounce)	3 tablespoons baking cocoa + 1 tablespoon shortening or oil
WHOLE MILK	1 cup	½ cup evaporated milk + ½ cup water